The Seven Feasts of Israel and the Messiah, 3rd Edition

Discovering Our Judean-Messianic Hebraic Roots

Ronald Jean, PhD

WestBow
PRESS®
A DIVISION OF THOMAS NELSON
& ZONDERVAN

WestBow Press books may be ordered through booksellers or by contacting:

WestBow Press
A Division of Thomas Nelson & Zondervan
1663 Liberty Drive
Bloomington, IN 47403
www.westbowpress.com
844-714-3454

Graphic of Africa map is partly retrieved from
https://pixabay.com/en/africa-map-african-political-35742/.

All other graphics are by the author.

Scripture taken from the King James Version of the Bible.

ISBN: 978-1-9736-5471-1 (sc)
ISBN: 978-1-9736-5472-8 (hc)
ISBN: 978-1-9736-5470-4 (e)

Library of Congress Control Number: 2019902799

Print information available on the last page.

WestBow Press rev. date: 12/06/2022

Dedication

—————⟞⊙⊙⊙⟝—————

This book is dedicated to my daughter, Diana.
This book is also dedicated to the completion of the
gospel work of Jesus the Messiah in the world.

Acknowledgments

My grateful appreciation to Dr. Sharon Samuels, Dr. K. Stepheon Weech, Jean Velace, and Magdalena Jean for looking over portions of the document and their editorial recommendations. All the graces to clients and friends who did not receive the level of attention I wanted to give them while performing this task. I thank God for their understanding.

"And the LORD answered me, and said, Write the vision, and make it plain upon tables, that he may run that readeth it" (Hab. 2:2).

Contents

Preface

Questions on the feasts have received increasing interest among Christians (Messianic). It is discomforting for some Judean Christians to leave their cultural practices and do as other Christians in the cessation of feasts. Some Christians believe that they have been ignorant about God's will for not practicing the feasts. As Christians, shouldn't we find a path to unite efforts to work for the common good? Shouldn't we be striving toward having a standard view? Hopefully, we can accomplish this by considering the topic of the feast through the lens of scripture.

There have been convolutions to the original divine names. The Tetragrammaton (YHWH) has been undisputed. However, its pronunciation has been the center of controversy. The versions that appear most credible are *Yahveh* and *Yahawah or Yahuwah*. They are used interchangeably in this book. The difference lacks significance for controversy. It is understood that the term "Christ" in Greek is a term that refers to a Greek king. The equivalent term in Hebrew is "messiah." "Christ," as adapted to biblical names, was converted from Judaism to the Greek language during the messianic movement. As for "Jesus," a conversion also took place. We know that the real name is Joshua (Heb. Yahawashi), which means the "salvation of Yah" (short for Jehovah in English). "Jesus" does not carry the original definition, but it is a transliteration from Yeshua, based on a Hebrew dialectal and an abridged application to the name Joshua. Some conscious Judeans think that the Jesus who the Christians are serving is a different person from two thousand years ago. Over time, the change involved a different person and a drastic image alteration. The old Northeast African Yahawashi's image has been changed to the modern Jesus we see in movies today. However, the name Jesus is a linguistic alteration of the original.

There are differences in culture between the Gentiles and the Jews. We should not expect the Judeans of ancient Israel to give up their New Year feast in recognition of the Gentile's New Year celebration. Do we expect them to accept the Gentile New Year and reject their own in return? The Christian rejection of biblical culture has caused a rift between Jews and Gentiles believers.

Before continuing to read, keep in mind the efficacy of prayer, humility, and willingness to live for God. These are the essentials for every Bible study. Reading for knowledge is useful for awareness. However, personal conviction is the work of the Spirit. It is therefore crucial that the reader prayerfully considers each section of this topic.

Another critical point in the discussion is the authority of the Bible. This thesis makes the Bible its primary authority on teachings and historical remarks. The Bible alone has become the source by which all Christian views are compared. Sometimes the scriptures' factual statements get reinterpreted or abrogated to align with one's interpretations of symbols and ritual practices. We must refrain from this practice. Scriptural and historical facts are unalterable. They should not be abrogated, ignored, or interpreted for an eisegetical alignment. This stance may not sound valuable until one meets up with those who have these difficulties.

As we gravitate toward defensiveness, it becomes effortless to formulate judgments via emotions. While we are defending a point, we don't stop to smell the roses. Sometimes our desire to be justified carries us away in a tunnel, where it becomes challenging to find our way out. Many times, we allow our circumstances to influence our understanding. Occasionally, the way we read a situation depends on our perception of the desired conclusion. We program our answers to reflect on our experiences and a projected outcome.

Christian unity has been the goal of many Christians. That integration can be achieved through the written Word, the Bible. Not all our spiritual friends believed in the Bible and the Bible alone as the sole source of light. For example, some are established by modern prophets, apostles, messiahs, and historical records as an additional or equal basis to the Bible. It is difficult to have unity in understanding when what most of our religious authorities can accept varies so greatly. Minor variations are acceptable; however, we can demonstrate love and tolerance amid variances. Although we speak from different spiritual perspectives, we can appreciate one another in agreement areas; we can love and respect one another despite our differences.

In part two of this book, we will look at God's plan for the dispersed and forgotten Israel. Among the forgotten are four notable remnants: the Lemba, the Ibos, the Ashanti, and the Falasha, some who are known to practice Judaism. This section takes you through the history of the dispersion from its first diaspora from Samaria to the descendants' present-day locations. Most of Israel is lost among the nations of Africa and was subsequently spread throughout the world. Israel is still in captivity and away from his homeland. In this section, we note most of the places where Israel is dispersed. This treatise is not a history book. Although this is not an exhaustive treatment on the subject, what is said is historically and biblically documented.

> "Therefore, seeing we have this ministry, as we have received mercy, we faint not; But have renounced the hidden things of dishonesty, not walking in craftiness, nor handling the word of God deceitfully; but by manifestation of the truth commending ourselves to every man's conscience in the sight of God." 2 Cor. 4:1-2.

However, the interpretation of history sometimes depends on the beholder. I recommend the Bible as the authoritative history book for telling Israel's story. To provide you with the evidence, most of my references are directly cited. In this type of controversy, it is needful for the statements to be directly quoted. I hope your reading will be mission accomplished.

In this edition you will encounter a new chapter on Israel's seasonal use of the calendar. This sequel has been added to bring clarification to Paul's statements in his epistle to the Colossians. Without this background, we will be left amiss to the necessary hermeneutics for deciphering the writer's intent. I hope that your consideration of this addition will bring the needed transparency for enhancing your understanding.

Chapter 1

───◄◦◦◦►───

The Ancient Feasts of the Lord

The Appointed Times

There has been a growing concern among Christians about the Feasts of the Lord (YHWH). Our species is a party type of animal. We love festivities. As sociable as we are, life would lack the spark of joy if we did not socialize regularly. It must be understood, though, that not all of us socialize in the same way. For some, it's talking; for others, it's playing a game. Still, some socialize on the philosophy of some unknown to bring about a resolution. For some, it is to watch; for others, it is to cheer or sing. If we are left unchecked, we will, "as it is written … sit down to eat and drink and rise up to play" (1 Cor. 10:7). Can we use these various forms of interest to celebrate the Lord's feast? Maybe not, but if we improvise to mimic the ancient feasts, perhaps we can celebrate without contaminating the holy order. Without improvisation, we are stuck with the Old Testament laws. As Christians, what should we do? Should the same names and dates be retained and modify the rest to taste? Should the ancient rituals be shadowed strictly (see Appendix C)? Or do we do nothing?

The term "feast," as presented in English, has various meanings in Hebrew (Pick, 1977). In Genesis 1:14, the Hebrew word for a feast is "mou-aide," meaning appointed time or fixed season or times of gatherings. In Genesis 26:30, the Hebrew term for a feast is "mish- teh." Here, it refers to a festival. In Exodus 10:9, the Hebrew term "khawg," as used for feast, designates a solemn meeting with sacred implications. In many other places in the English scriptures, these terms are used as homonyms. For example, *sun* and *son* or *hear* and *here* can only be differentiated in context while speaking or in writing. In Leviticus 23, both "khawg" and mou-aide are used for the term "feast." Any appointed time for anything can be termed a mou-aide. However, if a feast involves a solemn meeting with a sacred ceremony, it is called a khawg. If the feast is mainly about eating and having some fun, it is a "mish-teh."

Let the reader note carefully that the Sabbath is separate from the other feasts owing to purpose and origin (Lev. 23). While the other feasts are ruled by monthly (moon) cycles, which began on the fourth day of creation, the Sabbath's weekly period starts from the first day to the seventh day of creation. The moon's revolution around the rotated Earth, which began on the fourth day, marks our monthly cycle. The rotation of the Earth on its axis against the first created light, on the first day, marks the beginning of the weekly cycle, giving us a week of seven days. That is independent of all other seasons. The sun was created on the fourth day, not to begin a weekly cycle, but to add additional time and continue the seven-day week. As the sun replaced the work affected by the first light, the moon, on the other hand, began a cycle of months and years (Gen. 1:14–16). The heavenly bodies give us a clear indication of the time for the months and years. The separation between monthly and weekly feasts is shown in the listing of the feasts in Leviticus 23.

Memorials of Redemption

The feasts were not only celebrations but appointed tokens of God's love and foreshadowed a more magnificent demonstration through Jesus. In the days of ancient Israel, God appointed some feasts to illustrate the plan of salvation. The feasts were to teach the Israelites about Jesus, who would save them by an atoning sacrifice of himself. The scriptures declared: "For God so loved the world that he gave his only begotten Son that whosoever believe in him should not perish but have everlasting life" (John 3:16). For many centuries, this theme has been the vertebral column of Israel's ritual celebrations. As a type of the Messiah's work, the feasts were similar to the ancient animal sacrifices. The perfect example of this is the Day of Atonement on which participating Israelites' sins were forgiven; that event typified the day of deliverance from sin by the Messiah's death. The Greek for Christ (Messiah) is Χρίω, Crio; means "to rub the body or parts of it, to stroke it" (Grundmann, van der Woude, Hesse, 1964). This rub or strike means to anoint. The Anointed One died that we might have life. The feasts illustrate and point to how the sanctuary services, in the antitypical phase, were to be finished and the people cleansed.

These appointed feasts commemorated events that had taken place as the people of Israel left Egypt. Each appointed feast represented an event that had transpired through their journey toward the Promised Land. Later chapters explain how the celebrations were in response to what God did for Israel.

Requirements for Ancient Feasts

Most feast celebrations by some Jews and some Christians inadequately portray coherency with the law. Being inconsistent with the law, they are deficient in illustrating the lessons intended. A Christian who celebrates the old feast in their original intent, except for sacrifices, must include adherence to the rest of the law if the celebration will amount to more than just dates and fun. To only have dates and fun dismisses all the endeared lessons projected by these feasts. The biblical instructions for Messianics who wish to keep the feasts as originally intended are as follows:

The Passover (Heb. *Pesach*) was celebrated in the first month of the religious year. On the fourteenth day (daylight) before the evening drew nigh, all leavened materials were removed from the houses, including beers, wines, and sodas. On the same day, preparation of the unleavened bread (Heb. *matzot*) begins. At the end of the fourteenth day at sunset or shortly thereafter, a festive meal and the unleavened bread were consumed at one's private abode or in a small setting. Of the seven-day feast of unleavened bread, the first day must be celebrated as an attenuated Sabbath, likewise the seventh day. No leaven is to be present in the houses or in one's possession during these seven days. The family gathers together to celebrate this feast. If a nonbeliever is present, it must be made known that he may opt-out of the emblematic feast (Ex. 12).

On the next day after the seventh-day Sabbath, as a token of appreciation of the harvest gift, a meal-offering of the believer's firstfruits must be taken to the elders of his congregation before having breakfast. Most biblical authorities teach that the morrow after the feast Sabbath is the day referred to, the sixteenth of the month. However, since the Sabbath referred to by the scripture is the regular seventh-day Sabbath, Sunday is the time of the firstfruits' presentation. The elders will wave the gift before the Lord, the wave sheaf presentation (Heb. *Omer Noof,* Lev. 23:9–14). From Sunday, seven weeks are to be calculated to the Sunday after the last Sabbath for the fifty days of Pentecost (feast of weeks, Heb. *Shavuot,* Lev. 23:15–22). The Sunday after the last Sabbath will be made a non-servile Sabbath day. Two leavened loaves should be baked for this feast, and a modest offering brought to the elders for the goodness of the Lord (Ex. 34:22). That is the presentation of the wave loaves (Heb. *Lechem Noof*). These are the mandates for the spring festivals if we are to celebrate them with minimal instruction.

Very similar instructions are binding for the fall feasts (see Lev. 23:24). On the Feast of Trumpets (Heb. *shofar*), a meal offering by fire must be presented to the elders. That happens on the first day of the seventh month (beginning civil New Year, Heb. *Rosh Hashanah*). That day must also be celebrated as a non-servile Sabbath. Trumpets must be blown.

On the tenth day of this month is a feast of fasting and prayer for the Day of Atonement (*Yom Kippur*). It is the day of the Fast (Acts 27:9), day of the affliction of one's soul because the atonement is made on that day. It is the Day of Reconciliation. This day is a solemn seventh day–like Sabbath. It is a convocational day given solely to prayer; on this holiest day of Israel's year, worshipers must refrain from personal pleasures.

The Feast of Tabernacles (Heb. *Sukkot,* see Lev. 23:39–43; Neh. 8:15–18) is celebrated for eight days. During this time, Israel restrained from conveniences of regular abode to dwell in tents. That was a time of reflection on God's goodness and for bringing the convenience of daily comfort under the subjection of more challenging conditions. From the fifteenth to the twenty-second day of the month is camping out of one's dwelling place in a primitive setting. I had the privilege of sitting and discussing with some independent Messianic Hebrew Israelites who celebrate the feast this way. This state of affair can be best understood in the aftermath of a natural disaster. The first and the eighth days of this camping are Sabbaths. Those days are for solemn assemblies. Every person that is of the faith shall dwell in tents. Meal offerings must be brought to the elders.

In the absence of these minimal instructions, the feast day requirements are not accurately reflected. Sure! All these practices are rituals. To give an apparent authenticity, strict feast practitioners should observe the aforementioned ordinances as described. Indeed, the feasts were fulfilled in Jesus, and except for the feast commanded in His remembrance, the requirement to celebrate them may be optional while Israel is among the Gentiles. This is not to say that the feasts must not be celebrated if moderate improvising is adopted. Though the rest of the feasts may have no salvific implications, in the light of Judeo-Israelite cultural practice, it is preferable that we celebrate the feasts with some extemporization instead of pagan holidays. The truth is, these feasts, in their modifications, are better celebrated as a nation when God's people are in the Holy Land.

Chapter 2

Azazel and the Cross

Judeo-Christian Feast Celebration

As Israel had been instructed to celebrate the feasts in commemoration of their salvific experiences, Christians celebrate the feasts to commemorate Jesus's sacrifice. The Christian Passover, commonly called communion, memorializes the death of Jesus. Christians memorialize this time with Christ-centered rituals practiced as chronicled in the scriptures. Jesus' death fulfilled the Day of Atonement and Passover between the fifteenth and the eighteenth day in the month of Abib. The celebration signifies the Lord's sufferings, His broken body, and the removal of sins as an anniversary feast of salvation. From the fifteenth to the eighteenth day of the month Abib in AD 33 or 31 per chronicle tabulation, Jesus suffered and died for us. Because this event represents sanctification, the feet-washing ordinance of humility was added.

> Peter saith unto him, thou shalt never wash my feet.
> Jesus answered him, If I wash thee not, thou halth no

part with me... If I then, your Lord and Master, have washed your feet; ye also ought to wash one another's feet. For I have given you an example, that *ye should do as I have done* to you (John 13:8, 14-15).

If agreed that this added ritual should not be practiced owing to its symbolical representation, it should also be accepted that the same rule applies to the bread and the wine, seeing that they are likewise symbolic. The fact is, all the Lord's Supper rituals are symbolic. Our practice of the supper should be scripturally legal and personal. Much needed reformation should take place along this line. God is looking for legitimacy in our practice of the Lord's Supper. The Spirit works in us the willingness to follow the biblical prescription.

Numerous errors have been advanced creating an illusion about the Lord's supper. Instead of celebrating the feast as a supper, most people celebrate it in the morning or shortly after noon. Early Christians celebrated the Lord's Supper not as an afternoon meal or breakfast but in the evening; consequently, it has been called the Lord's Supper. The question becomes, is increasing the frequency of the ritual directly proportional to our relationship with the Lord? After Judas took the feast unworthily, Satan entered into him. Thus, it is illustrated that the supper was not designed to augment one's spirituality but to serve as a proclamation of a historical event. Since the feast is a memorial and a symbolic formality, it is celebrated annually. The Jewish sacred year commences around the time of the vernal equinox. Following the first full moon after the vernal equinox, the fifteenth day was the anniversary when our Lord celebrated His last supper. He was captured for trial at that time, which resulted in His being crucified on a tree. This night of capture and trial is celebrated in remembrance of His suffering and death. In light of these facts, there is a need to return to the Lord's Supper's true practice.

The symbolic ritual of Passover and the Day of Atonement has real meaning to the work Jesus did to save the world. They also have a profound connotation for the ancient Israelites. Jesus said that the bread represents His broken body. The unleavened bread typifies the purity of faith in Jesus's life and his disdain for sin. In ancient times, unleavened bread denoted the abruptness and hastiness in Israel's departure from Egypt (Deut. 16:3). This characterizes our immediate response in receiving salvation. The drinking of the wine epitomized the shedding of Jesus's blood. The foot-washing symbolizes the outcome of Jesus's sacrifice, which is our justification and sanctification. The slight conversions Jesus made to the celebration were not to change the time but to memorialize his final week in exchange for the departure from Egypt. God prefigured that the anniversary of the four days it took the children of Israel to leave Egypt would be the length of time of Jesus's sufferings, death, and resurrection. The story is beautifully illustrated in Exodus 12 and 13.

Antitypical Fall Festival Applications

According to Hebrews 9, Jesus fulfilled the ancient Day of Atonement rituals at Passover's time (Rom. 3:25, 5:11; 2 Cor. 5:19). The fall fasting festival was the most important and holiest festival of Israel's year. It coincides with the most important festival of Christian celebrations, the Christian Passover. To the Christian, Passover is a day of holy convocation. Although feast Sabbaths and fasting can be optional in the Christian celebration, there can be a non-servile Sabbath for Christians. The semi-Sabbath can be used for preparing the feast. This time reflects on the Day of Atonement which commemorates the actual removal of sins from the people of God (1 John 2:2, 4:10). As seen in verses 16 and 17 of John 3, atonement symbolizes forgiveness, reconciliation, and judgment. That day is a unique time for contemplation on the death of Christ. On the fifteenth day, a Sabbath is to be observed as a memorial of Jesus's suffering and death. As the scriptures declared, it is a time of introspection (1 Cor. 11:26–30). As Israel was required to do soul-searching for the Passover and Day of Atonement, Christians likewise should do the same. Since the New Testament lacks new delineations for celebrating the rest of the feasts, we can simultaneously observe these two feasts. The meaning of the two feasts and application are the same for those who wish to celebrate them separately. Anciently, the purpose of fasting was to accompany the process of reconciliation officiated by the Priest. From people to the priest, the whole process was about alignment.

Back in Egypt, the Passover and the Day of Atonement were essentially the same. Originally, they took place in the spring. The killing of the Passover lamb and the death of the firstborn in Egypt represents atonement and judgment. Remember, there was an investigation to remove leaven from the camp. That was a form of judgment. When the Passover took place, the people of God were "covered" or were passed over (atoned for by blood) to protect them from death (judgment).

In the typical sanctuary, the work of salvation was split in two. Since God wanted the service to represent the life of Jesus (the law) and the removal of sin, two festivals were instituted. These two timely festivals represented two events, namely the life of Jesus covering us with His life, and by His death the removal of sins. Remember, Jesus became sin for us (2 Cor. 5:21). Through His death, our sins were removed and vanished. The spring festival, like a canopy, represented a protective covering from sin. The Day of Atonement, in the fall, is for Christ's death on the cross through which He removed sins from His people. In the original setting, Egypt and its army represented sin. Symbolically, the Israelites were separated from sin at the death of the Egyptian army. Thus, the original spring event is represented by two festivals: spring Passover and fall Day of Atonement.

In illustrating this removal on the Day of Atonement, two goats were used—the Lord's goat and the scapegoat. In Hebrew, the scapegoat was called "aw-zazel," literally meaning "goat of removal." As a verb, the term can also mean to leave, forsake, or to lose (Whitaker, Brown, Driver, Briggs, Charles, 1997). Traditionally, the goat was taken to the wilderness and pushed off a precipice to its death (Lev.16:7–10, 15–16, 20–22, 34). This entire system of sacrifices was to last until the time of reformation (Heb. 9:10) spoken of in the following:

> Nor yet that he should offer himself often, as the high priest enters into the [most] holy place every year with blood of others; For then must he often have suffered since the foundation of the world: but now once in the end of the world hath he appeared to put away [removal] sin by the sacrifice of himself [the death of Christ] (Heb. 9:25–26).

This scripture states verbatim that Jesus's death is represented by the annual work of the high priest on the Day of Atonement.

Jesus is drawing us to him by the intervention of His Spirit (Eph. 4:12–17, 5:26–27; John 16:7–11).

Do the fall feasts represent works done at the end of this present world? As stated in the text in Hebrews 9, the end of the world is at the end of the Jewish sacrificial system, when sins were put away by the shedding of Jesus's blood. However, the complete eradication of sin in the people's daily lives by the anointing, as a latter component, is yet to finish its course. That will be a secondary, latter representation of the Day of Atonement. Through the centuries, this part has only been taking place partially. Thus, the antitypical Day of Atonement and the Feast of Tabernacle, which stretches back over two thousand years, embraces this church-wide latter component. The latter component is accomplished through the medium of the Holy Spirit in the life of the believer.

Jesus also fulfilled the Feast of Tabernacles as Immanuel. Additionally, the Father, through the Holy Spirit, made His abode (feast of Sukkot) with Jesus on earth. The latter-day component is when God dwells in us, and the church reflects God's perfect peace. The nations will be called to behold it, to celebrate the Feast of Tabernacles. They will behold it like the disciples beheld Jesus on the mount of transfiguration, prefiguring the latter-day feast of tabernacles (Matt. 17:1–17). Representatives of the nations will be taught how to live rather than how to celebrate with physical food.

The primary application of the fall feasts applies in the antitypical spring event. The fall feasts are shadows of the spring feasts. This way, the feasts will be shadows of Jesus, who they prefigured. Passover and the Day of Atonement can be celebrated together because they point to the same event, proving that both spring and the fall feasts point to one event—Jesus, the Messiah. We can celebrate the Feast of Trumpets in thankfulness to God for another New Year cycle in messianic faith. It also prefigured the last period of judgment. As we approach the time of executive judgment on the nations, we must sound the alarm to them. Although there is no New Testament protocol for celebrating most of the feasts; however, they should not be observed with the object of collecting money, as some churches do, but to spend monetary resources collected for recognizing them. Those of Judean Israelite roots should keep the feasts as a cultural mode of remembering their heritage.

Celebrating Pentecost is not as restrictive as was anciently since we are living in Pentecost. However, the focus for commemorating the day should be on giving the Ten Commandments and the gift of the Holy Spirit, who writes these laws in our hearts. The Spirit and the law were given on the day recognized as Pentecost. Christ in us through His Spirit is a continuous Feast of Pentecost. We can keep this feast by engaging in soul-winning for the Lord. That is what happened when the disciples received the Spirit on that day. One who complies with spiritual Pentecost receives a spiritual gift for ministering to those who are out of the church, and those who are immature in the faith. The gifts of the Spirit are mentioned in 1 Corinthians 12. We are not instructed how to celebrate ritualistic Pentecost anew. Christian ritualistic celebration of these feasts is done without observance of Sabbath days and respect to drinks and meats, only a timely celebration of the event in its relation to the messianic life of Jesus.

Chapter 3

⸺◦◦◦◦⸺

Christians and Legalism

Does God Require Rituals?

Does God want his people to fall prey to ritualistic festivals, as did the children of Israel? When Israel made a show of praises without an actual conversion of the soul, God responded with disdain upon the unwelcome service.

> I hate, I despise your feasts, and I will take no delight in your solemn assemblies. Yea, though ye offer me your burnt-offerings and meal-offerings, I will not accept them; neither will I regard the peace-offerings of your fat beasts. Take thou away from me the noise of thy songs; for I will not hear the melody of thy viols. But let justice roll down as waters, and righteousness as a mighty stream.-- Amos 5:21-24. cf. Psalms 50:7-23; Hosea 2:11.

The God we serve wants complete control over our lives, but this must be done entirely voluntarily. He wants our service and humility to serve His will. That is the only freedom that exists, to live within the joyful peace of the life-giver. This life can be ours only if our will is sacrificed for God through eternal commitment.

The ancient requirements for celebrating the feasts were for having a jubilant day and being educated by the rituals practiced. Christians who are mature in Jesus need not have the elements of rituals to teach them. However, some rituals (legal code) for Christians are authenticated and required from both the Old and New Testaments. The rituals serve for a proclamation to the world of God's requirements. Christians must not think all legal codes are abolished, and all structure and order are removed. Since the law is written in the heart, the rationale for the rituals are an open proclamation of work done internally.

One of the important festivals is the Feast of Tabernacles. This feast also represents the last great ingathering. This last ingathering is yet to occur (Zech. 14:16–19). Much of what can be said about this feast is beyond the scope of this book. When we are to keep this feast, new delineations will be given by the Lord. It will be celebrated after the last great ingathering has begun. Surely, as we are approaching the last harvest, it would be advantageous for the church to assemble on the original timing, to discuss and celebrate the meaning of this feast. Some aspects of the feasts were not meant to be celebrated while in captivity. The time will come when we will celebrate the Feast of Tabernacles anew.

Lessons on Christian Celebration

Although we know that the early church engaged in Passover and Pentecost, we have no New Testament delineation that they celebrated anything else. Remember, Paul fell short of encouraging the believers to accompany him to celebrate the feast with the Jews (Act 18:21). Scripture shows the feasts as shadows of events that reside in Christ. A shadow exists in partial obstruction of light. Once the light permeates the whole, the shadow disappears. Concerning the feasts, the scriptures state: "Let no man, therefore, judge [decide for] you in eating, or in drinking, or with respect to a feast day or a new moon or a Sabbath day [or Sabbath], which are a shadow of the things to come; but the body [the substance or reality of them] is Jesus" (Col. 2:16–17).

> So we also, when we were children, were held in bondage under the elemental principles of the world... However, at that time, not knowing God, you were in bondage to those who by nature are not gods. But now that you have come to know God, or rather to be known by God, why do you turn back again to the weak and miserable elemental principles, to which you desire to be in bondage all over again? You observe days, months, seasons, and years. I am afraid for you that I might have wasted my labor for you. -- Gal 4:3, 8-11.

In no uncertain terms, Paul said to the Jews that one should not judge another about the use of seasonal celebrations and not to celebrate holidays associated with foreign religions (2 Kings 21:6). To the Gentiles Christians, he commanded them to cease pagan holidays. The Christian feast is the life of the Messiah. If we fully believe in the Messiah, there will be no obligation to certain aspects of the ancient feast. Although it is lawful to celebrate the feasts' cultural aspect as Judean-Israelite heritage, the constraint of obligation for strict adherence to all the feasts' vernacular loses their application as we are scattered and lost among the nations. We must preach the gospel to Israel so that they may believe through the Spirit. When the gospel is preached free of the ancient sacrificial elements, the Spirit will do his work on prospective hearts.

While Peter was given to Judean ministry, Paul's was for the Gentiles, yet both men were known to mingle with Jews and Gentiles (Gal. 2:7, 8). There are some complications as to how Paul addressed the matter with Peter and the group. We will not look at the complexity at this time. Paul confronted Peter's hypocrisy (Gal. 2:11). By separating himself from the Gentiles that he may identify with the Jews, Peter had effectively parted from the truth (Gal. 2:13–14). Peter did not live according to the Gentiles but felt obligated at times to abide by Gentiles' customs and compelled others to follow suit. When the Judean zealots appeared, in fear, he swapped position (Gal. 2:14). Many Judean brethren who were with him were bamboozled into this trap (Gal. 2:13). While not living up to his principles to which he tries to convert another, Peter set the wrong example. That is an example of doing God's work by one's force and power (Zec. 4:6).

According to verse 19 of chapter 3, the law to which Paul refers is the sacrificial system and other symbolical laws. These laws were schoolmasters to bring us to the time of Christ. In chapter four, Paul gave examples of the lesson he taught in chapter three (Gal. 4:2, 22). In chapter five, he continues to say that Messianics are free from those elementary practices, including circumcision (Gal. 5:1–5). In this same chapter, he cautioned those who would misconstrue his words to create a license for immoral and unlawful behavior (vs. 13–26).

There are untenable reasons for feast celebrations. For some, it is to be holier. For others, it is to make another holier. Yet other's purpose is to keep young people from celebrating pagan holidays. Pagan holidays include Halloween, Easter, Christmas, birthdays, and Thanksgiving. As for the pagan holidays, it is not recommended that enlightened Christians get involved. Instead, Christians should have a yearly festival of Jesus's Passover. As more social gatherings are needed, we should accommodate other biblical feasts. Many religious leaders invent social exercises to keep their congregation from going off track. Such inventions are evidence of an underlying problem that cannot be solved by the undertaking. We should preach the gospel and set the right example with love (Matt. 5:16; Eph. 4:12, 13). More prayer sessions for more power over temptation and for a correct understanding of God's expectations are great strategies. Wouldn't that be a better way to increase Christian power? We celebrate the feasts for educational purposes. The Feasts times should be used to study the prophetic lessons associated with them.

The terms Easter and Passover need a bit of clarification. According to history, the only scriptural Sunday services are those immediately after Passover of the fifteenth day. Those Sundays were not meant to be regular service times. Israel celebrated that day for Wave Sheaf purposes. Biblically, it was not a regular day for convocation, but the temple doors were open for people to bring gifts and offerings to the priest. There was no weekly Sunday worship with the apostles. After the apostolic times, the church leaders celebrated Passover at the appointed time of Judean Passover.

The Gentile Christian churches, raised by Paul, eventually came into Passover controversy with the Judean Christians who were habituated with Peter. According to the historian Neander, the churches raised by St. Paul celebrated no feast days whatsoever. In concert with Polycarp, the churches of Asia minor observed the Passover according to Johannean tradition. As the controversies brewed between the two camps, an appeal was made to apostle John to authorized that the feasts must be celebrated strictly according to Judean chronology. Said Neander of John:

> As it regards him, it is in itself probable, that as he had been accustomed heretofore to celebrate the Jewish annual Festival, and as the feast of the Passover, which called to mind the great facts of which he had been an eyewitness, must have had a peculiar significancy for him, he may have introduced its celebration when he took up his permanent residence among the churches of that region. Thus it is explained how it happened that men were guided there wholly by the chronology of the Jewish Passover (Neander & Terrey, 1853, p. 297).

Athanasius, a Negroid church leader responsible for authorizing the New Testament books, adhered to this apostolic practice of celebration two hundred years later. "Easter," as a term, was used to represent the resurrection because Christ rose early on Sunday morning, a time used by the pagans to worship Easter, the pagan goddess of fertility. Easter is a pagan term. The church celebrated the resurrection at the time of Passover, the fifteenth day of the first month of the Judean religious calendar. Granted that the resurrection occurred at the approximate time the heathen celebrated Easter, some ventured to associate the resurrection with pagan Easter celebration. The group of Christians who waited on Sunday to celebrate the resurrection were more into Easter and resurrection celebration than Passover. The church after the apostles were struggling to maintain Judean apostolic tradition as seen in the following.

When *should we celebrate Easter?* Believers who lived in the eastern regions of the Roman Empire -including Polycarp, who tried to convince Marcion to change his mind celebrated the resurrection of Jesus *during* the Jewish Passover. In the western Empire, Christians waited until the Sunday *after* Passover to celebrate the resurrection. Both groups celebrated Easter with the ancient equivalent of a potluck dinner. So, each spring, some Christians found themselves feasting while others were fasting.

Thirty years after Polycarp visited Rome, the Easter dispute arose again. Victor was the new Roman overseer. At Victor's request, churches around Jerusalem began to observe the Roman pattern, but other eastern Christians kept following their earlier customs. In a letter to Victor, another leader in the eastern churches insisted that the apostles Philip and John had followed the eastern custom of celebrating Easter during the Jewish Passover. Still, Victor refused to back down. From his viewpoint, God had cursed the eastern churches. After Victor's death, most Christians ignored his rejection of the eastern churches. Today, churches whose heritage is rooted in the eastern Roman Empire still celebrate Easter during the Jewish Passover (Jones, 2009, p. 29).

The gospel's emphasis is on the suffering and death of Christ. However, it should be clear to all now as then that the Passover or Easter celebration was an annual event in the Judeo-Christian sense. It was never whenever you want to partake, but rather whenever you are partaking of it. The Wave-sheaf celebration, in the Christian perspective, is all-inclusive in the Passover celebration. Everything related to the death and resurrection of Jesus was celebrated at the appointed time of Passover.

Understanding Types and Shadows

The Day of Atonement and the Feast of Tabernacles have many extended applications for the last days. The atoning sacrifice of Christ fulfilled the Day of Atonement. This day also represents a separation of Christians from non-Christians (Ps. 1:5; John 16:8). The church, having fled from persecution from the Holy Roman Empire, leaving the large cities and finding themselves in groups in the wilderness, is typified by the Feast of Tabernacles. This escape from persecution will not eclipse a more elaborate fulfillment in the closing of earth's history (Zech. 14).

The Feast of Tabernacles typified Christ's life. Jesus said that foxes have holes and birds have nests, but the Son of Man has nowhere to lay his head. Dating the birth of Jesus by counting backward from the crucifixion, it is estimated that he was born in the month of the Feast of Tabernacles. This same time can be derived when considering the announcement of John the Baptist's birth. A detailed explanation of this can be found in the book *Christmas Catechism* (Richards, 1953). Jesus came to dwell among us at the time of the Feast of Tabernacles (John 1). The whole premise of the Feast of Tabernacles was for God to live in man through his Spirit.

Passover is celebrated anew to remind Christians of Christ's week of passion and that we have accepted the blood of Jesus at the new birth experience. The Feast of Trumpets celebration was typical of the announcement of the Messiah's coming by John the Baptist's preaching. They were all shadows of things to come (cf. Appendix B).

In Numbers 28 and 29, details for Leviticus 23:4–39 are presented. Enlightened Christians do not teach observance of the ordinances laid down in Numbers 28 or 29. These chapters explain the type of Christ who was to come. These ordinances are what Paul presented in Colossians 2:16, 17. However, in Numbers 28:9, 10, a special offering for the Sabbath is mentioned. This reference to the Sabbath is not an instruction to keep the seventh-day Sabbath holy but rather to offer the proper atonement for that occasion. The focus was atonement, thus separating the object, the Sabbath, from the subject, the sacrificial system. Based on context, the Sabbath mentioned in Colossians 2:16, though in the singular form, does not include the Sabbath in the Ten Commandments. It does not embrace all Sabbaths. The Sabbath of the Ten Commandments existed before sin and is said to be a holy physical rest. It is written as one of the Ten Commandments. The Sabbath mentioned in Colossians was given after sin entered the world. Those Sabbaths are associated with lunar holy days. Although lunar timing and gatherings are mentioned in Genesis 1:14, specific times and purposes were not given until after man's fall.

Shadows are not of the light, but they are unclear negatives of the light. To be precise, a shadow is antilight and predicts a version of the light. If the light is omnipresent, there will be no shadows to observe. The woman in Revelation 12, who is clothed with the light, has no shadow. Her entire being is beaming with light. This is the case of those who are clothed with the Spirit of Jesus. Considering Colossians 2:16, some say Paul was speaking concerning the austere lifestyle of the ascetic Jews. Paul warned the ascetic Jews of practicing their man-made restrictions. The scripture states that the festival days are, at least in part, shadows that found their fulfillment in Christ.

New Testament Feast Keeping

There has been some interest among Christians concerning the ancient feasts of Israel. Some believe that we should be keeping the feasts that ancient Israel kept. Are we in the position to keep the feasts the way Israel kept them? As we have seen, Israel was not always in the condition to keep the feast days even when it was a law for them to do so. When they kept the feasts in conditions undesired by God, he asked them to desist. As previously stated, the feasts are kept as a memorial. Ancient Israel had its memorials, so do Christians have Jesus Christ, whose presence is represented by the feasts.

Care must be taken not to acquire an unsubstantiated view. In Acts of the Apostles, very few scriptures mention the ancient feasts. Among them are Acts 18:21, 20:6, 16, 27:9, and 1 Corinthians 16:8. These scriptures are not justification for ancient feast keeping. Paul not asking the disciples to keep the feasts, and in some cases departing from them to be with the Jews at the time of the feasts, speak volumes to the fact that the Pauline Gentile disciples may not have celebrated the feasts. The following is a probable explanation of why Paul kept the feast with the Jews.

For though I be free from all men, yet have I made myself servant unto all, that I might gain the more. And unto the Jews I became as a Jew, that I might gain the Jews; to them that are under the law, as under the law, that I might gain them that are under the law; To them that are without law, as without law, (being not without law to God, but under the law to Christ,) that I might gain them that are without law. To the weak became I as weak, that I might gain the weak: I am made all things to all men, that I might, by all means, save some. And this I do for the gospel's sake, that I might be partaker thereof with you (1Cor. 9:19-23).

Do therefore this that we say to thee: We have four men who have a vow on them; Them take, and purify thyself with them, and be at charges with them, that they may shave their heads: and all may know that those things, whereof they were informed concerning thee, are nothing; but that thou thyself also walkest orderly, and keepest the law. As touching the Gentiles which believe, we have written and concluded that they observe no such thing, save only that they keep themselves from things offered to idols, and from blood, and from strangled, and from fornication. Then Paul took the men, and the next day purifying himself with them entered into the temple, to signify the accomplishment of the days of purification, until that an offering should be offered for every one of them (Acts 21:23-26).

Paul used conciliatory measures, disguising himself in Judean customs, obscuring his nonconformity to accomplish his mission. Should you continue to read the passage, you will discover that the concealment did not avail of his expectation.

Let Us Keep the Feast

Individually and corporately, Paul spoke of service done for God in hypocrisy (1 Cor. 5). Here, he refers to those services as leavened feasts. He wanted us to understand that Christian living is patterned after Christ, the true unleavened bread from heaven. Our lives should be mature in faith, spiritually represented by the Feast of Unleavened Bread. Unleavened and pure, the wine symbolizes the life of Jesus, poured out for our justification. When Christians keep this feast spiritually, they will not thirst for the presence of the Holy Spirit. Therefore, Paul said, let us keep the feast of sincerity and truth. Feast of sincerity refers to the spiritual feast. This spiritual feast is not said to eclipse a modified ancient feast celebration.

The church has forged doctrines that are AWOL from the scriptures (Matt. 24:45). Sometimes we let religious traditions rise above the holy scriptures; unfortunately, this has caused splinters in the church. However, if the focus is on the way, the truth, and the life, we will be harmonious co-workers with Christ.

Chapter 4

===○○○===

Memorial

Days of Jesus's Trials

Alterations to the Lord's Supper

The Lord's Supper is to be done in biblical alignment. When I became a Christian many years ago, I had no concern about the Lord's supper ritual. Like many of us, this was not my priority in early Christian development. Many doctrinal issues don't seem to matter in the infancy stage while trying to get a stronghold in the Christian faith. But as I grew, I began to question some of the things that were taught. I sought and asked for a standard and wanted to be motivated in the right direction. Christians do not ask how little they can do to align with God's will, but what will God have them do. At this point in our walk, we seek clarity and the way of the Master.

Some think that Christ reinvented everything to do with the Passover celebration. There is no question that Passover is an annual celebration. Jesus and the apostles celebrated it annually. Christ, referring to the Passover, told his disciples, "Do this in remembrance of me." To make people holier or to sell indulgences, many churchgoers have increased the frequency of the ritual. Instead of celebrating Passover in the light of the Lord's Supper, some have held Sunday services in commemoration of the resurrection. Celebrating the resurrection by a weekly day of worship is a church tradition for alignment with sun worship and Easter. We are told to celebrate the sufferings and the death of Christ. We are to celebrate the deliverance that springs from the blood spilled and the victory arose from the torment endured. By changing the Passover stipulations, the true intent and affect have not been satisfied.

In our defense, we use the scripture for support. "For as often as ye eat this bread, and drink this cup, ye do show the Lord's death till he comes" (1 Cor. 11:26). Two things are evident in this scripture: scripture did not say we ought to commemorate Christ's resurrection but his death! And the scripture is not saying how often we should celebrate the feast, but instead, whenever we are engaged in it, be cognizant of its premise. Its comprehension is not problematic, but when pledged to pioneers who made missteps, we tend to see the scriptures in an uncanny way rather than the natural, scriptural manner the event occurred. Being conditioned by tradition, our minds are likely to perceive a cloudy view of the original.

The Biblical Lord's Supper

When Paul traveled to the church in Corinth, he heard some reports about delinquency at the Lord's Passover feast. Paul was appalled by the rude manner the Lord's Supper was handled, so he addressed the immaturity that existed among the believers.

> For I received from the Lord that which also I delivered to you, that the Lord Jesus on the night in which he was betrayed took bread. (24) When he had given thanks, he broke it, and said, `Take, eat. This is my body, which is broken for you. Do this in memory of me.' (25) In the same way, he also took the cup, after supper, saying, `This cup is the new covenant in my blood. Do this, as often as you drink, in memory of me.' (26) For as often as you eat this bread and drink this cup, you proclaim the Lord's death until he comes. (27) Therefore, whoever eats this bread or drinks the Lord's cup in a manner unworthy of the Lord will be guilty of the body and the blood of the Lord. (28) But let a man examine himself, and so let him eat of the bread, and drink of the cup. For he who eats and drinks in an unworthy manner eats and drinks judgment to himself if he doesn't discern the Lord's body. For this cause many among you are weak and sickly, and not a few sleep. -- 1 Corinthians 11:23-30.

Another factor in the celebration is the customary meal offering. It was part of Israel's celebration that the Passover meal is eaten. This meal included a lamb, bread, bitter herbs, and a drink offering. The arrangement was known as the Seder or order that included the Haggadah, telling the deliverance story. Questions that were generally asked by children that night were: Why is this night different from all the other nights? Why do we eat bitter herbs? Why do we eat unleavened bread? The presider gave answers: this is the night of deliverance; the bread of affliction is baked in haste to leave the bitter bondage of slavery. The service was done in a particular order. The Festival of Matzoth is synonymous with the Feast of Unleavened Bread. The purpose was to celebrate the time of our freedom, which began the night of the Passover. This biblical tradition continued with the disciples. The exception is that a lamb was no longer served after Jesus died because Jesus replaced the sacrifices. When Jesus said, "With desire, I have desired to eat this Passover with you before I suffer" (Luke 22:15), he intended the celebration to be a way of comfort and spiritual strength for the events that were to follow. While enjoying the Passover meal with them, "Jesus took bread, and blessed it, and brake it, and gave it to the disciples, and said, Take, eat; this is my body" (Matt. 26:26; Mark 14:22). That indicates two meal services on the same night, one after the other. The first one was Passover, and the second was the New Passover emblem served by the Lord. According to John, after the first meal was served, there was a foot-washing intervention (John 13). These procedural inclusions conclude the basic service for the Christian festival.

As we have seen, there are two parts to the Lord's Supper. The disciples continued to celebrate the Lord's Supper with a potluck and by the emblem. The potluck was for festive purposes. The emblem represented the events of Jesus's trial and death. In the Christian sense, there is no Seder for the festive portion. However, there is a Seder for the emblematic portion. Paul, warning the Corinthians about the misuse of the festive portion of the feast, said:

> For in eating every one taketh before other his own supper: and one is hungry, and another is drunken. What? have ye not houses to eat and to drink in? or

despise ye the church of God, and shame them that have
not? What shall I say to you? shall I praise you in this?
I praise you not" (1 Cor. 11:21–22).

There is absolutely no question that this was supper and lots
of food was present. There were no meat offerings per se, but
rather it was a festive celebration. What have we done with this
festive celebration today?

On the night Jesus was betrayed, he celebrated the Passover.
He took bread and broke it, prayed, and said to his disciples,
"This is my body which is broken for you." Then he took the cup
in the like manner after they had eaten and said: "This is the new
covenant my blood … this is my blood poured out for you" (Luke
22:20). When these statements were made originally, Christ's
body had not yet been broken, and his blood had not yet been
poured out. When he said, "This is my body" and "This is my
blood," he could never have meant his literal body. Then he said,
"Do this in remembrance of me." "In remembrance" means not
in reality but a psychological panorama of the historical event.

We must understand and practice the Lord's Supper as
closely to the original instruction as possible. A person must be
sanctified, converted, or in terms of old Passover, "circumcised"
before partaking in the event. Each partaker's responsibility is
self-examination for compliance before taking the emblem. The
Lord's Supper does not increase one's spirituality any more than
baptism. They are both symbols of recollection. While baptism
celebrates the Lord's resurrection, the supper celebrates His
death. Paul's expression about Jesus's week of the trial was
chronological. "The same night" in the scripture indicates a
time of memorial that is the beginning of His sufferings for us.
His breaking of the bread is indicative of His intense sufferings

beginning with His arrest in that fateful last week. When we partake of the emblem, we memorialize the entire series of events from his arrest to His death. This memorandum is the responsibility of those who are entirely sanctified.

The Time Jesus Celebrated Passover

Does it make a difference when Passover is celebrated? After all, it is a ritual. Some believe that the supper should be celebrated on the day Jesus died; others, on the day it was originally appointed, and still others, on the annual date, He ate with His disciples. The question to ask is: Did Jesus partake of the Passover on the same day as did the Jews? To understand the scriptures about this question, we need to know that the terms "Passover" and "unleavened bread" were used interchangeably. In the New Testament, we can only differentiate them by the context rather than stand-alone words.

The Lord's Supper was timely. "Now before the feast of the Passover, when Jesus knew that his hour came that he should depart out of this world unto the Father, having loved his own which were in the world, he loved them unto the end" (John 13:1). Before the feast of the Passover, Jesus knew that His time had come to depart from this world. His contemplation was on His trial and love for the disciples. Unlike the other gospels, John did not mention the disciples' preparation but emphasized lessons on humility. The preparation for the Passover is before the feast of the Passover. The feast day of Passover happens at the beginning of the fifteenth day, the evening at the end of the fourteenth day. This fourteenth day is the fourth day from the eleventh day, which is called Palm Sunday. Since Israel could not have gathered Passover lambs on the Sabbath day, the gathering took place on either the ninth or the eleventh day of that year. Palm Sunday is known as the day of Christ's triumphant entry into Jerusalem when palm branches were laid before Him (Matt. 21). Israel was to hold their lambs from the tenth day to the fourteenth day. The lamb was to bond with the family and be cared for before it was killed. The phrase "Before the feast" mentioned in John 13:1 was when they were preparing for the Passover as declared in the other gospels.

"Jesus... six days before the Passover came to Bethany, where Lazarus was which had been dead, whom he raised from the dead" (John 12:1). Jesus was in Bethany on a Friday and had supper. "On the next day much people that were come to the feast, when they heard that Jesus was coming to Jerusalem" (John 12:12). Many people heard about Christ coming to the feast. They came to Jerusalem on the Sabbath or on a Sunday to meet Jesus. On Sunday, they "took branches of palm trees, and went forth to meet him, and cried, Hosanna: Blessed is the King of Israel that cometh in the name of the Lord" (John 12:13).

> Now the feast of unleavened bread drew nigh, which is called the Passover. The day of unleavened bread came, on which the Passover must be sacrificed (Luke. 22:1, 7). On the first day of unleavened bread, when they [Jewish Nation] sacrificed the Passover, his disciples asked him, 'Where do you want us to go and make ready that you may eat the Passover?' (Mark 14:12).

Events Before Passover   Six days before the Passover Jesus ...

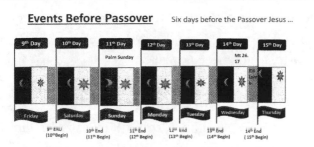

Jesus, six days before the Passover came to Bethany (John 12:1)

On the next day much people that were come to the feast; (John 12:12, Matt. 20:17-18)

They took palm branches and went forth to meet him (Matt. 21:1-11, John 12:13)

Events before the Passover

Anciently, the Passover meal was eaten on the first day of the Feast of Unleavened Bread, at the end of the fourteenth day.

In the first month, on the fourteenth day of the month in the evening, is The Lord's Passover (Lev 23:5). And ye shall keep it [lamb] up until the fourteenth day of the same month: and the whole assembly of the congregation of Israel shall kill it in the evening (Ex 12:6). They kept the Passover in the first month, on the fourteenth day of the month, at evening, in the wilderness of Sinai. According to all that the Lord commanded Moses, so the children of Israel did (Num. 9:5). *In the first month, on the fourteenth day of the month at evening, you shall eat unleavened bread, until the twenty-first day of the month at evening (Exodus 12:18). Seven days shall there be no yeast found in your houses,* for whoever eats that which is leavened, that soul shall be cut off from the congregation of Israel, whether he be a foreigner or one who is born in the land (Exodus 12:19). Moses said to the people,

> `Remember this day, in which you came out from Egypt, out of the house of bondage; for by strength of hand the Lord brought you out from this place. No leavened bread shall be eaten. (Exodus 13:3, Italics added).

Cloud-free, in no uncertain terms, the Passover lamb was killed at about sunset, near the end of the fourteenth day of the first month, and it was eaten at night, which began the new day. Exodus 12:18 teaches us how the days were counted and when the counting starts. When the scripture states, "The fourteenth day in the evening," it certainly meant starting from the beginning of the fifteenth day arriving on the twenty-first day for a total of seven days. Both the Passover and Feast of Unleavened Bread were celebrated together in the same meal and on the same days (Deut. 16:3; Ezek. 45:21–23). Furthermore, although the Passover lamb was killed on the fourteenth day in the evening, it is equivalently characterized by different lambs killed each day for the remaining six days.

Consequently, Christ did not have to die on the fourteenth day for a timely representation of the Passover lamb. On any of the seven days, there would be a perfect representation. All the gospel writers testify that Jesus was alive during the Judean feast of Passover.

> The day of unleavened bread came, on which the Passover must be sacrificed. (8) He sent Peter and John, saying, "Go and prepare the Passover for us, that we may eat. (9) They said to him, "Where do you want us to prepare?" (10) He said to them, `Behold when you have entered into the city, a man carrying a pitcher of water will meet you. Follow him into the house which he enters. (11) Tell

the master of the house, The Teacher says to you, where is the guest room, where I may eat the Passover with my disciples? (12) He will show you a large, furnished upper room. Make preparations there. (13) They went, found things as he had told them, and they prepared the Passover. (14) When the hour had come, he sat down with the twelve apostles (Luke 22:7-14). Now when evening had come, he was reclining at the table with the twelve disciples (Matt 26:20 cf. Mark 14:17).

We are assured that, conferring on these biblical records, Jesus was alive during daylight hours on the fourteenth day, when He directed His disciples to the city to prepare the Passover. As evening approached, initializing the fifteenth day, he sat with His disciples to eat.

Three Days and Three Nights and Night of Nights

As recorded in Matthew's gospel, three days and three nights and the Passover week timing, have received considerable attention among Christians. Some think that Christ's messiahship is reliant on these timely events. Since it is certain by testimony and prophecy that Jesus came to Earth, and since God was certainly in control of what happened to Jesus, His work or identity should not be challenged by the limited understanding of the facts we wish to convey.

According to the law, no one may eat the Passover ahead of schedule or after the fact but only at a designated time that God has fixed (Num. 9:6–11; 2 Chron. 30:15). The Passover was all about time memorial to the event. To celebrate it away from the designated time is to have a useless celebration. The grand purpose of the feast was to relive the scene to the day.

As you have already seen, there is overwhelming evidence that Jesus did not eat the Passover ahead of schedule. Consumption of the Passover meal at the thirteenth day's end or on the fourteenth day before evening conflicts with the law and the testimonies. According to the biblical record, Christ was on trial during the hours of the feast days. Some of the public trials were on the first feast day. There is an unrecorded recess of the trial. Jesus was released on the second day of the feast and was crucified, as John puts it, "at the Passover." One must understand that Passover begins at night. Passover occurred at the beginning of the fifteenth day, for it was the night when the Lord passed over the houses of the children of Israel to cover them while judgment passed through Egypt (Duet. 16:1). Since the prisoner was to be released at the Passover, it could only have been done during the daytime because it was in a public forum. Remember, only the first feast had to be during the night hours. Thus, it's not the time Jesus was crucified that needs to coincide with the killing of the first ancient Passover lambs, but the day He was captured and tried by the Jews.

As Paul so stated, on the same night Christ ate the Passover, He was captured. That night was more critical and unique than any other night. It was on this night that Jesus settled the terms and conditions to save humanity. On this night, Satan must unleash all the powers of hell to deter the purpose. When Jesus said, "With desire, I have desired to eat this Passover with you," it was a way to comfort and prepare for the subsequent events. Remember, He was heavily stressed (Matt. 26:37–39). "And there appeared an angel unto him from heaven, strengthening him. And being in agony, He prayed more earnestly: and His sweat was as it were great drops of blood falling down to the ground. And when he rose up from prayer and was come to his disciples, he found them sleeping for sorrow" (Luke 22:43–45). This is the memorial night; this is the night He would have us sit with Him (Duet. 16:3).

As the prophets declared, when torture, doom, and death lurked over the Savior, He was sore distressed. The Narrative below shows the anguish the Savior went through during the passion week.

Reproach hath broken my heart; and I am full of heaviness: and I looked for some to take pity, but there was none; and for comforters, but I found none. They gave me also gall for my meat; and in my thirst they gave me vinegar to drink (Psalm 69:20, 21).

He is despised and rejected of men; a man of sorrows, and acquainted with grief: and we hid as it were our faces from him; he was despised, and we esteemed him not. (v. 3). He was oppressed, and he was afflicted, yet he opened not his mouth: he is brought as a lamb to the slaughter, and as a sheep before her shearers is dumb, so he openeth not his mouth (v. 7). He was taken from prison and from judgment: and who shall declare his generation? for he was cut off out of the land of the living: for the transgression of my people was he stricken. (v. 8). Yet it pleased the LORD to bruise him; he hath put him to grief: when thou shalt make his soul an offering for sin, he shall see his seed, he shall prolong his days, and the pleasure of the LORD shall prosper in his hand. (v. 10)-- Isa. 53.

I gave my back to the smiters, and my cheeks to

them that plucked off the hair: I hid not my face from shame and spitting (Isa 50:6).

To the chief Musician upon Aijeleth Shahar, A Psalm of David. My God, my God, why hast thou forsaken me? why art thou so far from helping me, and from the words of my roaring? (2) O my God, I cry in the daytime, but thou hearest not; and in the night season, and am not silent. (3) But thou art holy, O thou that inhabitest the praises of Israel. (4) Our fathers trusted in thee: they trusted, and thou didst deliver them. (5) They cried unto thee, and were delivered: they trusted in thee, and were not confounded. (6) But I am a worm, and no man; a reproach of men, and despised of the people. (7) All they that see me laugh me to scorn: they shoot out the lip, they shake the head, saying, (8) He trusted on the LORD that he would deliver him: let him deliver him, seeing he delighted in him. (9) But thou art he that took me out of the womb: thou didst make me hope when I was upon my mother's breasts. (10) I was cast upon thee from the womb: thou art my God from my mother's belly. (11) Be not far from me; for trouble is near; for there is none to help. (12) Many bulls have compassed me: strong bulls of Bashan have beset me round. (13) They gaped upon me with their mouths, as a ravening and a roaring lion. (14) I am poured out like water, and all my bones are out of joint: my heart is like wax; it is melted in the midst of my bowels. (15) My strength is dried up like a potsherd; and my tongue cleaveth to my jaws; and thou hast brought me into the dust of death. (16) For dogs have compassed me: the assembly of the wicked have inclosed me: they pierced my hands and my feet. (17) I may tell all my bones: they look and stare upon me. (18) They part my garments among them, and cast lots upon my vesture (Ps 22:1-18).

As was Jonah in the belly of the fish, Jesus was barricaded by the hands of sinners. Jesus's prayer was like Jonah's on the bottom floor of the ship. Just as Jonah, for peace's sake, was willing to be thrown overboard, Jesus for our peace was willing to be barricaded by the hands of sinners. The suffering of Jesus and the experience of Jonah have a direct correlation. As the lamb was eaten on the fifteenth day, the same night the angel of death went through Egypt, Jesus likewise was captured by the hands of sinners. Here, they were "eating Him alive in the antitypical sense," before finally killing Him. That is like Jonah being thrown alive into the belly of the fish. They, being prefigured as the great fish, was the sign of His messiahship they were not prepared to accept. They were looking for a miracle. The event of the sign was their treatment of Him (Matt. 12:39–40). They were the ferocious fish that had swallowed up the Messiah (Matt. 26:24, 53–56,27:29–30, Mark 14:27, Luke 22:53, 24:16).

> And when the people were gathered thick together, he began to say; this is an evil generation: they seek a sign, and there shall no sign be given it but the sign of Jonas the prophet. For as Jonas was a sign unto the Ninevites, so shall also the Son of man be to this generation. The men of Nineveh shall rise up in the judgment with this generation, and shall condemn it: for they repented at the preaching of Jonas; and, behold, a greater than Jonas is here (Luke 11:29-30, 32).

Note carefully, Matthew's emphasis on Jonah's sign was for the suffering of Jesus at the hands of the Jews. Luke's focus on the sign was for the Jews' treatment of Jesus's message. From the time He was tried by the Jews to the time He was freed on resurrection day was three days and three nights. He was seized on our Wednesday at about 11:00 p.m. (current time). The official trial before the Sanhedrin started early in the morning on Thursday. Christ was resurrected on Sunday morning at about 5:00 a.m., and the women were at the tomb at about 5:30 a.m. However, the statement "Destroy this temple, and in three days, I will raise it up" only refers to the period from the point of death to resurrection. It is different than the sign of Jonah in the book of Matthew (12:40).

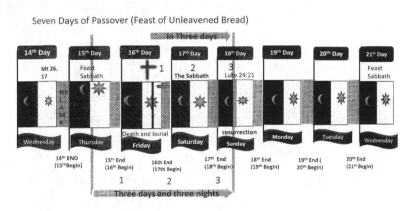

Seven Days of Passover (Feast of Unleavened Bread)

The resurrection: He appeared to the Ladies first Mark 16:9. He had not yet ascended to father; Touch me not John 20:17.
Luke 24:20 And how the chief priests and our rulers delivered him to be condemned to death, and have crucified him. 21 beside all this, to day is the third day since these things were done. 22 Yea, and certain women also of our company made us astonished, which were early at the sepulchre;

The Seven Days of Passover

In these dreaded days of Jesus's time, as the prince of suffering, He endured relentless torture to the pleasure of His worse enemies. He did it alone, and none stood with him. His suffering could have been avoided, but He accepted this way because the Father had traced this path for Him. He suffered this for the sins of humanity. Whatever our punishment should be, He needed to suffer on our behalf for our salvation.

The Passion Week and the Trials

The time of the Passover was approaching (John 11:55). About six days before the Passover, Jesus entered Bethany (John 11:12). He performed His miracle on Lazarus, which led many people to believe in Him (John 12: 11). That night, He ate supper at Martha's house, and there He was anointed (John 12:5).

On Palm Sunday, He arrived at Jerusalem to the Mount of Olives (Matt. 21:1–3). There He prepared for his triumphal entry. With many people believing in Him, He used that opportunity to cleanse the temple, which had been defiled by hypocrisy (Matt. 21:12).

He made His way toward the temple on Monday morning; He was hungry and did not find food on the fig tree. Thus, He cursed it. He proceeded toward the temple in the city, where He had a discourse about John the Baptist (Matt. 21:25). Then He began to speak to the leaders in parables (Mark 12:1; Matt. 22:1). After this, a discussion ensued through which an attempt was made to trap Him in His words (Mark 12:13). He silenced his opponents and denounced their hypocrisy (Matt. 23). Having left the temple, He predicted how it would be destroyed, not leaving one stone on another (Matt. 24). When the evening approached, He returned to the Mount of Olives (Luke 21:37).

On Tuesday morning, He returned to the temple to teach using parables illustrating His second return (Matt. 25). By this time, it was two days before the feast of the Passover. The priest then plotted how they might have Him put to death (Matt. 26:2–5). They did not want to kill Him on the first feast day because that day was a feast Sabbath.

Then Jesus went to Bethany to the house of Simon the leper, where He was anointed (Matt. 26:6). Following this, Judas planned Jesus' arrest (Matt. 26:14). On the same day, Jesus explained to His disciples, along with a Gentile inquirer, the requirements to become His disciple (John 12:20–26).

On Wednesday, when the Passover lamb was killed at approaching sunset, the disciples inquired of Jesus about the Passover's preparation (Matt. 26:17). He gave them instructions after sundown as they sat and ate the Passover (Mark 14:17). After the Passover supper, Jesus gave a discourse on humility and instituted its ordinance (John 13:2–4; Luke 22; John 13:5). According to Matthew 26:26–27, the Lord's emblematic meal was the last part of the Passover supper. After He rose from the table the first time, He instituted the ordinance of humility (John 13:4). Immediately after the disciples ate the meal, Judas left the scene to complete the betrayal (Mark 14:26–31; John 13:26). While Judas was out, Jesus taught lessons on humility. He assured them of His return and the promise of the Holy Spirit (John 14, 16). He warned them about the coming persecution, and He prayed for them (John 16, 17). Next, they sang some hymns and went to the Mount of Olives by way of the brook of Cedron to the garden of Gethsemane (Matt, 26:30, 36). It was there in the garden that Jesus's settled His victory. By this time, it was late at night when Christ began to pray. While the other disciples were left behind, He took three of them to pray with Him. Then He left the three behind to commune alone with the Father (Matt. 26:36–45). About two hours later, Judas arrived with a band of soldiers to arrest Jesus. Being bold and brave, Peter took out his sword and struck one servant of the high priest, taking off his ear. Jesus stooped toward the man and healed the broken ear. He told Peter to put away his sword and that if He needed help, He would call His Father and have His enemies disappear at will. Then all His disciples fled (Matt. 26:55–56).

The order of the events of Jesus's trials can be found in the *Holman Bible Atlas* (Brisco, 1998). First, He was led to Annas for a short preliminary hearing, and it was probably near to Caiaphas, the high priest (John 18:12–14). Then He was led to the Palace of Caiaphas, where many of the elders assembled (Matt. 26:57–68). "Then Jesus said unto the chief priests, captains of the temple, and the elders, which were come to him, be ye come out, as against a thief, with swords and staves? When I was daily with you in the temple, ye stretched forth no hands against me: but this is your hour, and the power of darkness" (Luke 22:52–53). Many witnesses testified falsely against Him, and the waiting mob abused Him.

On Thursday morning at about 6:00 a.m., the Jews had the first religious formal trial with the Sanhedrin (Matt. 27:1; Mark 15:1; Luke 22:66). Then later, they went in to see Pilate, possibly by 7:00 a.m. That trial was lengthy, so it took at least forty-five minutes. Afterward, he was sent to Herod (Luke 23:6–7). Herod's trial took at least one hour. After the trial at Herod's place, he was mocked and led away to Pilate once more (Luke 23:11).

Pilate took Jesus in for questioning; when he found nothing against Him, he took conference with the elders and informed them of his findings, which they opposed. Pilate offered to chastise Jesus and dismiss Him, but the elders insisted that Jesus should be crucified, and they would bear full responsibility. Meanwhile, Pilate's wife sent him a note about her nightmare of warning about his involvement. Having sufficient evidence to release Jesus and refused, Pilate had washed his hands as a gesture of innocent plea (Matt. 27:15–24). Finally, Jesus was sent away, mocked, and scourged at the maximum penalty. The scourging could have been completed by 12:00 a.m. on Thursday. By this time, the people were weak and hungry, and the crowd was dismissed. On the next day, at 8:00 a.m., He was led out to be crucified (Matt. 27:27–31; Luke 23:17–22).

According to Reese Chronological Bible, the fourteenth day fell on a Thursday, leaving only a short morning of two hours for four separate trials and two major events, all before the crucifixion (Reese, 1977). Some believe that the fourteenth day fell on a Wednesday of that week, allowing two days for all the trials and events.

On Friday, the crucifixion took place. One thing is clear; there were a Friday crucifixion and a Sunday early morning resurrection. These days were also Feast of Unleavened Bread times, which were called Passover by John's Gospel. That Sunday was a Wave-Sheaf day, presentation of the first fruits.

> The traditional view of a Friday Crucifixion has everything to commend it and nothing to contradict it. All the Gospels state that the day following the Crucifixion was Sabbath (Matt. 27:62; 28:1; Mark 15:42; Luke 23:56; John 19:31). All of the Gospels state that the women visited the tomb of Jesus on the day after the Sabbath that is, on the first day of the week, Sunday (Matt. 28:1; Mark 16:2; Luke 24:1; John 20:1). It was a common practice for the Jews to refer to a part of a day or a night as the whole day (Gen. 42:17-18; 1 Sam.

30:12-13; 1 Kings 20:29; 2 Chron. 10:5, 12; Esther 4:16; 5:1) (Ryrie, 1999, p. 326).

All the gospel writers who refer to Christ being released from prison stated that He was released at the time of the feast (Matt. 27.15, Mark 15.6, Luke 23.17, John 18:39). Thus, the crucifixion took place just about the middle of the feast week.

Jesus counted loss all earthly ties; through death, all heaven he may gain. With blessings and love as key, he opens his kingdom to you and me. Faith and selflessness were his garments. In pouring his soul, he gave his all. He rose on the third day to give life to all who follow him on the way. Jesus, Jehovah's salvation, died to free you and me from the power of sin by which we were all held sway.

Chapter 5

Days of Our Freedom

The Gospel's Account of the Crucifixion

There are opinions as to which day of the week the fourteenth day fell. The essential questions are: Was Christ crucified on the fifteenth day of the Feast of Unleavened Bread? Or was it on the sixteenth day, the following morning? Was Jesus in the grave or on the cross at the time the Passover lamb was killed?

While promoting a point of view, defensiveness serves as a face-saving attempt to protect one's reputation. One day while discussing a topic on evolution with a friend, I was disappointed because of the way he was driving the conversation. He did not show any form of objectivity. He pretended to try to convince me of the topic I knew a lot more of than he. Being more trained on the topic, I listened. Instead of listening and gaining some knowledge, he quickly tried to defend a widespread view about which he understood little. He was permitted to talk, and then the topic was changed. In life, we have to stop and smell the roses. We must take time to listen carefully to another's point of view. Some people harbor a fear of disenchantment. This fear is presented due to the lack of faith that God will lead and enlighten them further. I have often faced these difficulties with people of whom I differ and who are bent or hard pressed on surveying things in a particular way. Usually, these people do the majority of the talking and avoid taking questions about their analysis. If you get the opportunity to question them, they use topic diversion tactics to avoid learning or downgrade the issue's importance. The truth has a way of catching up; it's just a matter of time when they will have to decide on the path to follow.

Remember, the Passover lamb was sacrificed in the evening. Jesus was crucified in the morning, at least an eight-hour differentiation. John did not make use of the term "unleavened bread." John used the term "Passover." In John's day, Passover and Feast of Unleavened Bread were used interchangeably.

> Now at that feast, the governor was wont to release unto the people a prisoner, whom they would. (17) Therefore, when they were gathered together, Pilate said unto them, whom will ye that I release unto you? Barabbas, or Jesus which is called Christ (Mt 27:15,17; cf. Mark 15:6, Luke 23:17). "But ye have a custom that I should release unto you one at the Passover: Will ye therefore that I release unto you the King of the Jews?" (John 18:39).

Passover preparation for the fifteenth day began late afternoon on the fourteenth day or later that evening. The Passover was eaten at the time of the Feast of Unleavened Bread, about three hours after sunset. Since the term "Passover," as used by John, is, in fact, the Feast of Unleavened Bread on the fifteenth day, it synchronizes with the other gospels. Therefore, Christ was alive during the daytime on the fifteenth day, leaving the sixteenth day as the only possible crucifixion time.

The last key in this segment is the Sabbath. Let us look at the scripture:

> The Jews, therefore, because it was the preparation, that the bodies should not remain upon the cross on the Sabbath day, (for that Sabbath day was a high day,) besought Pilate that their legs might be broken and that they might be taken away (John 19:31). And that day was the preparation, and the Sabbath drew on. And the women also, which came with him from Galilee, followed after, and beheld the sepulcher, and how his body was laid. And they returned, and prepared spices and ointments; and rested the Sabbath day according to the commandment (Luke 23:54-56).

According to Matthew 28:5–7, the angel disclosed proof that Christ rose at Sabbath's end towards the dawn of the first day of the week. After seeing the empty tomb, the ladies left and met Jesus on their way to the disciples. Matthew is silent about the spices but states that the burial was complete. From Mark's standpoint (16:1–6), the reason the women went to the tomb was to anoint the body of Jesus with spices bought after the Sabbath. They either bought the spices Saturday night or early Sunday morning. The women went to the tomb when the Sabbath was past, on the first day of the week at the rising of the sun. According to Luke 24:1–4, precisely the same timing and idea are reflected as in Mark. In Luke 23:56, the women upon returning home from the burial prepared spices.

According to John 19:40, the body of Jesus was anointed

with spices after the crucifixion and before the Sabbath. John is silent on the women's purpose of going to the tomb verging on daylight Sunday (John 20:1–2). A possible conclusion is, they had run out of spices for the burial and needed more to continue their work on Sunday. Is it possible that Jesus's body was not adequately embalmed? Is it possible that the work had to be continued on the next workday near daybreak? Could this be the reason why the ladies went very early to continue where they left off? They certainly did not go there to guard the tomb or because they believed Jesus was going to be resurrected. Remember, everything about the burial was done with stress from the preceding events and in haste for the approaching Sabbath.

Furthermore, nothing in the law would have prevented them from completing their work on Jesus's body on a feast Sabbath. The feast Sabbath permits this sort of personal and voluntary labor. If this was a feast Sabbath, there would be no need for the ladies to work in haste for fear of encroaching on the Sabbath hours. The sabbath in question here must have been a seventh-day Sabbath. So, there may have been a reason for cleaning up left-over work on Sunday.

A misconception shared by some people is the utilization of Daniel 9:27 to show that Christ was crucified in the middle of the natural week, Wednesday. Almost all Bible students understand this prophecy as referring to a week of years, not literal days of the week. The text's times are for a long prophetic chain of events (Dan. 9:24–26). One week of years is seven years, and the middle of that is three and a half years. It is not biblically transparent why someone would use a literal week application for that verse.

The disciples possessed a range of experiences and interests. Mark was a disciple of Peter, who was an eyewitness. Luke carefully investigated many eyewitness accounts before reporting them with certainty. Luke was more interested in historical correctness and sequence than any other. John and Matthew were eyewitnesses of the events. None of the writers had complete detail but gave their accounts according to their experiences.

One question that stands out is: Isn't it unreasonable for the ladies to approach the tomb on Sunday morning to see Jesus if they were shown proof twelve hours earlier that He had risen? The inference that Jesus had been resurrected immediately at or around sunset Saturday night (beginning of Sunday) is inadmissible in all scriptures. Unambiguously, Mark, Luke, and John stated that the women went to the tomb on Sunday around daybreak to look for Jesus. Also, the women had not seen Him before that morning because, when He had risen, before ascending to His Father, He first appeared to the women. "Now when Jesus was raised early the first day of the week, he appeared first to Mary Magdalene, out of whom he had cast seven devils. Jesus saith unto her, Touch me not; for I am not yet ascended to my Father: but go to my brethren, and say unto them, I ascend unto my Father, and your Father; and to my God, and your God" (Mark 16:9; cf. John 20:17). If this "first day of the week" refers to Saturday evening at sunset, what happened with the ladies on Sunday morning? The truth is, this quote, as with every other similar quote, refers to the same event of the same time.

The Sabbath of the Holy Week

There is confusion among students of scripture concerning the Sabbaths contained in the Holy Week. There is a consensus that Passover of the holy week did not fall on the seventh day Sabbath. Therefore, the seven days of Passover will have three

Sabbaths, one seventh-day Sabbath, and the two feast Sabbaths. After reading about the Sabbath preparation day, mistakes are made by calling the Sabbath a festival Sabbath rather than the seventh-day Sabbath. If this Sabbath were a preparation for the Passover, John would have had no trouble saying so (as in John 19:14). What is often missed is, the preparation for Passover Sabbath is not as strict as for the seventh-day Sabbath. There are fewer restrictions for Passover preparation. Among them are killing the lamb, removing leaven, and baking unleavened bread. However, preparation for the seventh day Sabbath is different: all work must be finished, that no work may be done. For example, on feast Sabbaths, you can do cleaning around your home and cook. Doing these things on the seventh day Sabbath is not lawful.

The seventh day Sabbath fell on a Feast of Unleavened Bread day. That Sabbath was made high or associated with a high day. A high day is a feast day. The highest day in Judean circles is the Day of Atonement. During this Passover week, the Jews celebrated both the Earth's birth and its redemption in one celebration. They had to prepare for both the Feast of Unleavened Bread and the seventh day Sabbath. It is indeed a high day for rest and contemplation. According to Luke, "They rested the Sabbath according to the commandment." "The commandment" (Heb. *debar,* or word) here implies a set of instructions about the rest that festival Sabbaths lack. Notwithstanding, the Day of Atonement has a more serious protocol. As seen in the following quote of Josephus's works, Friday was known as the preparation time.

Caesar Augustus, high priest, and tribune of the people, ordains thus: Since the nation of the Jews hath been found grateful to the Roman people, not only at this time, but in time past also, and chiefly Hyrcanus the high priest, under my father (7) Caesar the emperor, it seemed good to me and my counselors, according to the sentence and oath of the people of Rome, that the Jews have liberty to make use of their own customs, according to the law of their forefathers, as they made use of them under Hyrcanus the high priest of the Almighty God; and that their sacred money be not touched, but be sent to Jerusalem, and that it be committed to the care of the receivers at Jerusalem; and that they be not obliged to go before any judge on the Sabbath day, nor on the day of the preparation to it after the ninth hour (Whiston, 1987, p. 436).

Friday evening was known as "the eve of the Sabbath." The day of the "preparation" is the *"paraskeue"* in Greek and "the first day before the Sabbath" in Hebrew. Those are the designations given to the sixth day. The Jews gave names only to two days of the week. Friday was called "the preparation," and Saturday was called "the Sabbath." The rest of the days of the week were called by numbers in connection to the "Sabbath" (week). The term *"Shavuot,"* in some instances, was used to mean a week or seven days. Strictly speaking, *"Shavuot"* is the term for weeks in Hebrew. *"Sheva"* is for a week (Gen. 29:27, 28). The Romans adopted Jewish naming of the days owing to the Roman Empire's Judean captivity (cf. Mark 15:42; Luke 23:50–56).

Another key factor in the events' timing is that the Jews did not want to have Jesus killed on the feast day. The purpose was not because they thought the day was so holy to them, but they feared an uproar among the people. The first day is not only a feast but also a feast Sabbath. Remember, the feast endured for seven days. The priests did not want the disturbance that the Messiah's killing would bring on the feast Sabbath. The second day of the feast is a normal workday. People going to their normal occupation serves as a fitting occasion for public display, avoiding large crowds. The first feast day events must be private, confined to a small group. To arrest Jesus subtly at any time was in concert with their purpose, but to have him killed would be better served on a regular feast day.

The Day of the Resurrection

On what day was Messiah resurrected? The best place to start is to look at the historical account. In John 20:1, the women went to the tomb on Sunday while it was yet dark. "Yet dark" forces the conclusion of the early morning. Dawn is the beginning of daylight. According to Luke 24:1, the women went to the tomb at "early dawn" on Sunday. Mark 16:2 states that the women went to the tomb on Sunday "when the sun had risen." In Matthew 28:1, the scripture says at the close of the Sabbath, "as it began to dawn" on Sunday, the ladies went to the tomb. The word "dawn" in Greek is *"epiphausko,"* which means to draw near or to begin to grow into light (see Luke 23:54 "drew on"). It is from the root word *"epiphaino,"* meaning to shine, be visible, give light, and make an appearance. The text can read as "immediately after the Sabbath at sunset, the ladies went to the tomb." Or it can be understood as, "when the Sabbath was past, the ladies went to the tomb at daybreak (daylight)" on the first day of the week. Either wording will satisfy the original text; the question is which reading satisfies the other gospel writers?

Or could we say only Matthew got it right? Depending on the text being treated, those in favor of prescheduled Passover are inclined to say that only John got it right. The same is said that only Matthew got it right for pre-sunset end of Sabbath resurrection. Most of the accounts clearly state that the women went to the tomb on Sunday morning when the day's lighted segment was approaching. Jesus had already risen, but when?

Counting days to the resurrection has been a significant concern for many expositors on the topic. One must keep in mind that the Jews counted the day as daylight hours. That is why Jesus said that a day consists of twelve hours. Twenty-four-hour days from even to even were only considered for special purposes. Just the mere mention of time as in Matthew 28 does not require an evening-to-evening reckoning. Concerning the rest of that day's record, John 20:17 stated that when Mary met Jesus on Sunday morning, He had not yet ascended and returned from the Father. After the same day's ascension and return, He met with two of His disciples on Emmaus's road. During their conversation, the disciples reiterated the scene since the trial and concluded: "This is the third day since these things had happened" (Luke 24:18–21). According to verse 29 of the same chapter, it was late in the day when the statement was made. Mark stated that Christ had "risen early first day of the week" (Mark 16:9). Thus, all these verses expose that Jesus had arisen just before full daylight on the first day of the week.

Concerning the soldiers who were to guard the tomb, several facts prove that Christ had to be resurrected on Sunday, just near daybreak. Because of the angels arriving at the grave, the soldiers who guarded the tomb died (Matt. 28:4). After leaving the tomb that Sunday morning, some of the tomb's watchers who survived reported what had happened (Matt. 28:11–13). The elders of the Jews instructed the soldiers to convey the idea that while they slumbered, the body was stolen. This propaganda must have an appearance of credibility; otherwise, it would have appeared to be a fabrication. If Jesus were not supposed to be in the grave throughout the night, long enough for the soldiers to need sleep, a different fabrication would have been employed. The soldiers had to know that Jesus was required to spend the dark hours of Sunday morning in the grave. They were to guard the tomb through the third day. If the third day ended on Saturday night immediately after sunset, what were they doing at the tomb on Sunday morning if He had already risen and the fourth day had arrived?

> And shall deliver him to the Gentiles to mock, and to scourge, and to crucify him: and the third day he shall rise again (Matt 20:19). Command therefore that the sepulcher be made sure until the third day, lest his disciples come by night, and steal him away, and say unto the people, He is risen from the dead: so the last error shall be worse than the first (Matt 27:64).

Therefore, Jesus was expected to be in the grave at least past midnight Saturday night. The idea that Jesus rose at the end of the Sabbath hours at sunset is discredited at every angle of scripture. The soldiers would not have needed sleep at that time. The third day must have included long dark hours when the soldiers would have been tired of watching through the night. This condition lends some credibility to the sleep fabrication originated with the Judean leaders.

Witnesses on The Third Day

Jews and the Soldiers

- Seal the tomb until the third day (Matt. 28:4).
- Reported that they were sleeping during the night (Matt. 28:11-13).

The women and the Disciples

- Ladies at Tomb: "in the end of Sabbath as it began to dawn (Mt. 28:1)" begin to dawn -means light approaching.

- "early dawn (Lk. 24:1)," early daylight

- "yet dark (Jn. 20:1)" light is advancing

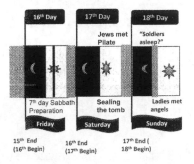

Witnesses on the Third Day

Since Jesus could not have been resurrected near midnight during the Sabbath hours, the only time left is Saturday around midnight or Sunday between 1:00 a.m. and 5:00 a.m. Besides all this, the feast day appointments show that Jesus, being the antitypical wave-sheaf, was resurrected on Sunday, the day the wave sheaf was waved before the Lord in the type, typifying Jesus as the firstfruits of those who died. The wave sheaf is presented on the morrow after the Sabbath (morning, see Judges 19:9; 1 Sam. 19:11). That day would be a Sunday morning according to the type. The wave sheaf represents the resurrection of Jesus, the firstfruits of the harvest of God's personal labor (1 Cor. 15:20). If one wishes to acknowledge the day of the resurrection, it is the Sunday of Passover week. Certainly, it was not a weekly worship day, and it was never a Sabbath day.

Segmental Timekeeping

There is a widespread postulation that the Jews commonly counted days for events as a twenty-four-hour period when the term "day" is used. The Jews counted part of a day as a whole day. A twenty-four-hour day is only regarded for special occasions such as Sabbaths and other celebrations. From creation, we know that a full day is twenty-four hours and starts at sunset (Ex. 20:8–11). If you worked on a project for three days, the last day you are working could be regarded as the third day since you have been working. If you wish to exclude the first partial day you worked, you will say: Today is the third full day since I worked on the project. Three days of light and part of the night can be concluded as three days of work. Days were never counted by twenty-four hours, but rather by chunks of hours in a day. Jesus said there are twelve hours in a day (John 11:9). Therefore, the word "day" in the Hebrew, Greek, or Aramaic was not commonly reckoned as a twenty-four-hour period on all occasions. Days were called by names, numbers, or both. Three days were regarded as three different names of days in the week regardless of the number of hours for an event.

You will see an example of segmental calculation in Ester 4:16–17, 5:1, where the people were told to fast for three days on Ester's behalf. She specified day and night. Secondly, she did not wait for twenty-four hours to elapse on the last day but went in to see the king on the third day of the fast. Although they could have continued to fast, the last day of the fast was the third day. Had it not been the third day since they were fasting, Ester would not have gone to the king. This situation is exemplary of how the ancient Jews counted time.

If we count the day of resurrection as one day and count

backward three days, we land on Friday, the day Jesus died. Those were three different days: Friday, Saturday, and Sunday. "Destroy this temple, and in three days, I will raise it up" (John 2:19). When considering the weight of evidence, this verse indeed cannot be construed to mean after three twenty-four-hour days.

Comparing John's and Luke's Account

First, we must establish that Luke was a scholar who painstakingly scrutinized many written and verbal accounts and interrogated many eyewitnesses before penning his account. Having had ample insight into all that transpired, it became his obsession to create an unprecedented and accurate report (Luke 1:1–4). He was more linguistically knowledgeable about Judean holidays and their contemporary associated usage than anyone living in modern times. He was equipped with Aramaic, Hebrew, and Greek. The Roman authorities with jurisdiction over Jerusalem had adequate knowledge of the Judean holidays. Luke didn't have to dumb down the standard Judean expressions as used in his day. When Pilate decided to release a prisoner on the day of the feast, he was not unacquainted with terms used by the Jews for the event. Some think that the feast mentioned at Barabbas's release was a casual feast unrelated to the Judean holidays. Every important feast had a name, especially if it was a well-known, customary event. The Jews had no popular customary feast around Passover week. To say that the feast mentioned at the time of Barabbas's release was not the Feast of Unleavened Bread is simply neither biblical nor historical. As we have seen, the record is not in some people's mysticism as interpretations have made it out to be.

According to Luke, the gospel says, "Now the feast of unleavened bread drew nigh, which is called the Passover" (Luke 22:1). Continues Luke, "Then came the day of unleavened bread, when the Passover must be killed" (Luke 22:7). The significance of verses one and seven is seen in the event placement of verse one, two days before the events of verse seven. Luke focused on the events of preparation, taking place before Jesus was arrested. Being acquainted with the correct timing of the Judean Passover, the disciples asked Jesus about preparing the Passover. By law, the Passover cannot be Passover unless it is eaten after the fifteenth day has begun. If it is eaten at some other time before, it is not Passover. Jesus said:

> And he said unto them, with desire I have desired to eat this Passover with you before I suffer (Luke 22:15). And the first day of unleavened bread, when they [Jewish nation] killed the Passover, his disciples said unto him, where wilt thou that we go and prepare that thou mayest eat the Passover (Mark 14:12, cf. Matt. 26:7)?
>
> And he sent Peter and John, saying, Go and prepare us the Passover that we may eat. And they said unto him, where wilt thou that we prepare? And he said unto them, Behold, when ye are entered into the city, there shall a man meet you, bearing a pitcher of water; follow him into the house where he entereth in. And ye shall say unto the goodman of the house, The Master saith unto thee, where is the guest chamber, where I shall eat the Passover with my disciples? And he shall shew you a large upper room furnished: there make ready. And they went and found as he had said unto them: and they made ready the Passover (Luke 22:8-13).

Now when the even was come, he sat down with the twelve (Matt. 26:20). And in the evening, he cometh with the twelve (Mark 14:17). And when the hour was come, he sat down, and the twelve apostles with him (Luke 22:14).

This same statement is found in John but without the details of the preparation. John's record leaped and showed the end of the preparation. After preparing the Passover, Jesus sat down with the disciples, waiting for the hour to initiate the celebration. None celebrated Passover from morning to morning because the law says it is celebrated from evening to evening. "Now before the feast of the Passover, when Jesus knew that his hour had come that he should depart out of this world unto the Father, having loved his own which were in the world, he loved them unto the end... And supper [preparation] being ended [made], the devil having now put into the heart of Judas Iscariot, Simon's son, to betray him" (John 13:1–2).

John's statement that says "before the Passover" has been the epicenter of misunderstanding for some. The premise of misunderstanding owes to that the claimants of the prescheduled Passover celebration create an untenable timetable leading to Jesus's crucifixion. Such timetable is subject to one's desired interpretation of antitypical application for the ancient Paschal Lamb sacrifice. The timetable they created for John 13, either twelve hours or twenty-four hours before the Passover, is difficult to find in scripture's text or context. It could have been neither of those periods. The preparation mentioned in John could have been about three hours before Passover. There is nothing in the text that precludes this time span for preparation.

John 13:1–2, cannot be used as a basis for the exact delineation of time for Jesus's celebration of the Passover.

Furthermore, the text says that Jesus continued curating for his disciples even to the time of the crucifixion. This time was a narrow moment when he exhibited an intensified love for his disciples (see vs. 1). Here, He was intensely focused on His life's last events while reassuring and comforting His disciples. Spending quality time with them and personal contemplation are the premises of the clause "before the Passover."

The translation in verse two of John 13 has some difficulty, as its meaning depends on one's assessment. The Revised Version says, "during the Supper." It is likely that Jesus rose at the beginning of the feast, washed feet, and then sat down at the feast (John 13:12). Verse two spoke of supper "being ended," but it should be translated as "supper taking place" (The Zondervan Cooperation, 1975, p.313). The Greek term for "generation" or "made or taking place" is "γίνομαι" (ginomai), the word used in the Greek New Testament. Supper being made or done does not mean they were done eating. It can mean that supper was in readiness. In verse four of the chapter, it states that "he rises from the supper," which means that He withdrew from the supper-ready area. After everyone's feet were washed (vs. 10), Jesus returned (vs. 12). The supper ended when it was late at night, between 8:00 and 9:00 p.m. (vs. 30). The creation of a twelve to twenty-four-hour gap between events from verse one to the Judean Passover time is not exegetical of John 13. This gap is a preconceived notion to rooter a prescheduled Passover.

The progression of events in John is the same as seen in the synoptic gospels; the disciples prepared for the feast *on the day of preparation for Passover* and *before* Passover hours arrived. The question remains, how early did they prepare? It could not be on the thirteenth day because that is not the day the lamb must be killed (Luke 22:7). It could not be during the night hours at the beginning of the fourteenth day (end of the thirteenth day) because of necessity; they would have to wait for the evening hours of the next day before partaking the supper (Matt. 26:20). This text in Matthew implicates the strictness in adherence to the ancient Passover law that one should not consume the Passover ahead of schedule. If Jesus consumed the Passover ahead of schedule, it would be needless to wait for the evening or any other time to arrive. Some of what is said here can also be found in the following quote:

> The next day was the first day of the Jewish Passover, and Jesus and his disciples prepared for the ritual dinner that evening. At sundown, they gathered secretly at the appointed place. Their mood was solemn as they ate the meal, commemorating the Exodus of the Jews from Egypt. Reclining on couches arranged around a low table, they drank wine and ate the bitter herbs and unleavened bread. Toward the end of the meal, Jesus took a piece of bread, gave thanks to God, broke it, and said, 'This is my body which is given for you. Do this in remembrance of me' (Luke 22:19). In the same way, he took a cup, saying, 'This cup is the new covenant in my blood. Do this, as often as you drink it, in remembrance of me' (1 Cor. 11:25) (Shelley, 2008, p. 10).

As we analyze John's record, he was not as meticulous with time and terms as the other writers. Comparatively speaking, he mentioned time rarely. Let us look at the times he mentioned.

> And it was the preparation of the Passover, and about the sixth hour: and he saith unto the Jews, Behold your King! (John 19:14). The Jews, therefore, because it was the preparation, that the bodies should not remain upon the cross on the Sabbath day, (for that Sabbath day was a high day,) besought Pilate that their legs might be broken, and that they might be taken away (John 19:31). There laid they Jesus therefore because of the Jews' preparation day; for the Sepulcher was nigh at hand (John 19:42).

About this same Sabbath day, the other writers spoke of it this way: "And that day was the preparation, and the Sabbath drew on" (Luke 23:54). "And now when the even was come, because it was the preparation, that is, the day before the Sabbath" (Mark 15:42).

It is essential to consider the events between the verses in John to identify if there could have been gaps in time. Verse 14 shows the last time Pilate saw Jesus. Immediately after that scene, he wrote on the tablet, Jesus, king of the Jews (vs. 19). Following this, Jesus was led to be crucified. According to verse 31, the following day was the Sabbath day. That Sabbath was a high Sabbath. Gaps are unapparent in John's account.

There are theories as to why that Sabbath was high but no scriptural proof. Which Sabbath was high? Being "high" can be said of any seventh day Sabbath upon which is also the Feast of Unleavened Bread. Or it could mean that the Sabbath fell on a high day, a feast day. The preceding day of that Sabbath is the same day as the day in verse 14, the preparation day. If one traces the same line of events as seen in the other gospels, it will make this manifest. The only absconded event in John's record is the hours of darkness that took place briefly on the same day.

The time of the embalming and burial needs clarification. According to verse 42, it was the Jewish day of preparation. The preparation day is the sixth day of the week, the day before the seventh-day Sabbath. "Then took they the body of Jesus, and wound it in linen clothes with the spices, as the manner of the Jews is to bury" (John 19:40). "And they returned, and prepared spices and ointments and rested the Sabbath day according to the commandment" (Luke 23:56). According to these two verses, the only logical conclusion is that they intended to finish their embalming work after the Sabbath. Thus, they went home to prepare more spices. This concludes the events surrounding our Savior's death. His trials were on Wednesday night, He died on a Friday afternoon, and He was resurrected on Sunday just before daybreak.

Chapter 6

━━◦◦◦━━

Scriptural Chronology of Jesus's Sufferings

Order of Events Verse by Verse

Six days Before Passover

I n this chapter, I thought to give a straight talk from the Bible. In this section, we will look at Jesus' passion week scriptural chronology. I seek to share with you all the pertinent references that map out the chronology leading to Jesus' death.

"Then Jesus, six days before the Passover came to Bethany, where Lazarus was which had been dead, whom he raised from the dead. There they made him a supper, and Martha served: but Lazarus was one of them that sat at the table with him. Then took Mary a pound of ointment of spikenard, very costly, and anointed the feet of Jesus, and wiped his feet with her hair: and the house was filled with the odor of the ointment. Then saith one of his disciples, Judas Iscariot, Simon's son, which should betray him. Why was not this ointment sold for three hundred pence, and given to the poor?" John 12:1-5

It must be understood that two events and two days are mentioned. Jesus came to Bethany on Friday and raised up Lazarus. And on the evening of that Friday, he had supper, which was the beginning of the next day, Saturday. The next day from the time they had eaten supper is Sunday, which we see in verse 12.

Events Occurred on Sunday

"On the next day much people that were come to the feast, when they heard that Jesus was coming to Jerusalem, Took branches of palm trees, and went forth to meet him, and cried, Hosanna: Blessed is the King of Israel that cometh in the name of the Lord" (John 12:12-13). "And when they drew nigh unto Jerusalem, and were come to Bethphage, unto the mount of Olives, then sent Jesus two disciples.... And the multitudes that went before, and that followed, cried, saying, Hosanna to the Son of David: Blessed is he that cometh in the name of the Lord; Hosanna in the highest. And when he was come into Jerusalem, all the city was moved, saying, who is this?" (Matt. 21:1, 9-10.; Mathew chapters 21-26).

Two Days Before the Passover (Tues.)

"Ye know that after two days is the feast of the Passover, and the Son of man is betrayed to be crucified. Then assembled together the chief priests, and the scribes, and the elders of the people, unto the palace of the high priest, who was called Caiaphas, and consulted that they might take Jesus by subtilty, and kill him. But they said, not on the feast day, lest there be an uproar among the people. Now when Jesus was in Bethany, in the house of Simon the leper, there came unto him a woman having an alabaster box of very precious ointment, and poured it on his head, as he sat at meat. But when his disciples saw it, they had indignation, saying, to what purpose is this waste?" (Matt. 26:2-8).

About Timing, Jesus   Two days before the Passover he said.........

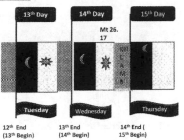

After two days is the feast of the Passover, and the Son of man is betrayed (Matt. 26:2)

After two days is the feast of the Passover, and of unleavened bread:
The priests and the scribes sought how they might kill him (Mark 14:1)

About timing, Jesus' statements

The Day Before the Passover (Wednesday)

"Now before the feast of the Passover, when Jesus knew that his hour was come that he should depart out of this world unto the Father, having loved his own which were in the world, he loved them unto the end (John 13:1). Now the first day of the feast of unleavened bread the disciples came to Jesus, saying unto him, where wilt thou that we prepare for thee to eat the Passover? And he said, go into the city to such a man, and say unto him, The Master saith, my time is at hand; I will keep the Passover at thy house with my disciples. And the disciples did as Jesus had appointed them; and they made ready the Passover." (Matt. 26:17-19).

Time of the Feast –Thursday Evening

"Now when the even was come, he sat down with the twelve" (Matt. 26:20). And supper being ended [made ready], the devil having now put into the heart of Judas Iscariot, Simon's son, to betray him...After that he poureth water into a basin, and began to wash the disciples' feet and to wipe them with the towel wherewith he was girded (Joh 13:2, 5). "And as they did eat, he said, Verily I say unto you, that one of you shall betray me. And they were exceeding sorrowful, and began every one of them to say unto him, Lord, is it I? .... And as they were eating, Jesus took bread, and blessed it, and brake it, and gave it to the disciples, and said, take, eat; this is my body. And he took the cup, and gave thanks, and gave it to them, saying, Drink ye all of it" (Matt. 26:21-22, 26-27). "When Jesus had thus said, he was troubled in spirit, and testified, and said, Verily, verily, I say unto you, that one of you shall betray me. Jesus answered, He it is, to whom I shall give a sop, when I have dipped it. And when he had dipped the sop, he gave it to Judas Iscariot, the son of Simon. And after the sop Satan entered into him. Then said Jesus unto him that thou doest do quickly.... Therefore, when he was gone out, Jesus said, now is the Son of man glorified, and God is glorified in him. If God be glorified in him, God shall also glorify him in himself, and shall straightway glorify him" (John 13:21, 26-27, 31-32, John 13-17).

The Brook Cedron in the Garden

"When Jesus had spoken these words, he went forth with his disciples over the brook Cedron, where was a garden, into the which he entered, and his disciples" (John 18:1).

"And when they had sung a hymn, they went out into the mount of Olives ...And he took with him Peter and the two sons of Zebedee, and began to be sorrowful and very heavy. Then saith he unto them, my soul is exceeding sorrowful, even unto death: tarry ye here, and watch with me. And he went a little further, and fell on his face, and prayed, saying, O my Father, if it be possible, let this cup pass from me: nevertheless, not as I will, but as thou wilt" (Matt. 26:30, 37-9). Jesus answered, I have told you that I am he: if therefore ye seek me, let these go their way: That the saying might be fulfilled, which he spake, of them which thou gavest me have I lost none" (John 18:8-9). Now he that betrayed him gave them a sign, saying, Whomsoever I shall kiss, that same is he: hold him fast. And forthwith he came to Jesus, and said, Hail, master; and kissed him" (Matt 26:48-49).

Appearance Before the Priest

"But Peter followed him afar off unto the high priest's palace, and went in, and sat with the servants, to see the end. Now the chief priests, and elders, and all the council, sought false witness against Jesus, to put him to death; (Matt. 26:58-59). "And led him away to Annas first; for he was father-in-law to Caiaphas, which was the high priest that same year" (John 18:13).

Appearance before Caiaphas

"Now Annas had sent him bound unto Caiaphas the high priest. To all the chief priests and elders" (John 18:24). When the morning was come, all the chief priests and elders of the people took counsel against Jesus to put him to death" (Matt. 27:1).

First Appearance Before Pilate

"And when they had bound him, they led him away, and delivered him to Pontius Pilate the governor Matt. 27:2. Then led they Jesus from Caiaphas unto the hall of judgment: and it was early; and they themselves went not into the judgment hall, lest they should be defiled; but that they might eat the Passover" (Joh 18:28).

To Herod

"And as soon as he knew that he belonged unto Herod's jurisdiction, he sent him to Herod, who himself also was at Jerusalem at that time" (Luke 23:7, cf.8-12).

Second Appearance Before Pilate

"Then Pilate entered into the judgment hall again, and called Jesus, and said unto him, Art thou the King of the Jews?

"But ye have a custom that I should release unto you one at the Passover: will ye therefore that I release unto you the King of the Jews? Then cried they all again, saying, Not this man, but Barabbas. Now Barabbas was a robber" (Joh 18:33 39-40). "Now at that feast the governor was wont to release unto the people a prisoner, whom they would. ...And they had then a notable prisoner, called Barabbas...When he was set down on the judgment seat, his wife sent unto him, saying, have thou nothing to do with that just man: for I have suffered many things this day in a dream because of him" (Matt. 27:15, 16. 19).

The Scourging of Jesus

"Then Pilate therefore took Jesus, and scourged him" (John 19:1). Then released he Barabbas unto them: and when he had scourged Jesus, he delivered him to be crucified.

.... And after that they had mocked him, they took the robe off from him, and put his own raiment on him..." (Matt. 27:26, 31).

Third Appearance Before Pilate

"When Pilate therefore heard that saying, he brought Jesus forth, and sat down in the judgment seat in a place that is called the Pavement, but in the Hebrew, Gabbatha" (John 19:13).

Led Away to be Crucified

"Then delivered he him therefore unto them to be crucified. And they took Jesus, and led him away" (John 19:16). "And it was the third hour, and they crucified him" (Mark 15:25). "Now from the sixth hour there was darkness over all the land unto the ninth hour" (Matt. 27:45).

The Preparation and the Sabbath

"And it was the preparation of the Passover, and about the sixth hour: and he saith unto the Jews, Behold your King!" (Joh 19:14). "And that day was the preparation, and the Sabbath drew on" (Luke 23:54). "And they returned, and prepared spices and ointments; and rested the Sabbath day according to the commandment" (Luke 23:56). "Now the next day, that followed the day of the preparation, the chief priests and Pharisees came together unto Pilate" (Matt. 27:62). "Command therefore that the sepulcher be made sure until the third day, lest his disciples come by night, and steal him away, and say unto the people, He is risen from the dead: so, the last error shall be worse than the first" (Matt. 27:54).

Christ in the Passover

According to Gill (1746-1763), the text in Deuteronomy indicates a continual Passover for seven days (Ezek. 45:21–23). This refers to the rest of the seven-day offerings for Passover. The other regular offerings were differentiated as peace offerings. The seven days of Passover daily offerings have the same force as the Passover lamb. This can be seen in the following:

> Observe the month of Abib, and keep the Passover unto the LORD thy God: for in the month of Abib the LORD thy God brought thee forth out of Egypt by night. Thou shalt therefore sacrifice the Passover unto the LORD thy God, of the flock and the herd, in the place which the LORD shall choose to place his name there. Thou shalt eat no leavened bread with it; seven days shalt

thou eat unleavened bread therewith, even the bread of affliction; for thou camest forth out of the land of Egypt in haste: that thou mayest remember the day when thou camest forth out of the land of Egypt all the days of thy life (Duet. 16:1-3).

'Seven days shall ye eat unleavened bread therewith;' with the Passover; this plainly shows, that by the Passover in the preceding verse is not meant strictly the Passover lamb, for that was eaten at once on the night of the fourteenth of the month, and not seven days running, and therefore must be put for the whole solemnity of the feast, and all the sacrifices of it, both the lamb of the fourteenth, and the Chagigah of the fifteenth, and every of the peace offerings of the rest of the days were to be eaten with unleavened bread (Gill, 1746-1763, Deuteronomy/16.htm)

Deuteronomy's text indicates a continual Passover for seven days, which has the same meaning, purpose, and force as the Day of Atonement and the fourteenth day Passover lamb. As you will note from the scripture, the Passover offerings continued throughout the seven days. Thus, when John stated that it was the Passover's preparation on a Friday, he referred to the unleavened bread, the daily Passover arrangements, and the seventh-day Sabbath (John 19:14, 13, 42).

But ye shall offer an offering made by fire, a burnt-offering unto Jehovah: two young bullocks, and one ram, and seven he-lambs a year old; they shall be unto you without blemish; and their meal-offering, fine flour mingled with oil: three-tenth parts shall ye offer for a

73

bullock, and two-tenth parts for the ram; a tenth part shalt thou offer for every lamb of the seven lambs; and one he-goat for a sin-offering, to make atonement for you. Ye shall offer these besides the burnt-offering of the morning, which is for a continual burnt-offering. After this manner, ye shall offer daily, for seven days, the food of the offering made by fire, of a sweet savor unto Jehovah: it shall be offered besides the continual burnt-offering, and the drink-offering thereof" (Num. 28:19-24).

The purpose of the Passover existing on the fourteenth day is, the Passover lamb was killed on the evening of that day at twilight. The unleavened bread is prepared late afternoon of the fourteenth and eaten on the fifteenth. We must note that there is no eight-day feast with Passover and unleavened bread. The first of eight days is preparation only. The seven days included both preparations and the feast. Each day of the seven days is regarded as part of the Passover (Num. 28:16–18).

The fourteenth day Passover lamb was special. It sets up the symbolism of deliverance. Now, the lamb was captured to be killed, and it was killed that night at dusk. Jesus was captured the same night and was on trial to be put to death. His sufferings began that night. He said, "Ye know that after two days is the feast of the Passover, and the Son of man is betrayed to be crucified" (Matt. 26:2). This time of capture is what happened anciently. It can be noted here that the Passover lamb was eaten only after dusk after the fourteenth day ended. None of the Passover lamb's leftovers were to remain for the morning (Num. 9:12). Jesus was tried by the Jews during the night and was deployed in the morning to the Gentiles. "Then led they Jesus from Caiaphas unto the hall of judgment: and it was early." It was daylight when they got to the judgment hall, and they may have had to wait until the governor was ready.

This trial could have started at approximately 7:00 a.m. According to James Strong's concordance, early morning coincides with the fourth watch of the night, from 3:00 to 6:00 a.m. (Strong, 1990). Some may contend that these are not official times. True, the Jews' desperation to get rid of Jesus did not bow to any rule except the fear of the people. Remember, it was on one of the feast days and the Sabbath they went in to see Pilate for sealing the tomb. From the platform of scripture, there is no confusion as to the events that occurred and when they happened.

The difficulty in dealing with the types is in our preferential selection of certain events to coincide them with an antitype. For example, to say that Jesus must spend three days and three nights in the grave as Jonah spent three days and three nights in the belly of the fish and that Jesus must die on the first day of Passover between two evenings is not prophetic, nor does any scripture state such things. These applications are personal and selective extrapolates of the types. Not looking first at the New Testament scriptures' historical record to see what can be applied, some rush to the same act as the Muslim apologists to discredit the resurrection of Jesus. By doing this, the truth is sold for thirty pieces of mistakes. Our opponents are lined up to buy up the errors we are ready to sell. The second paragraph, in the following quote, shows how it works.

> Most Christians learn from an early age that Jonah was preserved in the huge fish by a miracle of God; and they understand the language of Jonah's second chapter as

figurative with regard to death. Rare, "urban-legend," type examples of men swallowed by sharks or other large fish are drawn upon from far and wide to prove the possibility of such. While nothing is impossible for God, was Jesus alive in the tomb?

The followers of Islam are quick to pick up on this widespread, Christian approach to the book of Jonah (stressing Jonah's preservation) to argue for the "Swoon Theory." In a debate between Ahmed Deedat and Josh McDowell in south Africa, Deedat called out to his followers in the crowd about Jonas state in the whale, and they answered, "Alive!" Then he asked about Jesus state in the tomb, and they again responded, 'Alive!' (Cox & Easley, 2003, p. 329).

Sometimes, one's desired perspective for his expected outcome of biblical types become his interpretational rubric of the events. This should not be. We should let the scriptures speak for themselves. As I have said from the beginning, we should trust the biblical record and its historical application of the types. I hope I have demonstrated that to you in this book. I must say that all those who have put forth their noble effort and time to show something different have attempted a brave undertaking to get a clearer vision of the truth. Even with the mistakes of some, we are afforded another opportunity to look into the Messianic church's great Judean truths. We do not need to be divided; we learn, understand, and are convicted at different pace. The peace we have received from the Messiah far outweighs our lack of understanding of this topic's elusive areas. You must understand the truth concerning what is written. The entire record is not completely clear about John's sixth-hour statement with the trials' duration times. According to Campbell's Bible, hours could have been counted by blocks of time.

I hope you have a better understanding of the events surrounding the death of Jesus and a greater appreciation of the salvific work done for us. To me, the Bible is clear on the subject. I hope the same for you as you consider all sides of the issue.

Although we may not celebrate the feasts according to the old pattern, they should be recognized as Israel's cultural heritage. As Israel is waking up to their loss of cultural heritage, their recognition of the feasts is admissible. The feasts recommended for the Messianic church are Passover, Feast of Weeks, Feast of Trumpets, and Hanukkah. Other feasts celebrations may vary depending on a leader's implication and setup. In place of general cultural norms, such as birthdays, Gentile New Year's, Christmas, Easter, Halloween, and Thanksgiving, the divine feast celebrations should mark our deployment. During these feasts' times, we can assemble to learn about the culture and heritage of ancient Israel and prophetic insights that the feasts convey, each feast according to their times. We can also have a potluck, and theatrical role-play of the ancient events. The church should have a budget and a special program for these celebrations. Those with ancient Israel roots should welcome the following three feasts: September for a civil New Year, December for the Feast of Dedication, and Passover. It is a shame how people spend so much money to celebrate an important occasion in their lives, but the Judean church, as a people, has no culture to rejoice over. Really?

Claiming Your Freedom

For all that Yahawasha (Jesus) has done for us, we ought to let Him be our guide. His guidance calls for a personal relationship with Him. This relationship is not dependent on group relations or ego trips in knowledge. This relationship asks for humility inspired by the Spirit of Jesus. This humility in Christ will break from the soul all ties to self-sufficiency puffed up by knowledge. It will permit us to yield freely to the Most High. Remember, it is the Spirit who guides and convicts to repentance, not a good argument, even if it is convincing. Our prayers should be to have faith in God.

If you have not given your life to Jesus, this day could be your day of remembrance. If you will, you can bow in prayer and ask God to forgive you. Confess to God that you have come to accept what the death of Yahawasha means to you and how much He suffered for your sins.

When we accept Yahawasha's saving grace as a gift, we can live for His cause eternally. You must acknowledge that this gift was in no way earned by you or by any other sinner, and you do not owe anyone devotion for your redemption. This day of your commitment is your new day. It can start today if you wholeheartedly pray this prayer to Yahawah in the name of His Son, Yahawasha. There is no other name given among men by which we can be saved and receive peace.

This prayer happened to me back in the summer of 1982. The Lord has kept me steady in His peace ever since. The peace of Yahawasha can be yours. After my conversion, the Lord proved himself to me with signs and wonders. This experience can be cultivated in you through his Spirit. May Yahawah (YHWH) keep you and bless you abundantly.

Chapter 7

—◉◉◉—

The Lord's Rest

Are You Overworking?

Although we are cognizant of the need for rest, we often allow ambition, fame, and power to triumph over this physiological necessity. Failure to accept one's physical limitations is intemperance and insobriety. One summer, about twenty-five years ago, I was taking a class in Florida. The class had approximately forty-five students. We met three times a week. Since it was a semester-long program, the information was intense. Most of us in college taking certain classes could identify with the quick attempt to absorb bulks of information. We were told of our responsibility for the day of the exam. It was our duty to know how much studying time needed to pass the exam. As adults, we prefer to be working than learning to serve. For some of us, while we are learning, working remains a necessity for survival. Thus, many of us find ourselves under the intense pressure of many responsibilities.

One of my classmates during a conversation, expressed the hardship she was facing between school and work and how time was limited. As it was nearing the end of the semester, the responsibility of catching up on studying and accomplishing several tasks took its toll. A group of students decided to meet off schedule to catch up on some required study. They had to decide on which day to meet.

Among them were Jewish, Christian, and unchurched folks. Most of them decided that Saturday would be a good day. Before making the final decision, I spoke up and said Saturday is a sacred religious holiday for rest and convocation. A Jewish lady in the group asked, "You don't do anything on Saturday?" I replied, "No, it's a rest day, to recuperate, relax, and lay aside the concerns of all secular matters." "What religion is that?" she asked. She was told of the church I attended. Elated about her discovery, she expressed her desire to join. She continued by saying: "I need time off too; it must be good being in your religion." I smiled because little she knew that it is not as mechanical as she seemed to think. One cannot keep the Sabbath holy if he is not holy. Afterward, she expressed how difficult it was to find twenty-four hours of the week to donate to tasks unrelated to life's secular and casual concerns. At the end of the conversation, she came to realize that the rest day was not particularly for sleeping but rather a religious celebration with God and a joyous occasion for fellowship among believers. The Sabbath is for rest from secular matters.

The day itself is holy and sacred, regardless of whether one accepts it as such. Why? How can a day be holy? It is so because God said so. It is God's righteousness that makes the day holy. The lady forgot that an attempt to do God's will by the letter in one's strength creates difficulty keeping the Sabbath holy. By the letter of the law, one who is not holy cannot keep the Sabbath holy, much less to keep it by the Spirit.

The Sabbath is not a day for finding one's pleasure, but

rather an active occasion for those whose joy is in the God of salvation. To have a day like that is to have some preparation made for it. It is like having a party. During the party, it is not the time you are washing dishes, cooking food, setting up chairs, or concerning yourself with nonemergency situations in the battle for survival. Think about it. You are in a state of mind pretending that nothing except your recuperation exists. This is the only way you can relish your party. This same principle works for the Sabbath day. When we enter the spiritual rest in Jesus (Heb. 4:1–11), we will find it natural to enter the holy physical rest (Ex. 20:8–11). To enter the spiritual rest, you must make certain preparation too. This preparation involved learning who you are as a sinner, where you come from, and where you are going (Luke 13:25–34).

Another familiar term we use for rest is holiday. In holidays, we rest (stop) from our normal occupation. We do so by refreshing ourselves, celebrating whatever the occasion may be. Sometimes when you find yourself doing something too much, you get bored and need to be refreshed. This refreshment may mean different things for different people. For an athlete coming from a race, he needs two things. One, he needs people who are going to cheer for him. Two, he needs rest with a cup of cold drink. A champion athlete needs not only these but also a party to satisfy a refreshment from his labor.

On the other hand, a student may need to sleep to refresh himself from studies. He does not require a party or cheerleaders. He may need food and exercise to wear off the stress of studying. A sedentary occupant needs a brisk walk for her Sabbath. In every case, there may be a different need. Therefore, rest to the satisfaction of labor requires demarcation of limits and purposes. We need to know the amount of rest, the goal, and the necessary actions for satisfaction. Sometimes we make slaves of ourselves in the name of financial security. We work day and night to occupy ourselves with problems. We pile up bills to keep up with the Joneses. Most of us can't save much unless we are rich. We ask the question: When is it time to take a break? The Bible has the answer.

In Genesis, the Bible says that the Sabbath was created for refreshing from labor. It would look awkward for God to bless the Sabbath day at creation time and permit Adam to work and not celebrate the blessing with Him. On the first day after the day Adam was created, he communed and learned directly from his Maker. He did not work on that day. He also learned of the importance of that holiday and its insignia. The devil has taken this need of rest from the church. Unwittingly, by abolishing the Sabbath, the church has paved the way for promoting the evolutionary philosophy of Darwinian religion.

A Break for the Big Boss

In a ritualistic fashion, God took his break on the seventh day. To be sure God did this, we read the following:

> And on the seventh day God ended his work which he had made, and he rested on the seventh day from all his work which he had made. And God blessed the seventh day and sanctified it: because that in it he had rested from all his work which God created and made (Gen. 2:2–3). For in six days the LORD made heaven and earth, the sea, and all that in them is, and rested the seventh day: wherefore the LORD blessed the Sabbath day, and hallowed it (Ex. 20:11). It is a sign between me

and the children of Israel for ever: for in six days the LORD made heaven and earth, and on the seventh day he rested and was refreshed (Ex. 31:17). For he spake in a certain place of the seventh day on this wise, And God did rest the seventh day from all his works (Heb. 4:4).

There is a common thread in all these verses giving us the reason for the seventh day Sabbath. This day marks a time of cessation from physical labor, at which time, God celebrated His accomplishments. The Most High was refreshed, and He sanctified the day for a holy purpose. This seventh-day cycle is holy unto the Lord. He simply made it an insignia of His power, authority, and love. He set it apart that it may not be classed as other days. The Sabbath is neither regular nor like other days. It is a different dimension of time from all other cycles of time known to man. Apart from Earth's rotation, it has no natural derivative. It is a divine cycled time that depicts the Sabbath of God Almighty. This declaration for the seventh day has nothing to do with any human experience but God's desire for Sabbath. Jesus said that God extended the day to the human family for their benefit.

Now to answer the question of whether Adam kept the Sabbath. Of course, he did. No scripture states that Adam broke or kept the Sabbath. According to Jesus, the Sabbath was made for Adam (man) and *all* his descendants. Considering that God wanted to celebrate the Sabbath with His creatures, Jesus said, the Sabbath was made for mankind (Mark 2:27). Consequently, the first Sabbath celebrated was with Adam's full knowledge; this obvious fact exposes the truth that God would not have left Adam and Eve out. As God declared the creation story to Adam of how He placed celestial bodies in motion to calibrate time, it would be illogical for Him to be silent about the sacredness of His last creation—the Sabbath, a sacred independent timepiece in the time cycle.

No! Not for a second would God bypass the time to bond and declare to Adam that His work was done and the time of the Almighty's Sabbath comes, the last act of creation, the act of the seventh-day Sabbath. The seventh day of the weekly cycle, the official one in Eden, given to Moses, having its hourly differences in time zones, is the only Sabbath recognized by God with the blessing for each of its time zones. It is a commandment of the sign of ownership.

Sabbatical Classifications

It is necessary to treat the Lord's rest separately. Some believe that the seventh-day Sabbath of creation week and the feast Sabbaths of lunar timing work as one commandment. Although they are in the same worship-laws category, they are in separate subcategories. They are in the same general worship category as the Old Testament dietary and purification laws. As a subcategory of worship, the Sabbath is separated from the other feast days seen in Leviticus 23.

> And the LORD spake unto Moses, saying, (2) Speak unto the children of Israel, and say unto them, Concerning the feasts of the LORD, which ye shall proclaim to be holy convocations, (3) Six days shall work be done: but the seventh day is the Sabbath of rest, a holy convocation; ye shall do no work therein: it is the Sabbath of the LORD in all your dwellings. (4) *These are the feasts of the LORD, even holy convocations, which ye shall*

proclaim in their seasons. (5) In the fourteenth day of the first month at even is the LORD'S Passover. (6) And on the fifteenth day of the same month is the feast of unleavened bread unto the LORD: seven days ye must eat unleavened bread. --Lev. *23:1-6.* Italics ours.

Observe that the Sabbath is an appointed time, a feast (*mou-aide* in Hebrew). Also, observe that it is separated from the main list owing to its nonlunar timing (vs. 3). The seventh day Sabbath, in this chapter, is classed among holy convocations. Unlike the other feast days, it is not regulated with meats and drinks. There is no food or drink association with the Sabbath. The Sabbath is not a part of other festival days for four reasons: 1) it is governed only by the weekly cycle; 2) it was instituted before sin; 3) God blessed it as sacred before sin; and 4) it was engraved among the Ten Commandments, the law to be written in our hearts.

Consequently, it is not a shadow for solving the sin problem, but it serves as a model for our anointing due to its sanctification. The transgression of the Sabbath instruction is incompatible with God's character. After He worked, He rested. The Sabbath as an appointed time started with the original week beginning with day one.

If one is at odds with any of the Ten Commandments (ten words), naturally, he will be at odds with the rest of them. Some people attempt to spiritualize the Ten Commandments' to avoid the conscious conviction of breaching them. This act is done in vain because once the Sabbath is spiritualized to eradicate its practical application; similar efforts are employed to do away with the rest of the commandments' valuable lessons.

The Sabbath mentioned in Colossians 2:16 refers to the

yearly festival for monthly regulated Sabbaths. In the original, it reads "or Sabbath" (Westcott & Hort,1881). On the surface, it may appear to be all Sabbaths, but the context does not support that. While God told the Israelites to cease keeping Sabbaths associated with the lunar holidays, all the Ten Commandments, including the Sabbath, were still required (Amos 5:21–24; Isa. 1:11–14; Neh. 13:15–18). The purpose of lunar Sabbaths was for celebration; however, the seventh day weekly Sabbath is for temperance, which is the fruit of the Spirit, the righteousness of God. The yearly lunar Sabbaths were shadows of Jesus, who has given us spiritual rest. The term "Sabbath" itself means "rest or cessation from labor." It is also used to designate week (Heb. *shavooa* or *shavout)* of seven days. The way to know which Sabbath is referred to is to study the context carefully, prayerfully, and logically.

Some try to fuse all the Sabbaths into one type of commandment and timing system. The feast Sabbaths are of lunar timing, but the seventh-day Sabbath is a weekly cycle belonging solely to the idea that God made the world in six days. The first day of creation, not the fourth day, begins the creation's weekly cycle. The fourth day of creation was to mark time for other gatherings. Those specific gatherings and their associated events were given to Israel in the light of messianic salvific tutors (Heb. 9:7–10). However, the seventh day Sabbath was known to all mankind. Some of Israel's remnants in Iboland and Ghana in West Africa recognize Israel's God as the God of the seventh day. They still recognize the same Saturday as the Sabbath, and the God of it is the one they worship. V. T. Houteff (1942) gave a fitting explanation in the booklet, "The Sign of Jonah," where he not only explained how the three days and three nights work but also had this to say about lunar seventh-day Sabbath-keeping:

> A lunar sabbath must necessarily coordinate with both lunar and solar time. But a sabbatical month (28 days) falls 1-1/2 days short of a lunar month (29-1/2); and a sabbatical year (12 x 4 = 48 weeks; 48 x 7 = 336 days) falls 18 days short of a lunar year (354) and 29 days short of a solar year (365). So at the close of each sabbatical year, the lunar Sabbath-keeper, in order to keep time with the weekly cycle, as well as with the rotation of the earth and of the moon, would have to make the earth stand still 29 days and the moon 18 days (Houteff, 1942, p. 34).

It is impossible to keep a lunar Seventh day creation Sabbath. There is also the subjective calculation of feasts times and calendric adjustments among the Israelites to determine times of feasts. The Sabbath is set from creation and is independent of subjective computations.

The Sabbath has kept Israel in recognizing the great God of creation. God is the almighty Creator. No matter what religion teaches, the weekly Sabbath testifies about the Creator. The Sabbath is the seal of God's mark of authority and domain. The fourth commandment explains God's domain. It does not speak to Israel only but all of mankind. Yes, even to the sons of the stranger.

Justification Through Christ

When we are complete in Jesus, He removes from us the burden of being lost. He gives us the comfort of justification and empowers us to sanctification. He eliminates the handwriting (sentences) that was against us, exonerating us of charges.

While the yearly lunar Sabbaths represent our justification, the seventh-day Sabbath represents our sanctification, anointed for a holy purpose. This commitment is seen in our daily walk with Jesus by faith. The seventh-day Sabbath is a picture that illustrates our sanctification (Heb. 4:4). Thus, it cannot be obliterated or modified by the coming of Jesus. While the yearly feast Sabbaths were shadows, the seventh-day Sabbath isn't. The purpose of the shadows was to forecast the plan for reparation. Since the seventh day Sabbath was in existence before sin, it cannot symbolize a fractured object.

Our justification is a declaration, substituting our status quo to the standard that God desires. Justification requires us to confess our sins and believe that God will change our status. Justification has nothing to do with whether you are charitable, hate your neighbor, or lived as an adulterer. None of one's good or bad works can qualify or disqualify him from receiving justification. The catch is, justification does not come alone. Trailing justification is your sanctification, dedicating you to the service of God. Just as Jesus died (Passover) to save you, God expects you to follow through with obeying His Ten Commandments by the Spirit (feast of weeks). If you are serving yourself and Satan with bad works, it is your proof that grace and justification is of no benefit to you.

Creation's Interminable Signature

The Sabbath existed before the law was given to man (Gen. 2:1–3), before the Exodus (26:5), and before God made the Old Covenant at Sinai (Ex. 16, 19:5–8). The Sabbath was not of the Old Covenant but engrafted as an adjunct. There was no written covenant when the Sabbath was made and set apart as holy during the creation week. So blessed and sacred is the Sabbath that it would take a direct commandment to change its status. The Sabbath cannot become elusive by implication (Num. 23:20). It is for these reasons that the New Covenant has not made the Sabbath obsolete.

The seventh day was the last creation of God on creation week. We heard of the gap theory interpretation about Genesis 1, 1:2. This theory explains that the term "day" in Hebrew, as used in this context, means a period of opaqueness versus clarity and that there was a major gap between verse one and the rest of the verses in Genesis chapter 1. Regardless of how one wishes to interpret the Genesis record of creation, if scripture explains scripture, Moses's inspired interpretation for what took place during creation week is superior to the gap theory. His record is found in Exodus 20:8–11. The weekly cycle of twenty-four-hour days is independent of all solar system bodies except earth. The sun was created on the fourth day, not to begin a weekly cycle but to mark its continuation. While the sun replaced the work that was already affected by the first light, the moon, on the other hand, began a cycle of months and years (Gen. 1:14–16).

The history of the second-century church shows how church members in Rome kept the first day of the week instead of the seventh day. This change was done upon the premise that the resurrection of Jesus took place on Sunday. During those times, the Judean name of days was not yet officially paganized. Name of days was counted by numbers from the Sabbath. That made it impossible to adopt a lunar-based weekly cycle since the moon does not set a fixed weekly cycle of days, a twenty-eight and twenty-nine-and-a-half-day month. From Jewish to Roman, the order of days in the weekly cycle of seven days remained unbroken. Regardless of how one changes dates, months, and years, the weekly cycle remains unaffected.

Was the Cessation Cycle for All?

Some written papers were trying to prove that the Sabbath is only for Israelites who came out of Egypt. Well, those original Israelites lasted only for a few generations. How about the Gentiles who came out of Egypt with Israel? Were they included in the Sabbath commandment? The more profound question is, how about the Gentiles who did not come out of Egypt but later joined the Israelites? The Bible has the answer. "Ye shall have one manner of law, as well for the stranger, as for one of your own country: for I am the LORD your God" (Lev. 24:22; c.f. Ex. 12:49; Num. 15:16).

> Also the sons of the stranger, that join themselves to the LORD, to serve him, and to love the name of the LORD, to be his servants, everyone that keepeth the Sabbath from polluting it, and taketh hold of my covenant; Even them will I bring to my holy mountain, and make them joyful in my house of prayer: their burnt offerings and their sacrifices shall be accepted upon mine altar; for mine house shall be called a house of prayer for all people.-- Isa. 56:6-7.

The Almighty's intent in Deuteronomy 5:15 was not to make the Sabbath Egypt-exodus dependent but asked His people to reciprocate by doing something for Him. The Sabbath commandment was to exclude none. Not only animals but even the ground had to observe a Sabbath too.

The Lord of the Sacred Rest

Without a doubt, we know that Jesus observed the Sabbath according to the law (John 8:46). He was never accused of doing manual labor on the Sabbath. The Jews in His day had burdened the Sabbath with many protective rules beyond the law. There are three situations presented where Jesus dealt squarely with that problem.

The Cornfield. In this situation, two facts stand out clearly: Jesus did not plan the event, and He did not go through the cornfield for self-satisfaction. When accused, He did not conclude that the Sabbath was changed, old, or abolished (Matt. 12:5, 8). Jesus said He is Lord of the Sabbath (Mark 2:27). Neither was Jesus breaking the Sabbath as claimed by His accusers. Jesus's passing through the cornfield on a single occasion out of necessity and allowing His disciples to take some free corn is not sufficient grounds for accusing Him of Sabbath-breaking. By citing similar Judean circumstances in the Old Testament for His defense, Jesus sustained His innocence. He said the law appears to have been broken, and He was not guilty; the situation was circumstantial. Jesus was not saying we can, on our authority or circumstances, work on the Sabbath.

Healing. Jesus made it transparent that it was general understanding He had not broken any law by healing the man on the Sabbath. Jesus did not herald an anti-Sabbath defense. He concluded the argument by saying that the Sabbath given to mankind was for his benefit. According to Jesus, there is no law against saving one from distress through volunteer service when it comes to healing on the Sabbath (Matt. 12:11; Mark 3:4; Luke 13:14–17, 14:3–4; John 7:22–23). Therefore, Jesus did what was lawful to do on the Sabbath (Mark 3:4). However, this is not saying that healing routinely replaces the Sabbath rest.

Pick up Thy Bed. One of the defenses used against the Sabbath is that Jesus broke the Sabbath (John 5:18). The reference that is usually used by some preachers is John 5. In consideration of the context, the claim is not apparent. The Pharisees sought to kill Jesus not only because He had healed a man, but He had the man parading God's power by picking up his bed and walk on the Sabbath day. The reason for picking up the bed was not to make the man work but to draw attention, engaging him with others, thus declaring God's power. In that context, the Pharisees saw the display as work, a violation of the Sabbath law. If these acts were breaking the Sabbath, Jesus would have acknowledged it and used a valid circumstantial defense compatible with the Old Testament. Instead, He stated that His Father works, and so does He. His Father healed the man, and He directed the display of the Father's power. What was the type of work involved? Was it common labor? The Sabbath was not created as a hindrance for relieving suffering or obscuring a declaration of God's glory.

Was not the physical Sabbath rest created to be a blessing? Jesus had made this so clear that no one should take issue with the Sabbath. The Pharisees knew full well that Jesus was not guilty of breaking the Sabbath. He stated that His Sabbath work was authenticated in the Old Testament in concert with the established custom. The Old Testament agrees with Jesus's action on the Sabbath. Does such a fact invalidate the physical rest in Old Testament times? There are rudimentary arguments some people use to lure others into believing something false about the Sabbath. In the Old Testament, none were guilty of saving a suffering animal on the Sabbath. Neither did such service invalidate Sabbath-keeping. The Old Testament stipulates a cessation of manual labor from secular matters. Making statements on behalf of the gospels that Jesus broke the Sabbath for its invalidation is not biblical.

Jesus taught proper Sabbath-keeping. In Luke 23:56, we see that Jesus's followers kept the Sabbath according to the law after He died. If He taught, in word or practice, not to rest on the Sabbath, why were the disciples keeping it after the crucifixion? Jesus's mission was to make the Sabbath enjoyable and free from man-made rules. It was not His mission to convert or spiritualize the Sabbath. He did not come to abolish the law or to reduce our obligation to it but to fulfill it, to make it more honorable.

The Apostolic Rest

Over the centuries, the church has been struggling with the Sabbath question. From AD 31 to about AD 96, when John wrote the Revelation, the Sabbath controversy between Jews and Christians was quiescent. The paucity of argument on the issue was due to the disciples' customary use of the Sabbath.

"And when the Jews were gone out of the synagogue, the Gentiles besought that these words might be preached to them the next Sabbath. And the next Sabbath day came almost the whole city together to hear the word of God" (Acts 13:13–15, 42–44; 16:13, 18:4). If the disciples were known to keep Sunday regularly for the resurrection, there would be no need to keep the Gentiles waiting for the next Sabbath—a whole week. This case is especially important to note since the upcoming meeting was not predicated on a Judean synagogue, and the Jews were not collaborating.

When John wrote the Revelation by AD 96, the apostolic Christian church's custom was Sabbath-keeping. There could not have been any change to the Sabbath before AD 70 when Jerusalem was under siege—an event referred to by Jesus in connection with the Sabbath commandment (Matt. 24:20).

Sunday and the Apostolic Church

The first meeting of the disciples mentioned was on a Sunday afternoon. The gathering was related to fearing the Jews (John 20:19). The last recorded Sunday gathering was Paul's farewell assembly recorded in Acts (20:7, 8, 11). The breaking of bread, in this situation, is synonymous with having a regular meal. This gathering was a picnic, not Holy Communion (Luke 24:35; Acts 2:42, 46). This meeting, lasting until midnight, proves that it was not a Sunday morning church service but a late afternoon Sunday picnic.

The Sunday gathering referred to in 1 Corinthians 16:1–2 was clearly for individual aggregation of gifts. The location of this treasury is not clear. The text states:

> Now concerning the collection for the saints, as I have given the order to the churches of Galatia, even so do ye. Upon the first day of the week let every one of you lay by him in store, as God hath prospered him, that there be no gatherings when I come.

Each person was to amass a reserve by placing things that needed to be picked up by Paul next to himself. There is nothing in the original text, permitting one to believe that the storage was a place for convocational worship. If this gathering could have taken place on a church day, and if Sunday were a church day, this instruction would have been unnecessary. The implication of this instruction admits a time-consuming and laborious element. Had this been a church day, they would have naturally gathered their contributions beforehand. Sunday was a regular workday. After the apostles died, the early church fathers, without any biblical authority, were involved in Sunday worship. Since the church is not a democracy, the early church fathers had no biblical right to change the messianic Judean culture. Paul spoke of the danger of making changes as follows:

> Take heed therefore unto yourselves, and to all the flock, over the which the Holy Ghost hath made you overseers, to feed the church of God, which he hath purchased with his own blood. For I know this, that after my departing shall grievous wolves enter in among you, not sparing the flock. Also of your own selves shall men arise, speaking perverse things, to draw away disciples after them. Therefore watch, and remember, that by the space of three years I ceased not to warn every one night and day with tears (Acts 20:28-31).

In the apostles' days, Sunday was a worship day for the believers in Mithra, the sun-worshiped god. Naturally, it was a day of inactivity for most pagans. However, it was a regular workday for Christians. As seen in the text, in 1 Corinthians, the church worked to amass contributions in their private abode, waiting for the apostle to arrive for pickup. The apostolic Judeo-messianic church did not celebrate the resurrection of Jesus by observing a weekly service day but worked every day except on the seventh day.

The Church and the Lord's Day

As seen earlier, the church Jesus left on Earth used Sunday for work and personal pleasure and Sabbath for worship. Ensuring the biblical quiescence of the change of the Sabbath, I quote from *The Summa Theologica,* the most authoritative literature on doctrine in the Catholic church, to wit:

> In the New Law, the observance of the Lord's day took the place of the observance of the Sabbath, not by virtue of the precept but by the institution of the Church and the custom of Christian people. For this observance is not figurative, as was the observance of the Sabbath in the old Law. Hence the prohibition to work on the Lord's Day is not so strict as on the Sabbath: certain works are permitted on the Lord's day which was forbidden on the Sabbath, such as the cooking of food and so forth (Aquinas, 2007, *Article four: Question 122).*

Sunday is the first day of the week, and Saturday is the seventh day of the week. According to St. Thomas, Sunday is not the Sabbath, and that Sunday "Sabbath" rules do not originate from the scriptures but tradition. He also stated that Sunday keeping is a tradition of the post-apostolic era. This man-made rulership is an example of what Jesus talked about in Matt. 15:3, 9, 13–14. Among the pagans, in apostolic times, Sunday was known as the day of the sun god. Between AD 100 and 200, as the church continued to grow, Sunday came to be adopted as "the Lord's

Day." Justin Martyr (AD 130–165), a church father who studied in Rome, wrote:

> But Sunday is the day on which we all hold our common assembly because it is the first day on which God, having wrought a change in the darkness and matter, made the world; and Jesus Christ our Savior rose from the dead (Martyr, 130-165, pp.75–76).

Sunday keeping, from the inception, proceeded from pagan religions. Pagans, as a rule, kept Sunday in honor of the sun god. The early Christian fathers joined the pagans in Sunday keeping. Initially, the Sabbath was the typical Christian day of worship until it was supplanted by Sunday keeping. While Sabbath-keeping was rampant among Christians in the early days (AD 31–150), those in Rome and Alexandria began to observe Sunday in the latter part of this period. Through the years, the Romans made Sunday a Christian festival day for worship in honor of the resurrection. Out of disdain, they made the Sabbath a day of fasting. By these acts, the Sabbath was effectively transferred to Sunday.

In both the pages of history and the holy scriptures, the early church's custom is Sabbath observance in memorial of creation. It is unscriptural to assume that the church did not routinely meet on the Sabbath. Paul died at the hands of Nero in AD 67. Jesus spoke of the Sabbath in connection with an event that took place in AD 70. He also said that the Sabbath was made for mankind. He could have easily said, "God gave the Sabbath to you for your fathers' sake," as He said for circumcision, but instead, He said that the Sabbath was made for mankind, Jews and Gentiles alike. We can now see that the apostolic stance, history, and scripture stand as one on the subject.

If Sunday keeping was not part of the Christian church during apostolic times, when did it creep into the church, and for what reason? Some say the disciples were Jewish, so in their immaturity, they kept the Jewish Sabbath. Is it not an affront remark and insulting the truth to call the Sabbath a Jewish Sabbath? Paul labored hard to keep the church from falling back into Judean rituals for achieving salvation. It is doubtful that all of Paul's labor was done in vain. In any event, there is no biblical record of controversy between the Jews and the Christians about breaking the Sabbath. There is no biblical record of Paul telling the church to cease keeping the seventh day Sabbath. As can be noted, there are many Judean and Christian controversies after the ascension of Jesus recorded in the New Testament. The seventh day Sabbath is not one of them.

Hardinge (1973), a historian on the Celtic church and the Sabbath, revealed some very useful information about the Sabbath history.

> Soon after the founding of the faith, Gnosticism and Mithraism raised tensions in Christian thinking. Gnostics 'celebrated the Sunday of every week, not on account of its reference to the resurrection of Christ, for that would have been inconsistent with their Docetism, but as the day consecrated to the Sun, which was, in fact, their Christ'. The influence of Mithraism tended in the same direction, for, as G.L. Laing declared rightly: 'Our observance of Sunday' as the Lord's Day is apparently derived from Mithraism. The argument that

has sometimes been used against this claim, namely, that Sunday was chosen because of the resurrection on that day, is not well supported' (Hardinge, 1973, pp. 75-76).

On Saturday, the Gospels and other portions of the Scripture shall be read aloud." Neander remarks that this canon is open to two interpretations. It may mean that on Saturday, as on Sunday, the Holy Scriptures shall be read aloud in the church, and therefore solemn public service shall be held; and Canon 49 is in favor of this interpretation. It was also the custom in many provinces of the ancient Church to observe Saturday as the feast of the Creation" (Hardinge, 1973, p. 310).

Because it was difficult to make a clean break, the Sabbath was kept alongside Sunday for a few centuries. The Sabbath was still the only authentic day of worship until Rome declared it a Jewish Sabbath. Sabbatarian Christians were called Judaizers. As noted below, Rome discouraged Sabbath-keeping by enforcing fasting on that day and enacting laws that forbade fasting on Sunday.

Neander suggests ...that it was the custom in many parts of the ancient Church to keep every Saturday as a feast in commemoration of the Creation... Neander also suggests that possibly some Judaizers read on the Sabbath only the Old Testament (Catholic Encyclopedia, 2007, Synod of Laodicea Canon 16, 49).

Those churches, however, which were composed of Jewish Christians, though they admitted, with the rest, the festival of Sunday, yet retained also that of the

Sabbath; and it was from these that the custom became general in the Eastern church of distinguishing this day, as well as Sunday, but exclusion fasts and by standing position in prayer; while in the Western, and especially in the Roman church, where the opposition against Judaism predominated, the custom, on the other hand, grew out of this opposition, of observing the Sabbath also as a fast day. This difference in customs became striking whenever members of the Eastern churches past their Sabbaths in churches of the West (Neander & Torrey, 1853, pp. 296-297).

The Roman church made Sunday a strict Sabbath and Saturday a working day. Some Protestants have approved this transfer while accepting the Ten Commandments as binding. Even when paganized with Sunday keeping, the Roman church believes that the Ten Commandments were not abolished; however, most Protestants believe they are. Today, those who do not believe Sunday to be a strict Sabbath use it as a convenient day of worship. Historically, Rome fabricated Sunday in place of the Sabbath. As noted in the following, through the progressive years, Sunday keeping became international law. Constantine moreover placed Sunday under the protection of the State [Edict of 321 A.D.].

It is true that the believers in Mithras [Sun-worshiped god] also observed Sunday as well as Christmas; consequently, Constantine speaks not of the day of the Lord, but of the everlasting day of the' sun. According to Eusebius, the heathen also was obliged on this day to go out into the open country and together raise their hands and repeat the prayer already mentioned a prayer without any marked Christian (*Catholic Encyclopedia*, 2007, Art. "Constantine the Great).

No one shall fast on Sunday, nor may anyone absent himself from church during Lent and hold a conventicle of his own (Hefele, & Von, 1876, p.293).

Christians shall not Judaize and be idle on Saturday but shall work on that day; but the Lord's day they shall especially honor, and as being Christians shall if possible do no work on that day. If, however, they are found Judaizing, they shall be shut out from Christ (Hefele, & Von, 1876. *p. 316*).

At the beginning of the fifth century Socrates (+ 445) wrote of the situation as it then existed: "Although almost all churches throughout the world celebrated the sacred mysteries on the Sabbath of every week, yet the Christians of Alexandria and at Rome, on account of some ancient tradition, have ceased to do this" (Hardinge, 1973, p. 76).

Pope Gregory (+ 604), as champion of Roman usages, had upheld the careful observance of Sunday and had stigmatized any respect for the Sabbath as Judaizing. In a letter to the Roman people, he wrote: "It has come to my ears that certain men of perverse spirit have sown among you some things that are wrong and opposed to the holy faith, so as to forbid any work being done on the Sabbath day. What else can I call these but preachers of Antichrist, who, when he comes, will cause the Sabbath day as well as the Lord's day to be kept free from all work."

Theodore of Tarsus (+ 690),... drew up seven canons

to deal with the keeping of Sunday. "Those who despise the Lord's day and neglect the appointed feasts of the church of God." Theodore prohibited all labor on the Lord's day and forbade all fasting on it. One canon ruled: "If he fast out of contempt for the day, he shall be abhorred as a Jew by all the Catholic churches" (Hardinge, 1973, p. 85).

Until it was adopted from the sun-worshiping pagans, what is now called Christian Sabbath was originally pagan and had no relationship with Christians. Even after the lapse of many decades, the church was still holding to the Sabbath. Things changed through the centuries, and the Sabbath was abolished from Christian practice and replaced by Sunday. However, antinomianism (against the law) was not part of the Roman church per se. Neither was antinomianism part of the early Christian church. Today, antinomianism becomes fashionable among protestants. In the desire to please large crowds, Sunday-observing churches are trapped by the defense of antinomianism.

Chapter 8

———⊂◦◦◦⊃———

Antinomianism and the Christian

How to Understand the Law

In concert with many Christians, antinomianism is the basis for discarding the Sabbath. The term means without the law. Believers in antinomianism feel that the Spirit's inner workings convicting you of sin and your request for forgiveness are all-sufficient. Antinomianism precludes the necessity of righteous living. In support of antinomianism, some religious teachers blew out of proportion statements made by the apostle Paul. Unfortunately, and unwittingly, some missteps are made when reading the Pauline epistles. These missteps are made when attempting to avoid laws written in the Old Testament, the only authoritative canon of the apostolic church (Matt. 12:24; Luke 24:27, 32, 45; John 5:39, Acts 17:11; Rom. 15:4).

Another reason for the missteps in comprehending the Pauline epistles is that some chapters or parts of Paul's epistles are discussions on previously discussed matters or are responses to issues observed by him or reports he obtained. Therefore, although contexts may not be expressly written, the truth can be rightly calculated by prayer, though with some difficulty at times.

Peter states that some parts of the Pauline epistles were not for newborn babes or older believers who were not fully grounded. Most of Paul's writings must be taught to those who lack experience. A novice needs the help of a mature believer who is Spirit-filled to support a heaven-guided understanding. According to Peter, a misinterpretation of Paul's writings can lead to the destruction of the soul. To think that when Paul refers to the law, embraces the entire spectrum of the law is a mistake. Concerning Paul's writings, Peter said: "As also in all his epistles, speaking in them of these things; in which are some things hard to be understood, which they that are unlearned and unstable wrest, as they do also the other scriptures, unto their own destruction" (2 Peter 3:16). It is not the best advice for a novice to start with Paul's epistles without an experienced teacher. At times, even professional ministers need lots of prayers and careful study to understand Paul's epistles.

Unless guided by the Spirit, it is easy to misunderstand the Pauline epistles. Some revisions of antinomianism theory include a concept of separation in the requirement for separate salvation. Some believe that good works will save the body, and separately, the soul is already saved by grace. They believe the latter happens by faith alone, regardless of the believer's lifestyle. For some, this is the basis of the belief "once saved always saved." Promoters of this view use Paul's first epistle to the Corinthians, chapter 5, to teach that the unruly and law-breaking Christians were forever saved. Again, this concept is derived because of a misunderstanding of Paul's writings. The scriptures teach that the work we do for God in ignorance is worthless and receives no credit, but the worker will be rescued in discovering the truth.

The Old Testament Multifaceted Law

The controversy in Paul's day centered on the Jews' desire for Christians to keep all the laws in the Old Testament as a premise for salvation. Secondly, there were concerns that some Christians had been deceived into believing the Jewish teaching that salvation was obtained by observing the law. Although the Old Testament speaks flatly against this, Jewish leaders held this concept to mandate obedience from the people. The disciples had set out to combat this teaching.

The law of the Israelites had many parts. The scope of this book is inadequate to subcategorize all the laws and writings of the Old Testament. However, to determine the continuing validity of Old Testament laws, we must consider each case's context and conditions. When this is done, no law will be abolished without reason, and no law will be practiced that has completed its purpose. Notice how most churches accept the Old Testament's tithing law but do not accept other laws with similar allocation. They claim that tithing predates Moses. So do many other laws they feel have been abrogated. The Israelites were a self-contained nation without the advancement of the technology we have today. They had laws in place for both medical precautions and societal organization. They had judges and laws for judging their society. Their laws were for the reflection of God's character. There were international laws and rules of combat. Most of the Gentiles did not have this commonwealth.

Some of the laws, as mentioned earlier, can be made

international. For example, to a great degree, the United States of America uses some of these laws to rule American society. We use the law of debtors and capital punishment. All civilized societies use the law of handwashing and medical isolation. No one questions the hospitals for keeping parts of Moses's laws. If they don't keep Moses's laws, at least in part, and we get sick as a result, we would want to sue the practitioners for unfair medical practice. When the doctor tells a hypertensive patient to stop eating pork and harmful fats, or a person with diabetes to stop eating refined carbohydrates, or a nurse to wash her hands between seeing patients, we do not say no. However, we thought to be no longer under such rituals or legalisms. Instead, in good judgment, we insist that these principles are to be maintained. They are not empty rituals or legal codes as some would have it. They are kingdom principles. These laws have received general acceptance in our society. God's laws are a blessing to all people.

Morality for the Israelites was not the same as for the Gentiles. The moral code of the heathen is substandard to the life of Jesus. The only code of morality acceptable to Jesus is what's written or implied in the Bible. Those who have problems with God's standards have not entirely surrendered their lives to the life of Jesus. It is a way of feeling saved without making a full surrender of their way of life to Jesus. They were taught to feel saved by grace while living in their kingdom. Bible principles are not a conglomerate democratic code deriving from a pagan or heathen origin.

There were other laws, symbolic in nature, prescribed by God to the Israelites. Because of transgressing the written moral code, laws were established to teach the Israelites about salvation from sin. These added laws were symbolical. The symbolical laws were the sanctuary, the annual feasts, and circumcision; symbolical priesthood expressions were worn. Priests and others wore special clothing for remembrance. For example, the priestly robe, the tallit, the fringes, and the mezuzah were all symbolical expressions of the priestly role and their association to the ancient sanctuary.

Not all the laws had the same conditional requisition. The Jews in the Old Testament times did not observe all the judicial laws or all the sanctuary laws during captivity. They were required to keep the Ten Commandments always. The Ten Commandments were not made for cherry-picking, redaction, or conversion. Each of them has the same force, importance, and moral value (James 2:10).

Three of the Ten Commandments have no time limit and were instituted in a sinless world. The three are: Jehovah, the one and only God, the Sabbath is on the seventh day of creation week, and marriage is one man to one woman. These laws were made with the Earth. Pursuant to Earth's unrenewed existence, these laws are unalterable and non-negotiable. Some may say, in Genesis, these were not written or commanded. When Jesus referred to the marriage law authenticity, He pointed to Genesis when laws were not written (Matt. 19:8). Notice that in this case, Jesus did not refer to the Ten Commandments on table of stones. The implied law, by example, had a stronger, more foolproof authenticity than the written law. Imagine our leaders today trying to teach Jesus that the marriage law was not valid in Genesis because it was not written on tablets of stone, or that homosexuality and polygamy were all valid for the same reason. Although polygamy was under God's permissive will, in the Old Testament, it was not part of His perfect will (1 Tim. 3:2). Ignorance of the law does not invalidate its need or existence. While some laws have their limits and conditions, others are timeless.

Trusting in a Guide

The dismissal of the responsibility for thinking for oneself in spiritual matters is the greatest of all sins. Some wish to control their audience by thinking for them. It is very lucrative when you think for someone else. It is robbery to ascent to the desire to think for others or to control their thinking. A huge majority have no time to pray and spend personal quality time in the Word to check if what they are told is biblical; they approve by word or deed whatever a leader leads them into. Their taste for spiritual things is immature. There is a phobia for discovering the truth. The only winner in this state of affairs is the enemy of truth. The heavenly borne counsel concerning this matter is found in the following quote from the book, *The Great Controversy*:

> But God will have a people upon the earth to maintain the Bible, and the Bible only, as the standard of all doctrines and the basis of all reforms. The opinions of learned men, the deductions of science, the creeds or decisions of ecclesiastical councils, as numerous and discordant as are the churches which they represent, the voice of the majority—not one nor all of these should be regarded as evidence for or against any point of religious faith. Before accepting any doctrine or precept, we should demand a plain "Thus saith the Lord" in its support.
>
> The truth and the glory of God are inseparable; it

is impossible for us, with the Bible within our reach, to honor God by erroneous opinions. Many claims that it matters not what one believes if his life is only right. But the life is molded by the faith. If light and truth are within our reach, and we neglect to improve the privilege of hearing and seeing it, we virtually reject it, we are choosing darkness rather than light.

'There is a way that seemeth right unto a man, but the end thereof are the ways of death.' Proverbs 16:25. Ignorance is no excuse for error or sin when there is every opportunity to know the will of God. A man is traveling and comes to a place where there are several roads and a guideboard indicating where each one leads. If he disregards the guideboard and takes whichever road seems to him to be right, he may be ever so sincere, but will in all probability find himself on the wrong road. (White, 1888, pp.459, 461-462).

The Sabbath and the Law

There are four anti-Sabbath camps. One camp believes that the Sabbath is still binding because it is part of the eternal law, but the church democratically has the right to make changes in the law. Therefore, the Sabbath is now on Sunday, the first day of the week. The next camp believes that the Sabbath is part of the ceremonial laws and, therefore, was abolished with similar laws in the Old Testament. The third camp believes that the Sabbath is governed by the lunar calendar and is not on the seventh day of the weekly cycle from the first day of creation. The last camp believes that the Sabbath is still binding and that the Ten Commandments are still good, but that the Sabbath rules are now spiritual; therefore, the day is no longer sacred. Some people take 2 Peter 3:8 out of context and believe that the Sabbath is one thousand years long. Below is the nations' way of defining Sabbath:

> Sabbatarianism, doctrine of those Christians who believe that Sunday (the Christian Sabbath) should be observed in accordance with the Fourth Commandment, which forbids work on the Sabbath because it is a holy day. Some other Christians have contended that the Fourth (or Third in some systems) Commandment was a part of the Hebrew ceremonial, not moral, law. They believe that this law was entirely abolished by Jesus Christ, whose Resurrection on the first day of the week established a new kind of day, characterized by worship rather than absence of work (Encyclopedia Britannica (n.d.), Art. Sabbath).

These ideas from the various camps are not clear from the scriptures. The interpretations are less than canonical (Ezek. 4:12–14). Jesus said He did not come to destroy the law but to fulfill it. The true interpretation is: Jesus came to make what existed more precise and entirely apprehensible. Sure, fulfilled could mean to "accomplish" or "to make whole." It equally means to "fill up, to add more, or to meet up to expectation." In this context, the Savior made it clear that abolish, remove, or change was not His intent (Matt. 5:17–20). Therefore, there is no biblical premise for teaching abolished or reduced as the purpose of Jesus's statement. "For to be carnally minded is death, but to be spiritually minded is life and peace. Because the carnal mind is enmity against God: for it is not subject to the law of God, neither indeed can be" (Rom. 8:6–7). Isn't it carnally minded, teaching that the law must be reductively reinterpreted, changed, or abolished?

Is there a change in the law from the Old to the New Testament? The difference that exists is in the provision of salvation (Heb. 7:11–12). In this provision, there is a substitution. Hebrews 7–9 and Matthew 5 outline the changes and how they took place.

According to the scriptures, "The law is holy, and the commandment holy, and just, and good" (Rom. 7:12; cf. John 15:10; Rev. 14:12). Why abolish that which is holy, just, and good? In the same chapter, sin is known as the transgression of the law. According to Romans 6:23, "The wages of sin is death." What happens if the law is abolished? Well, there would be no more sins to be forgiven, no more death to be feared, and all of mankind's actions would be law-free and sin-free. Who then is the leader in the lawless gospel movement? Isn't it the enemy? According to him, "Do as you please shall be the whole book of the law." It serves his purpose when all the laws are interpreted as a universal generalization that removes all explicit practicality. However, God is holy, and so is the law in the Old and New Testaments. Although the law cannot give life in any sense, its purpose is to aid the novice in the steps toward holy character and give meaning to the kingdom of the Holy Spirit. The Spirit and the law work as a unit.

The Holy Spirit's work is to transcribe those laws in the mind of natural Israel (Heb. 8:7–12; 2 Cor. 3:3). Israel knew of the commandments from paper or stone, which is the first step. Most of them did not take the second step to have the law in their hearts through the Spirit. Gentiles cannot have all the law written in their hearts without first learning it all from paper or stone (Rom. 8:7). Before children of Israel lost their culture, they needed only to have the law written in their hearts. The purpose of the law written by the Spirit is to create Israel's holy nation with all the Gentiles who will join them. This transcription happens through the call of truth in those who are willing to believe.

Salvation by faith alone without the law is not a New Testament doctrine per se; instead, it is an Old Testament doctrine resurfaced with stronger emphasis. No one in the Old Testament was saved by keeping the laws. Neither those who kept the law had any more earned credits than those who were the worst of sinners. All of mankind's right doings were always as filthy rags. The Old Testament speaks firmly against the belief of being saved by keeping the law (Hab. 2:4; Gen. 15:6). You may ask, how about this scripture? "But before faith came, we were kept under the law, shut up unto the faith which should afterward be revealed" (Gal. 3:23), and "for the law was given by Moses, but grace and truth came by Jesus Christ" (John 1:17). Because we had no hope with the law, Jesus had become the perfect law for us, and by believing in his life, death, and resurrection, we are free from sins that are past (Rom. 3:25). By believing this, we are free from the penalty of breaching the law and are empowered to live in the law, free from condemnation. This freedom is not the one practiced by the Gentiles, as explained in 2 Peter 2. Grace allows you to move into the law's apartment without ambivalence. Thus, you are dead to the law. God justifies not by the law but by Jesus's sacrifice, those who take him as their Savior (Rom. 2:3, 3:20, 31).

One of the most misunderstood texts on the subject is Galatians 3:24–25. "Wherefore the law was our schoolmaster to bring us unto Christ, that we might be justified by faith. But after that faith is come, we are no longer under a schoolmaster." Paul's purpose was to treat the problem of being Jewish in practices while affiliating with Gentiles who became Christians. Peter and some members of the early church were found in hypocrisy for approving this partition. When the dust settled, Paul drew his conclusion by saying that the truth is not "fork-tongued." If you live as a sinner of the Gentiles, you cannot use that as the premise for attracting the same. We are all one group and have one doctrine in Jesus (Gal. 3:27–29).

The whole law was a protective guidepost to secure and carry us to the arrival of the Messiah. The laws allowed us to have a connection with God, not necessarily salvation. Some of those connections were moral, and others were symbolical and prophetic. Now that Christ has come, we are no longer preserved by a guidepost for safeguarding. As belonging to the law, no! We are under Jesus, the living law demonstrated. To be sure that he was not speaking of abolishing the laws, Paul says:

> But if, while we seek to be justified by Christ, we ourselves also are found sinners [breakers of the Law], is therefore Christ the minister of sin [promoting breaking of the Law]? God forbids. For if I build again the things [sin] which I destroyed, I make myself a transgressor. For I through the law am dead [nothing against me] to the law, that I might live unto God. I am [my old anti-law self] crucified with Christ: nevertheless I live; yet not I, but Christ liveth in me: and the life which I now live in the flesh I live by the faith of the Son of God [not mine], who loved me, and gave himself for me" (Gal 2:17-20).

In Galatians 3–4, Paul's lucidity is, salvation had never been obtained by keeping any law at any time. Paul's strafe was not with the Old Testament law, but rather with the Jews' concept of salvation.

Was Jesus a breaker of the law? Was He a sinner? Was He found violating any of the Ten Commandments? Or was it written in His heart? Did the commandments arrest him? Or was He in compliance? "By the law is the knowledge of sin" (Rom. 3:20); "whosoever shall keep the whole law, and yet offend in one point, he is guilty of all" (James 2:10). He said to the Jews, "Which of you convinced me of sin? And if I say the truth, why do ye not believe me?" (John 8:46).

It is unfortunate and tragic that most Christians believe that the ancient church was not concerned with the way people lived their lives. They believe that the gospel has nothing to do with the way people eat, dress, or carry on in their bodies. Isn't the church its own kingdom and culture? Shouldn't it have its own rules? Christians like to fit-in as an integral part of the kingdom of this world. There is a bowing down to the devil's trade-off. If we worship the devil in deeds while giving lip service to Jesus, we will obtain the kingdom of this world. Christians are at the forefront, blessing many unscriptural deeds. Contrary to Christianity, the messianic doctrine is a continuation of the Judean culture, teaching a person about public comport, hygiene, health, moral values, and interpersonal relationships.

One Sabbath-keeping sister said that her experience in traversing from Sunday church to the Seventh-day Adventist church had been a cultural shock. Back in her church, everything goes. Since salvation is already obtained, it renders void the need for laws and judgment. She further attests that the church's culture was the same as with the public. According to her, the church keeps pace with diverse cultural norms. There is no question that the world's culture is changing, and sometimes for the worse, and most Christians change with it.

Apart from the sacrificial system and symbolic representations of the ancient priest, Christian living has more do's and don'ts than the law. The real Christian doctrine outlines every step. Isn't it time Christians stop and think about what the Christian doctrine consists of? Isn't it time they come out from under the world and receive the teachings of Jesus? If we were following Jesus, there would be a huge boycott of many industries—clothing, medical, and food. We should not be surprised! The kingdom of the Gentiles promotes Gentile kingdom principles. Everything goes downhill. Is Christianity a Christianized Gentile kingdom? Christians need to leave that kingdom and step up into Jesus's messianic kingdom by precept and example.

Rightly Dividing the Word

By using 2 Corinthians 3:7, 9, some feel that strict compliance with the Ten Commandments is unchristian. This Gentile-minded sentiment is due to the commandments on stone referred to as the "ministrations of death" and "condemnation," which is "done away with" and "abolished" (vs. 11, 13). Paul is not attempting to convey that the Ten Commandments themselves are obsolete or vestigialized, but rather the way they were emphasized to be observed by the Jews. That is, instead of being reminded of them by the two tables of stone, we should have the whole ten, by the Spirit of God, engraved in our minds as a guide to righteousness. The process of engravement begins by reading and being instructed as one grows to maturity. We are not asked to invent or reinvent the commandments. Neither will the Spirit reinvent them. Should the Spirit reinvent them? By what criteria would we test the spirit? If the Spirit leads us, the commandments will not be ministrations of death, but instead, they will be administered by the Spirit. We should no longer be servants of sin and condemnation but of the Spirit after whom we walk free (Rom. 8:5–9; Heb. 8:8–10). No! We are not free from living the law but free from being under its condemnation, a gift from God.

Some feel that the Old Testament's Sabbath and dietary laws are legal codes from which Christians are exempt. They use Romans 14 as well as other scripture to show this. A close analysis of Romans 14 reveals that Paul's issue was not with what is written in the law but rather with his brethren's desires. Isn't it a mistake to think that Paul, in that chapter, takes issues with the law (Rom. 7)?

There is a spiritual rest mentioned in scripture (Isa. 28:7–12; Matt. 11:28–29; Heb. 4). This rest refers to cessation from breaking the law, a cessation from sin in the practical life. This work refers to one's effort to keep God's law. We are asked to cease this labor. Instead, the Spirit of God should be the driving power to work the law through us. As you may note from reading Hebrews 4, though this rest had not been attained, it was available in the Old Testament while the Sabbath commandment was still in force. Therefore, the spiritual rest (Heb. 4) does not eclipse the physical sanctified rest in the law (Ex. 20:8–11).

Before trusting any teaching, we must analyze its views. Some leaders who are authorized by the masses may not know what they are teaching is wrong. I have spoken to people who said they rest their whole faith in a present-day prophet or an apostle. They said they do not know theology, and they can only trust the one leading them. They have affirmed there is no necessity to study or share views with anyone who disagrees with what they have been taught. Their security is the responsibility of those who teach them. Is this real security? Unfortunately, many pastors and teachers have an affinity for such converts. Many will fall victim to this tragedy because they have not received the grace of Jesus who is the way, the truth, and the life. They lack personal experience and a real relationship with Jesus.

Today can be your day. You don't have to trust in your good works or a man to lead you. The Holy Spirit is here to abide in us if we receive Jesus as our personal Savior. Will you trust only in Him as your Lord and Savior?

Chapter 9

The Ten Words of God

Relativism or Standard?

Interpretation of texts is usually influenced by cultural norms, tastes, and personal beliefs of the reader. The nuances of interpretation are directly dependent on the amount of symbolic language used in a text or the writer and the reader's cultural differences. For example, the US Supreme Court was established to interpret the Constitution. Their job is to bridge the cultural gap and transcend time and conditions to provide a homogeneous understanding between two cultures—the culture of the 1800s versus today's culture. When we speak of God, these factors are also transcended to understand God's intent correctly. To that end, we may be under the empathy of the author.

Why ten? Aren't there 613 laws in the Old Testament? Is the Ten special? The answer is yes. The way they were delivered testifies to their specialty. "These words the LORD spake unto all your assembly in the mount out of the midst of the fire, of the cloud, and of the thick darkness, with a great voice: and he added no more. And he wrote them in two tables of stone and delivered them unto me" (Duet. 5:22). The day the commandments were delivered was a special inaugural holiday (Ex. 19:10–19). It was a day of a special display of divine power and holiness unto the Lord. It was a day of the divine constitution's ratification, written twice by God's finger (Ex. 31:18, 32:16, 34:1). That is the day of Pentecost, the day the Spirit of God delivered His law on Mt. Sinai. Moses went to receive it twice; each time, he spent forty days and forty nights fasting (Duet. 9:11). The two tables of stone were placed separately from the other laws (Duet. 10:2). They were placed inside the Ark of the Covenant overlaid by the mercy seat (Ex. 25:21). Do you think God will use the Ten Commandments to determine who in our time get the plagues and who doesn't (Mal. 4:1–4)? The scriptures saith:

> Who shall not fear thee, O Lord, and glorify thy name? for thou only art holy: for all nations shall come and worship before thee; for thy judgments are made manifest. And after that I looked, and, behold, the temple of the *tabernacle of the testimony in heaven was opened*: And the seven angels came out of the temple, having the seven plagues, clothed in pure and white linen, and having their breasts girded with golden girdles" (Rev. 15:4-6, cf. Rev. 11:19).

There are some popular unbalanced interpretations of the Ten Commandments. Not everyone interprets the law the same way. A piece of literature I read states that the Old Testament commandments are negative, thou shall not's, whereas Christ's commandment is love. For some, understanding love is derived from concepts arising from their spirit and not from tables of stone. For example, commandments one and two about having other gods or praying to idols are not conclusive. Some think it is not bad to have other gods. You should not make idols gods, but only that they can be used as mediums representing God or to get to God. Some believe and teach that the seventh commandment does not fully express real love. A woman should be able to share her husband or a wife herself. Accordingly, the true meaning of "thou shall not commit adultery" is spiritual.

Concerning commandment four, some think that the "rest" is spiritual and Sabbath is not literal. A literal Sabbath is too legalistic. According to some, the fourth commandment shows that we should ignore the whole ten. According to the theory of evolution, the biblical record is held in question. The seven days of creation may not be real. As one of the US presidents said, it all depends on how you interpret the Genesis account.

Eliminating life, according to some, is insignificant to the commandment. They claim that inspiring wars and killing the unborn is not truly a desire to kill. They contend that life is not truly life if the struggle for existence outweighs the benefits. Causing depression in people is what is meant by the commandment. Killing is significant only when you kill spiritually; that is, to kill one's spirit or to cause depression. These misinterpretations about the Bible are occasionally heard from those uncomfortable with its precepts. These views are not the standard for understanding the Judeo-Christian faith. Although some of these views are in concert with the various cultural norms, they are not true and do not reflect the love of Jesus. God has provided better things for those who are born of the Spirit.

It is more difficult to misinterpret the rest of the commandments. These residual commandments may not be altered or spiritualized in any way. Among them are: Thou shall not steal, thou shall not take the name of your God in vain, thou shall not bear false witness, thou shall not covet, and honor thy mother and thy father. Notwithstanding, we find the religious leaders in Christ's day managed to misinterpret the parent-honoring commandment.

> But he [Jesus] answered and said unto them, why do ye also transgress the commandment of God by your tradition? For God commanded, saying, honor thy father and mother: and, He that curses father or mother, let him die the death. But ye say, whosoever shall say to his father or his mother, it is a gift, by whatsoever thou might be profited by me; And honor not his father or his mother, he shall be free. Thus have ye made the commandment of God of none effect by your tradition. Ye hypocrites, well did Esaias prophesy of you, saying, This people draw nigh unto me with their mouth, and honors me with their lips; but their heart is far from me. But in vain they do worship me, teaching for doctrines the commandments of men (Ma*tt*.15:3-9).

Like some "grace alone" misappropriations of today, the religious leaders in Jesus's day had much grace attached to their parent-dishonoring transgression, provisional to their traditional misapplication of the law. These warnings are given that we may be sober in our understanding of God and how we transmit that understanding to others. We must take caution when repeating an original message. We must not pass ambiguity as certainty. Declaration of ignorance is better than hopeless hope.

These warnings are not given so that we should be critical of God's servants; rather, they are given that we may be cautious and constructive in our criticisms. Be patient, kind, and fair to all who you think may be in error. We all, at one time, have made some errors. We always want others to be patient with us during our times of ignorance. Some people may have hidden agendas, but care must be exercised during the interpolation of judgment. As Messianics, we cannot sit on the sidelines and say nothing about the distribution of hopeless hope. We need to pray for wisdom. Sometimes, silence for the moment is golden.

> We henceforth be no more children, tossed to and fro, and carried about with every wind of doctrine, by the sleight of men, and cunning craftiness, whereby they lie in wait to deceive; But speaking the truth in love, may grow up into him in all things, which is the head, even Christ (Eph. 4:14, 15). Prove all things; hold fast that which is good (1 Thess. 5:21). Beloved, believe not every spirit, but try the spirits whether they are of God: because many false prophets are gone out into the world (1 John 4:1).

The Facets of the Law

The word "law" in the New Testament applies to different aspects and the whole of the law. The entire law is referred to as the Torah or the Pentateuch, the first five books written by Moses. There are many types of laws in the Pentateuch. Our obedience to all of them is not required due to dispensation and other conditional limitations. The explanation of the Ten Commandments law in Deuteronomy and Leviticus do not all apply to all time and conditions. All laws are of love, hope, and peace. There is no law that was not by God's love.

The Ten Commandments were written by the finger of God twice. God did not suffer a man to write it; he did not want help in its interpretation or intent. The Ten Commandments' explanation is found throughout the book of Deuteronomy and Leviticus; they are elaborated with specifications that need to be taught. This type of education is crucial because the Israelites had the mind of Gentiles, or heathens —a mind-set that needed to be changed to kingdom living. God gave them commandments (Heb. *mitsvah*), statutes (Heb. *khook-eem*), decrees, and judgments (Heb. *mishpot-eem*). Though these words appear to have similar meanings, they are used to designate different law parts. The commandment laws explain God's relation to mankind and spell out mankind's responsibility. The statute stipulates how a person should recognize his responsibility to God and how he needs to approach Him. These laws express God's holiness and how we should relate to it; besides, they show how God would have mercy on us. The judgment laws deal with how a person should relate to his fellowmen. These are the ways the law was understood.

Some of these laws were fulfilled in Jesus by substitution; others, Jesus fulfilled by adding more regulations, making them more difficult to the sinful nature. Other laws were self-canceling because they were contingent on Israel's independence and their conditional relation to God—for example, stoning. The classification of laws as moral and ceremonial is elementary and does not reflect the biblical classification. This classification usually lends itself to opinion in determining what is moral and what is a ritual. Using this rudimentary classification, we classify the unpalatable as ritual, legalism, and ceremonial to escape the inevitable. This classification mode creates a haven, a conscience-free hideout for our sin problem. Knowing that the Ten Commandments are God's handwriting and dictation; is it safe to tamper, reinterpret, or rationalize things written therein?

The Pillars of Love—Holy, Just, and Good

"What shall we say then? Is the law sin? God forbids. Nay, I had not known sin, but by the law: for I had not known lust, except the law had said, thou shalt not covet. Wherefore the law is holy, and the commandment holy, and just, and good" (Rom.7:7, 12).

Why should one claim that the Ten Commandments are abolished when, in truth, they are still acceptable to all Christians? Why would a Christian not comply with the first three commandments? Should they disregard the fifth through the tenth commandments as they do the fourth? If they were all genuinely abolished, why consider them still valid? Some Christians reinterpret the second commandment because they use earthly representation as a medium when praying. Those who have experienced the Lord's call accept all of God's commandments. Without reinterpretation for artificial alignment, the entire Ten Commandments (Heb. *eser haDabar*, the ten utterances) are synonymous with the life of Christ. Jesus did not break any commandment of God. He said that he kept all the commandments (John 8:46; James 2:10).

One: "And what agreement has the temple of God have with idols?" (2 Corinthians 6:16). "You shall worship the LORD your God, and Him only you shall serve" (Luke 4:8):

Two: "They... changed the glory of the incorruptible God into an image made like corruptible man--and to birds and four-footed animals and creeping things" (Romans 1:22-23). "And I fell at his feet to worship him. And he said unto me, see thou do it not: I am thy fellow-servant, and of thy brethren that have the testimony of Jesus: worship God: for the testimony of Jesus is the spirit of prophecy" (Rev 19.:10).

Three: "But above all things, my brethren, swear not, neither by heaven, neither by the earth, neither by any other oath: but let your yea be yea; and your nay, nay; lest ye fall into condemnation' (James 5:12). "Do not they blaspheme that worthy name by the which ye are called?" (Jas 2:7).

Four "And pray that your flight may not be in winter or on the Sabbath" (Mat 24:20). "The Sabbath was made for man, and not man for the Sabbath. Therefore, the Son of Man is also Lord of the Sabbath" (Mark 2:27). "And they returned, and prepared spices and ointments; and rested the Sabbath day according to the commandment" (Lu 23:56). "And when the Jews were gone out of the synagogue, the Gentiles besought that these words might be preached to them the next Sabbath" (Acts 13:42).

Five: "Children obey your parents in the Lord, for this is right. 'Honor your father and mother,' which is the first commandment with promise: that it may be well with you and you may live long on the earth' (Ephesians 6:1-3). You know the commandments: Honor your father and your mother" (Luke 18:20).

Six: "You shall not murder (Romans 13:9). You have heard that it was said to those of old, 'You shall not murder,' and whoever murders will be in danger of the judgment. But I say to you that whoever is angry with his brother without a cause shall be in danger of the judgment" (Mat 5:21-22).

Seven: "But now I have written to you not to keep company with anyone named a brother, who is sexually immoral" (I

Corinthians 5:11). "Neither... adulterers, nor homosexuals... will inherit the kingdom of God" (I Corinthians 6:9). "Whoever divorces his wife and marries another commits adultery against her. And if a woman divorces her husband and marries another, she commits adultery" (Mk 10:11-12).

Eight: "You shall not steal" (Romans 13:9; cf. Luke 18:20).

Nine: "You shall not bear false witness" (Romans 13:9; of. Matt 19:18).

Ten: "You shall not covet" (Romans 13:9; cf. Mark 7:22-23).

Some people use the exclusion principle to eliminate the fourth commandment. They claim that Jesus told the young rich ruler about the necessary commandments for salvation and excluded those that were unnecessary. In one of the references in question, only five were mentioned (Matt. 19:17–20). Can we disavow commandments one through four and yet inherit eternal life? Some people pray with image mediums; others believe there are many ways to God, and still others think polytheism is just as good. Since Jesus did not mention one's unique relationship with God, can we use the exclusion principle to worship any god? If the answer is no, then the fourth commandment can't be excluded. The exclusion principle has only recently become popular in Christian thought. Among the new adaptations are women in worship without head coverings; invalidity of Sabbath; latter-day seven-year tribulation period; women wearing pants; and tattooing the body. These are new societal norms. Some Christians are still offended by some of these practices. These cultural parameters have only been recently accepted as part of normal Christian thought. Even at the transatlantic slave trade, the white Christian slave masters still believed in strict fourth commandment observance, restricting work on the Sabbath (Mannix & Crowley, 1962). The exception was, they were taught that Sunday was the Sabbath. The question should be asked: "On what path are we?"

Better Name Than Sons

"He that turns away his ear from hearing the law, even his prayer shall be abomination" (Prov. 28:9).

> Finally,(For not the hearers of the law are just before God but the doers of the law shall be justified) ...Let us hear the conclusion of the whole matter: Fear God, and keep His commandments: for this is the whole duty of man. For God shall 'bring every work into judgment, with every secret thing, whether it be good, or whether it be evil...Blessed are they that do His commandments, that they may have right to the tree of life, and may enter in through the gates into the city. For without are dogs, and sorcerers, and whoremongers, and murderers, and idolaters, and whosoever loveth and maketh a lie (Rom. 2:13, Eccles. 12:13, 14, Rev. 22:14, 15).
>
> Blessed is the man that doeth this, and the son of man that layeth hold on it; that keepeth the sabbath from polluting it, and keepeth his hand from doing any evil. Neither let the son of the stranger, that hath joined himself to the LORD, speak, saying, The LORD hath utterly separated me from his people: neither let the eunuch say, Behold, I am a dry tree. For thus saith the LORD unto the eunuchs that keep my sabbaths, and choose the things that please me, and take hold of my covenant; Even unto them will I give in mine house and

within my walls a place and a name better than of sons and of daughters: I will give them an everlasting name, that shall not be out off. Also the sons of the stranger, that join themselves to the LORD, to serve him, and to love the name of the LORD, to be his servants, every one that keepeth the sabbath from polluting it, and taketh hold of my covenant; Even them will I bring to my holy mountain, and make them joyful in my house of prayer: their burnt offerings and their sacrifices shall be accepted upon mine altar; for mine house shall be called a house of prayer for all people. The Lord GOD which gathereth the outcasts of Israel saith, Yet will I gather others to him, beside those that are gathered unto him (Isa. 56:2–8).

PART II

Chapter 10

Judeo-Israelite Messianic Roots

The Gospel to Israel

The gospel is salvation to Israel. The conventional mode of viewing the gospel compared to God's plan has been amiss. The Messiah's church preaches a third of the gospel. Consequently, Israel has not been exposed to the full gospel. Many of the titles placed in front of the various churches about being apostolic, full gospel, and so on are good advertisements. However, there is a need to be rooted in truth.

The gospel to Israel comes in three phases. The first phase is the reception of the Savior, who brings everlasting righteousness (Dan. 9:24). The Messiah came two thousand years ago and declared that salvation is of Yahudah (Judah). The second phase of the gospel is about Jacob's descendants who accepted the gospel and their brethren of Jacob's seed who followed suit. The third phase of the gospel is concerned with Israel's regathering in the land God gave to Abraham, and with them, all the Gentiles who accepted the gospel during the latter-day ingathering.

Paul declared that the salvation tree is rooted in Israel.

Salvation from sin comes through the Messiah, the critical person in the restored kingdom of David. Most of Israel was spiritually blinded, and they were rejected at the first advent of the Messiah. Subsequently, the fathers and the children who ate sour grapes had their "teeth... set on edge." Their acceptance of the gospel happens mainly toward the latter part of the two thousand years after their due course of punishment.

With the ingathering time wrongly placed, the disciples asked Jesus if the kingdom were to be restored to Israel in their day. The kingdom they perceived was the restored kingdom of David in Palestine, not the spiritual aspect demonstrated by the life of Jesus. Jesus replied to their question by saying: "It is not for you to know the times or the seasons, which the Father hath put in his own power" (Acts 1:7). The answer to that question is a definite no with the condition that they would not know the time of the return of the kingdom to Israel ahead of the reception. The writer of Hebrews wrote that the church looks to Jerusalem, which is above. This view is true for both his time and ours. Besides, as the fulfillment for this Jerusalem is incomplete, Israel has the promise of the New Covenant in Jeremiah 31. The promise of the Abrahamic territory in the restoration is the last string of the gospel to be fulfilled. "This gospel of the kingdom [restoration of Israel] shall be preached in all the world, then shall the end come." We often leave out Israel to whom the gospel came to restore. No! not spiritual Israel but the legitimate seed of the house of Israel. This entire gospel of restoration is found in Jeremiah 31. As an introduction, I will quote a few important verses.

Is Ephraim my dear son? is he a pleasant child? for since I spake against him, I do earnestly remember him still:

therefore, my bowels are troubled for him; I will surely have mercy upon him, saith the LORD (Jer 31:20).Upon this I awaked, and beheld; and my sleep was sweet unto me (Jer 31:26).And it shall come to pass, that like as I have watched over them, to pluck up, and to break down, and to throw down, and to destroy, and to afflict; so will I watch over them, to build, and to plant, saith the LORD (Jer 31:28).

In those days they shall say no more, the fathers have eaten a sour grape, and the children's teeth are set on edge (29). But everyone shall die for his own iniquity: every man that eateth the sour grape, his teeth shall be set on edge (30). Behold, the days come, saith the LORD, that I will make a new covenant with the house of Israel, and with the house of Judah (31): Not according to the covenant that I made with their fathers in the day that I took them by the hand to bring them out of the land of Egypt; which my covenant they brake, although I was a husband unto them, saith the LORD (Jer. 31:28–32).

If those ordinances depart from before me, saith the LORD, then the seed of Israel also shall cease from being a nation before me forever. Thus saith the LORD; If heaven above can be measured, and the foundations of the earth searched out beneath, I will also cast off all the seed of Israel for all that they have done, saith the LORD (Jer. 31:36–37).

For the children of Israel shall abide many days without a king, and without a prince, and without a sacrifice, and without an image, and without an ephod, and without teraphim: Afterward shall the children of

> Israel return, and seek the LORD their God, and David their king; and shall fear the LORD and his goodness in the latter days (Hosea 3:4–5).

Some of us rush to credit this fulfillment to the return during the Persian Empire. The new covenant did not happen then. The Gentile church believes that all the great promises made to Israel and their return is spiritual and only incidentally apply to Israel. The truth is, some of the "believing" Gentiles' descendants, at one point, were slave masters of the scattered seed of Jacob. The promises are made for ancient Israel and their descendants and only incidentally apply to the believing Gentiles.

The Israelites: The People of the Land

The Bible is replete with prophecies made to the children of Israel. To be moderately engaged on this topic, it is incumbent upon us to consider the people with whom the covenant was made. Israel's relegation, as referred to in the covenant promises, is owed to their disobedience. Other prophecies refer to irrevocable blessings through grace. These prophecies demand that we give attention to the historical genealogy of Israel as a people. We are not speaking of endless genealogies that provide useless prophetic information, but useful clues that trace Israel as a people and give insight into their eschatological deliberation. Romans 9, 11 and Revelation 7, compounded with other scriptures, provide clues for the validity of genealogical discussion. These prophecies and their prophetic and punitive allocations span our time and beyond. As noted in the following, God has associated His name with the children of Israel, and He will bless them.

The LORD bless thee and keep thee: The LORD makes his face shine upon thee, and be gracious unto thee: The LORD lift up his countenance upon thee and give thee peace. And they shall put my name upon the children of Israel, and I will bless them (Num. 6:24–27).And now, Israel, what doth the LORD thy God require of thee, but to fear the LORD thy God, to walk in all his ways, and to love him, and to serve the LORD thy God with all thy heart and with all thy soul, to keep the commandments of the LORD, and his statutes, which I command thee this day for thy good? Behold, the heaven and the heaven of heavens is the LORD'S thy God, the earth also, with all that therein is. Only the LORD had a delight in thy fathers to love them, and he chose their seed after them, even you above all people, as it is this day (Duet. 10:12–15).

To whom was He talking? Was it a group of Egyptian-resembling individuals who took up residence in the land of Canaan after many years of slavery in Egypt? The children of Israel were to inherit the blessings given to them through Abraham. After Jacob had his sons, he suffered deprivation related to the perceptive loss of his youngest son. The barouche of his misfortune was brought upon him by his sons, who sold their brother to the Egyptians. They manufactured a story of a wild beast that had torn their brother. Though Semitic in origin, the children of Israel were forced to live among Ham's children, the Egyptians. The enslavement appeared to be of consequence for the suffering imposed on their father.

The children of Israel had many laws: circumcision, the Sabbath, monotheism, oblation laws, and the Noahic hygienic laws of clean versus unclean (Gen. 7:2). Other laws were communal, such as marriage, how to treat your neighbor, and so on. Although some of these laws were not enforced during their sojourn in Egypt, the knowledge of them was common among the Israelites. While these laws were not given to Israel until after the Exodus, most of them were known to the Egyptians and predated Moses (Gen. 26:4–5; Job 22:22, 23:12).

Israel was part of the technological progress of the ancient world. The seed of Abraham, beginning with Isaac, sojourned for 430 years (Gal.3:16–17). They went into Egypt for 215 years and were servants there. They were involved in learning and contributing to Egyptian culture. They were forced to endure slavery in the burning sun for eighty of those years (Resse & Klassen, 1977). The time of Israel's stay in Egypt has received a plethora of plausible explanations. Still, the Septuagint, in the Genesis record, has an alternate rendering of the verses related to this topic (Exo. 12:40).

Like the Egyptians, Israel's only conspicuous protection during servitude was their melanin-ladened cover, but they had just gotten darker through the hot sun of Egypt. The scripture below is a descriptive example of what outdoor slavery's effect can have on an already person of color.

> Look not upon me, because I am black because the sun hath looked upon me: my mother's children were angry with me; they made me the keeper of the vineyards, but mine own vineyard have I not kept (Song 1:6). My skin is black upon me, and my bones are burned with heat (Job 30:30). Judah mourneth and the gates thereof languish; they are black unto the ground; and the cry of Jerusalem is gone up (Jer. 14:2). Their visage is blacker

than a coal; they are not known in the streets: their skin cleaveth to their bones; it is withered, it becomes like a stick (Lam. 4:8).

Moses's Israelite roots were naturally camouflaged among the Egyptians when he was taken to be the son of Pharaoh's daughter. From Joseph's time to Moses, it was natural, not only for Moses, but the whole Israelite nation to resemble the ancient Egyptians. In those days, the Hykos ruled Egypt (Hindson, 2003). These newcomers were a group of mixed races and cultures. They ruled Egypt for a short period.

In Acts 21:37–38, Paul was asked by a Roman soldier if he spoke Greek. From the outward appearance, Paul did not look like a Grecian. In Paul's days, some Grecians were generally mulattos, some white, and others were black. Paul was born a Roman citizen (Acts 22:25–28) and a natural-born Israelite (Rom. 11:1). Israelites did not resemble Grecians, but rather Egyptians and Ethiopians (vs. 38). Back in those days, the Israelites can go unnoticeable among the Egyptians during times of Roman persecution. This situation occurred with Jesus. Egypt was a Roman territory; however, Jesus was sent to Egypt to be disguised among the Egyptians and away from Roman persecution (Matt. 2:15).

Race and color do not matter when it comes to God's love, but racial profiling of the seventeenth century was indicative of social classification of skin color that resulted in disenfranchisement to certain groups. Our modern history of enslavement, prejudice, and racial injustice proves that it is inextricably a moral and spiritual issue. This statement is not meant to judge anyone negatively but to highlight an allocation achieved through ignorance and misinformation. The issue of injustice has not always been an issue of color. The Egyptians enslaving the Israelites is an example of black-on-black crime. Even among the Israelites were intertribal wars. In today's societies, we have plenty of interracial prejudices and classism exemplified among groups of people.

Although the Messiah's gospel was accepted by some Judeans and afterward the Gentiles, God did not forget the people to whom the promises were made. Paul told the Gentile converts not to boast against Israel's natural branches because they were borne by them (Rom. 11:18). While both original Israel and Gentiles possessed Samaria in Jesus's day, He was careful not to include the "proselytes" of the Samaritans as the original children of Israel. He told his disciples not to preach to them. According to Jesus, the Gentiles who accepted Judaism are not natural Israelites, to whom the promises were made.

Besides, the mothers' lineages do not make up for the male lineages of Israel. Therefore, a group of Gentile men mixing with Israelite women will not produce Israelite descendants but Gentiles, offspring of the stranger. Since Timothy's father was a Gentile, he is a Gentile messianic. To be of Israel's lineage, at least half of his recent ancestral lineage must come from patriarchal Israel, and his early descendants will continue with the Israelite family.

In our time, as in the early days of the church, Gentile messianic will inherit the promises through the Judean-Israelite messianic believer: "Salvation is of Yahudah." Although salvation is ethnological, it extends to all with love. God has not cast away his original people. They, too, need to be grafted to the tree of Israel. Some of the original stock returning to God through the Messiah will bring salvation to the world (Rom. 11:12, 15–16). God accepts them again but as messianic Israelites, a final remnant according to the election of grace.

Israel's remnant from the parent stock are those whose main lineage, historically, culturally, and prophetically, are traceable to Israel (Jacobs & Farrar, 2016). God has not forgotten the lineage of Israel (Rev. 7). The natural branches are still from the stock of Jacob. It is said about those who are saved: "Let people serve thee, and nations bow down to thee: be lord over thy brethren, and let thy mother's sons bow down to thee: cursed be every one that curseth thee, and blessed be he that blesseth thee" (Gen. 27:29).

Israel on Mistaken Identity

Most Christian organizations who adhere to the seven-year future tribulation theory (pre, mid, and post) believe that God has a unique position for Israel. They believe this for Israel because of the prophetic statements made for the seed of the house of Israel. There are original Jews, and there are Jewish converts. The blessings are for the original descendants and only incidentally if at all, apply to converts. Although some may be part of it, the Jews, who are not natural Israelites through ancestry, cannot complete the promise.

For this reason, a two-state solution has been heralded as the only viable solution to the Middle East crisis concerning Jerusalem. The recent repatriation of some Ethiopian Jews is commendable. The Ethiopian Jews' historical and regional connection to Israel can be traced to aboriginal ancestry. This gives the unrelated Zionist and European Jews some authenticity by association. That is, holding the "skirt of him who is a Jew."

What do we say about the Israelite kingdom in Africa, in Negro land? What do we say about those of that stock taken on slave ships to the Americas, West Indies, and Europe by force?

139

An early 1747 map of Africa's west coast shows a region known as the "kingdom of Judah," from which slaves were taken, sold, and scattered to the Americas.

> In a 1790 edition of the "Memoirs of the Reign of Bassa Ahadee, King of Dahomey" by Robert Norris a map was portrayed which was a direct eye-witness account by the English and French. On the map they designated the town of Whydah as the "Country of the Jews". The town is called "Juda" or "Ouidah". The Portuguese call this town "Ajuda". The people today in this town still pronounce their town in their native tongue as "Judah" (Jacobs & Farrar, 2016, p. 9).

What do scriptures declare concerning the lost and scattered of Israel? Do they become part of Gentile ancestry by accepting the messianic or Muslim faith? Or would they be grafted into the olive tree upon conversion to the messianic gospel as natural branches? Would the gospel make God's promises to dispersed Israel void? Didn't Paul say that there is neither Jew nor Gentile? Are we not one in the Messiah? The following quotes shed light on these questions.

> For there is no difference between the Jew and the Greek: for the same Lord over all is rich unto all that call upon him. For whosoever shall call upon the name of the Lord shall be saved (Rom. 10:12-13).
>
> For as many of you as have been baptized into Christ have put on Christ. There is neither Jew nor Greek, there is neither bond nor free, there is neither male nor female: for ye are all one in Jesus. And if ye be Jesus', then are

ye Abraham's seed, and heirs according to the promise (Gal. 3: 27-29).

And have put on the new man, which is renewed in knowledge after the image of him that created him: Where there is neither Greek nor Jew, circumcision nor uncircumcision, Barbarian, Scythian, bond nor free: but Christ is all and in all. Put on, therefore, as the elect of God, holy and beloved, bowels of mercies, kindness, humbleness of mind, meekness, longsuffering (Col. 3:10-12).

God *hath not cast away his people which he foreknew*. Wot ye not what the scripture saith of Elias? how he maketh intercession to God against Israel ... (7) What then? Israel hath not obtained that which he seeketh for, but the election hath obtained it, and the rest were blinded. (11) I say then, *Have they stumbled that they should fall? God forbid*: but rather through their fall salvation is come unto the Gentiles, for to provoke them to jealousy. (25) For *I would not, brethren, that ye should be ignorant of this mystery, lest ye should be wise in your own conceits; that blindness in part is happened to Israel, until the fulness of the Gentiles be come in.* (28) As concerning the gospel, they are enemies for your sakes: but as *touching the election, they are beloved for the fathers' sakes.* (29) For the gifts and *calling of God are without repentance* (Rom 11:2, 7,11,25, 28, 29). [Italics added].

The first three citations' overarching premise is to express the need for love and oneness among believers in Jesus. There is no intent to defeminize women or to make an Israelite a non-Israelite, but only to say that our love in the gospel makes us of one body—the body of Jesus. Though there is diversity, we are one in Jesus. Concerning the last quote, God remembered His people, the Israelites to whom the promises were made. He recognizes them for their fathers' sake. Since their blindness was temporary, their place in the gospel as chief administrators shall be rekindled. God still has a unique calling for the remnant of Jacob. The mystery of Israel's blindness and recuperation is little understood among theologians. This is because they are not looking at the people whom God has chosen. The healing of Israel is like raising the world from the dead—a new era in time, a new beginning. The time of the Gentiles is ending, and the time of Israel is commencing.

The Divine Allocation

God's plan for ancient Israel was for them to be the head, not the tail, but in the curses of Deuteronomy 28, there is a mention of being the tail. Israel is under the curse. The main curse is one of blindness, complete ignorance (Jer. 17:4). Generally, they are not at the head of the other nations. They are the tail. They are still scattered among the nations.

> What advantage then hath the Jew? or what profit is there of circumcision? Much every way: chiefly, because that unto them were committed the oracles of God. For what if some did not believe? shall their unbelief make the faith of God without effect? God forbid: yea, let God be true, but every man a liar; as it is written, That thou mightest be justified in thy sayings, and mightest overcome when thou art judged (Rom. 3:1-4).

And the LORD shall make thee the head, and not the tail; and thou shalt be above only, and thou shalt not be beneath; if that thou hearken unto the commandments of the LORD thy God, which I command thee this day, to observe and to do them (Deut. 28:13).

For thou art a holy people unto the LORD thy God: the LORD thy God hath chosen thee to be a special people unto himself, above all people that are upon the face of the earth. (7) The LORD did not set his love upon you, nor choose you, because ye were more in number than any people; for ye were the fewest of all people: (8) But because the LORD loved you, and because he would keep the oath which he had sworn unto your fathers, hath the LORD brought you out with a mighty hand, and redeemed you out of the house of bondmen, from the hand of Pharaoh king of Egypt. (9) Know therefore that the LORD thy God, he is God, the faithful God, which keepeth covenant and mercy with them that love him and keep his commandments to a thousand generations; (10) And repayeth them that hate him to their face, to destroy them: he will not be slack to him that hateth him, he will repay him to his face. (11) Thou shalt, therefore, keep the commandments, and the statutes, and the judgments, which I command thee this day, to do them...Thou shalt be blessed above all people: there shall not be male or female barren among you, or among your cattle. (15) And the LORD will take away from thee all sickness, and will put none of the evil diseases of Egypt, which thou knowest, upon thee; but will lay them upon all them that hate thee. (16) And thou shalt consume all the people which the

LORD thy God shall deliver thee; thine eye shall have no pity upon them: neither shalt thou serve their gods; for that will be a snare unto thee. (17) If thou shalt say in thine heart, These nations are more than I; how can I dispossess them? (18) Thou shalt not be afraid of them: but shalt well remember what the LORD thy God did unto Pharaoh, and unto all Egypt (Deut. 7:6-18).

The first citation clarifies that God is not disposing of His promises made to natural Israel. However, He will keep His promise of an exuberating judgment on His people and their reward after repentance. In the second and third citations, God promised ancient Israel of their elevation above the nations (Isa. 2:1–4). How could God make some (Gentiles, non-Israelites) servants and some of Jacob's descendants administrators? How could Jesus call the Greek woman a "dog" (Mark 7:27)? The woman recognized God's sovereignty (Rom. 9:17–23) and agreed to the charge. The charge was not to disparage her but to show that her place was not among royalty (Matt. 20:23). God punishes Israel through the dispersion and then decided to give them a prominent position in His work (Rom. 10:12). He will restore Israel to their original place if they accept the gospel. However, the scriptures have this to say concerning the non-Israelite people:

Blessed is the man that doeth this, and the son of man that layeth hold on it; that keepeth the sabbath from polluting it, and keepeth his hand from doing any evil. (3) Neither let the son of the stranger, that hath joined himself to the LORD, speak, saying, The LORD hath utterly separated me from his people: neither let the eunuch say, Behold, I am a dry tree. .... (6) Also the sons of the stranger, that join themselves to the LORD, to serve him, and to love the name of the LORD, to be his servants, every one that keepeth the sabbath from polluting it, and taketh hold of my covenant; (7) Even them will I bring to my holy mountain, and make them joyful in my house of prayer: their burnt offerings and their sacrifices shall be accepted upon mine altar; for mine house shall be called a house of prayer for all people. (8) The Lord GOD which gathereth the outcasts of Israel saith, Yet will I gather others to him, beside those that are gathered unto him. (9) All ye beasts of the field, come to devour, yea, all ye beasts in the forest (Isa. 56:2-9).

It is not always necessary for one to be born in Jacob to join the twelve tribes. Though not of the genealogical race, a real convert by personal experience with God, into Judaism was a proselyte of Israel (2 Chron. 6:32, 33). Conversely, a Gentile who is a convert through parental or political expediency is not an Israelite but a Gentile proselyte. In the messianic dispensation, for a Gentile to join Israel, they must do it through Jesus (Yahuwahsha). Most of the Samaritan Jews of Jesus's time and today's European Jews are examples of Gentile proselytes.

Jesus brought deliverance to literal Israel. God wants to save them. "And so all Israel shall be saved: as it is written, there shall come out of Sion the Deliverer, and shall turn away ungodliness from Jacob. For this is my covenant unto them [Israel], when I shall take away their sins" (Rom. 11:26–27). "All Israel" refers to the saved Judeans in the apostles' day and those of the diaspora. God is bound to the remnant of Israel's lineage by promise. As recorded by Jeremiah, Jesus came to deliver Israel from their sins by the New Covenant. The gospel being accepted today by original and scattered Israel fulfills the call of God to them "for it is without repentance."

Chapter 11

---ⓐⓐⓐ---

Hosea: The Prophet of the Diaspora

Joint Venture between Israel and Judah

The kingdom of Israel was divided into two separate kingdoms between Rehoboam, son of Solomon, and Jeroboam, son of Nebat, around 945 BC. The history of the divided kingdom is found in 2 Kings 12. Before the division, the kingdom of Israel consisted of twelve tribes. After the separation, ten of the tribes were called the children of Israel among other names, and two tribes were called the children of Judah. The children of Judah, some of Levi, and some of Benjamin were the southern tribes of Palestine in Judea. The children of Israel possessed the northern portion of Palestine in Samaria. The southern tribes were ruled by Rehoboam and the northern tribes by Jeroboam.

At first, Israel's tree continued with Judah and Israel's original children and grew accordingly (Acts 2:5–7). After the crucifixion of Jesus, most of Judah was rejected; some of them were accepted and grafted into the original tree. When Christ started His ministry, He forbade His disciples from entering the Samaritan cities or any city of the Gentiles. They were sent to the house of Israel. The Hellenized people of Samaria in Jesus's day were not of the House of Israel; although they made claims to it, Jesus did not recognize them as Israel. After the church harvested a large number from Israel, it was commissioned to disseminate its message to all. The church then was known as the twelve tribes scattered abroad (James 1:1). When this statement was made, it referred to Israelites who were scattered, not the newly added Gentiles. However, the message was for all.

When Jesus commissioned His disciples to go after the lost sheep of the house of Israel, it was not without meaning. After the division of Israel and Judah in 945 BC, many of the Israelites had contentions. Some of them were disgruntled by the way Jeroboam handled the spiritual aspect of the kingdom. Because of various agents of mismanagement, there were two permanent departures from Israel into Judah. In about 944–942 BC, Jeroboam changed the priesthood. The faithful priests were replaced by those who wanted to worship idols. That caused a rift in the kingdom. The result of this split was an exodus to Judah as seen below.

> And the priests and the Levites that were in all Israel resorted to him out of all their coasts. (14) For the Levites left their suburbs and their possession, and came to Judah and Jerusalem: for Jeroboam and his sons had cast them off from executing the priest's office unto the LORD: (16) And after them *out of all the tribes of Israel* such as set their hearts to seek the LORD God of Israel *came to Jerusalem*, to sacrifice unto the LORD God of their fathers. (17) So they strengthened the kingdom of Judah, and made Rehoboam the son of Solomon strong,

three years: for three years they walked in the way of David and Solomon. 2 Chron. 11:13-14, 16-17.

In about the year 912 BC, king Asa, king of Judah, was known in Israel for his discrete connection with God's intent. That led many of the Israelites into Judah, producing the second exodus.

> And he gathered all Judah and Benjamin, and the strangers with them out of *Ephraim and Manasseh, and out of Simeon*: for they fell to him out of Israel in abundance when they saw that the LORD his God was with him. (10) So they gathered themselves together at Jerusalem in the third month, in the fifteenth year of the reign of Asa. (12) And they entered into a covenant to seek the LORD God of their fathers with all their heart and with all their soul (2Chron. 15:9-10, 12).

The third departure from Israel to Judah took place in 725 BC, just before Israel went into the Assyrian captivity (Hos. 1:6). This exodus appears to be a visit. The text below mentions a return to their cities. This return can be to the cities in which they were in Samaria as presented in the following:

> Nevertheless, divers of *Asher and Manasseh and of Zebulun* humbled themselves and came to Jerusalem. (12) Also, in Judah, the hand of God was to give them one heart to do the commandment of the king and of the princes, by the word of the LORD. (18) For a multitude of the people, even many of Ephraim, and Manasseh, *Issachar*, and Zebulun had not cleansed themselves, yet did they eat the Passover otherwise than it was written.

But Hezekiah prayed for them, saying, the good LORD pardon every one (25) And all the congregation of Judah, with the priests and the Levites, and all the congregation that came out of Israel, and *the strangers that came out of the land of Israel*, and that dwelt in Judah, rejoiced.... Now when all this was finished, all Israel that were present went out to the cities of Judah, and brake the images in pieces, and cut down the groves, and threw down the high places and the altars out of all Judah and Benjamin, in Ephraim also and Manasseh, until they had utterly destroyed them all. Then all the children of Israel returned, every man to his possession, into their own cities (2 Chron. 30:11-12, 18, 25; 31:1). [Italics ours]

Judah, as the leading tribe, went into Babylonian captivity in 606 BC. The Bible certifies that all the tribes were in this captivity. Of those who returned from the Babylonian captivity in 458 BC were many Israelites. "And there went up some of the children of Israel, and of the priests, and the Levites, and the singers, and the porters, and the Nethinims, unto Jerusalem, in the seventh year of Artaxerxes the king" (Ezra 7:7; cf. Neh. 11:3; 1 Chron. 9:2–3; Matt. 4:13–16; Luke 2:36). By the time of Jesus, Judah and some of Israel became one nation. This unity is evident by the Judean-Israel captivity in the regathering Judah during the Persian Empire. Four hundred years later, during the time of Jesus, Israel had multiplied Jacob's seed in and around Jerusalem and in the surrounding nations. Since all of them did not receive Jesus, in fulfillment of Hosea 1:10 and Isaiah 10:22–23, a remnant was to be saved (Rom. 9:24–25).

One must note that Paul spoke of the Israelites from among the Gentiles using Hosea 1. It refers to those Israelites of the diaspora. The ones on whom God had "no mercy" were the ten tribes. Not only was God calling those of the diaspora but also Gentiles who would call on His name. Those whom God called "not my people" were Judah. It was prophesied of Judah's rejection as a nation when Jesus uttered the words: "Behold your house is left unto you desolate ... Now when she had weaned Loruhamah, she conceived, and bare a son. Then said God, Call his name Loammi: for ye are not my people, and I will not be your God" (Hos. 1:8–9). This rejection was only temporary (Matt. 23:39; Luke 13:35).

The Dispersion of Israel

Because of the wickedness committed by kings of the ten-tribe kingdom, God commanded vengeance on the house of Ahab for killing His prophets. The house of Jehu was called to carry out God's mission of retribution against the house of Ahab. That happened in the valley of Jezreel. During those days, subsequent kings of Israel continued to disobey the laws of the Most High. God then began to cut down the number of the people of Israel by creating a departure from them to the two tribes. After many converts transferred to Judah, the ten-tribe kingdom ceased from being a kingdom before the Lord. The next step was to extricate them from the land, as seen in Hosea 1:6. The first act of the dispersion can be understood from the following:

> And the LORD said unto him, Call his name Jezreel; for yet a little while, and I will avenge the blood of Jezreel upon the house of Jehu, and will cause to cease the kingdom of the house of Israel. And it shall come

to pass at that day, that I will break the bow of Israel in the valley of Jezreel. And she conceived again, and bare a daughter. And God said unto him, Call her name Loruhamah: for I will no more have mercy upon the house of Israel; but I will utterly take them away" (Hosea 1:4-6).

And they transgressed against the God of their fathers and went a whoring after the gods of the people of the land, whom God destroyed before them. (26) And the God of Israel stirred up the spirit of Pul king of Assyria, and the spirit of Tilgathpilneser king of Assyria, and he carried them away, even the Reubenites, and the Gadites, and the half-tribe of Manasseh, and brought them unto Halah, and Habor, and Hara, and to the river Gozan, unto this day (1Chron. 5:25, 26).

That act took place about 734 BC. Israel remained in captivity of Assyria and the cities of the Medes. The second act of the dispersion is presented in the following:

In the twelfth year of Ahaz king of Judah began Hoshea the son of Elah to reign in Samaria over Israel nine years. (2) And he did that which was evil in the sight of the LORD, but not as the kings of Israel that were before him. (3) Against him came up Shalmaneser king of Assyria, and Hoshea became his servant and gave him presents. (4) And the king of Assyria found a conspiracy in Hoshea: for he had sent messengers to the king of Egypt, and brought no present to the king of Assyria, as he had done year by year: therefore, the king of Assyria shut him up and bound him in prison. (5) Then the king of Assyria came up throughout all the land, and went up to Samaria, and besieged it three years. (6) In the ninth year of Hoshea, the king of Assyria took Samaria, and carried Israel away into Assyria, and placed them in Halah and in Habor by the river of Gozan, and in the cities of the Medes. (13) Yet the LORD testified against Israel, and against Judah, by all the prophets, and by all the seers, saying, turn ye from your evil ways, and keep my commandments and my statutes, according to all the law which I commanded your fathers, and which I sent to you by my servants the prophets. ... (17) And they caused their sons and their daughters to pass through the fire, and used divination and enchantments, and sold themselves to do evil in the sight of the LORD, to provoke him to anger. (18) Therefore, the LORD was very angry with Israel, and removed them out of his sight: there was none left but the tribe of Judah only (2 Kings 17-1-13, 17-18).

The foregoing history took place in 721 BC. Concerning the final fall of Israel, scripture states:

Behold, the eyes of the Lord GOD are upon the sinful kingdom, and I will destroy it from off the face of the earth; saving that I will not utterly destroy the house of Jacob, saith the LORD. (9) For, lo, I will command, and I will sift the house of Israel among all nations, like as corn is sifted in a sieve, yet shall not the least grain fall upon the earth. (10) All the sinners of my people shall die by the sword, which says, 'the evil shall not overtake nor prevent us' (Amos 9:8-10). My God will cast them away because they did not hearken unto him: and they shall be wanderers among the nations (Hos. 9:17). Cf. Hos. 8:8). Samaria shall become desolate; for she hath rebelled against her God: they shall fall by the sword: their infants shall be dashed in pieces, and their women with child shall be ripped up (Hos. 13:16).

The children of Israel who escaped the sword went to two places, Egypt and Assyria. "Ephraim also is like a silly dove without heart: they call to Egypt, they go to Assyria" (Hos. 7:11). "They return, but not to the Most High: they are like a deceitful bow: their princes shall fall by the sword for the rage of their tongue: this shall be their derision in the land of Egypt" (Hos. 9:3; cf. Hos. 7:16; Isa. 31:1–2; Jer. 44). Most of these Israelites protected their lineage, people, and culture as some worshipped God in colonies in lands of their sojourn.

The consequence of Israel leaving Palestine resulted in heathens taking over Samaria in lieu of the children of Israel. These Gentiles mirrored the religion of the Jews by incorporating Judean practices into their culture. The Samaritan (Gentiles) had insufficiently accepted Judaism for Israelite classification. Jesus commissioned his disciples to refrain from proselytizing the Gentiles or the Samaritans. These Samaritans were descendants of the same Gentiles from 721 BC and the Helens from Greece who shared in Israel's culture. As these Gentiles possessed Samaria, Israel was scattered in the northeast and to the south. The following quote reveals how it all went down:

> And the king of Assyria brought men from Babylon, and from Cuthah, and from Ava, and from Hamath, and from Sepharvaim, and placed them in the cities

of Samaria instead of the children of Israel: and they possessed Samaria, and dwelt in the cities thereof. (25) And ,so it was at the beginning of their dwelling there, that they feared not the LORD: therefore the LORD sent lions among them, which slew some of them. (26) Wherefore they spake to the king of Assyria, saying, the nations which thou hast removed, and placed in the cities of Samaria, know not the manner of the God of the land: therefore, he hath sent lions among them, and, behold, they slay them, because they know not the manner of the God of the land. (27) Then the king of Assyria commanded, saying; carry thither one of the priests whom ye brought from thence; and let them go and dwell there and let him teach them the manner of the God of the land. (28) Then one of the priests whom they had carried away from Samaria came and dwelt in Bethel, and taught them how they should fear the LORD. (29) Howbeit every nation made gods of their own and put them in the houses of the high places which the Samaritans had made, every nation in their cities wherein they dwelt. (30) And the men of Babylon made Succothbenoth, and the men of Cuth made Nergal, and the men of Hamath made Ashima, (31) And the Avites made Nibhaz and Tartak, and the Sepharvites burnt their children in fire to Adrammelech and Anammelech, the gods of Sepharvaim. (32) So they feared the LORD and made unto themselves of the lowest of them priests of the high places, which sacrificed for them in the houses of the high places. (33) They feared the LORD, and served their own gods, after the manner of the nations whom they carried away from thence. (34) Unto this day they do after the former manners: they fear not the LORD, neither do they after their statutes, or after their ordinances, or after the law and commandment which the LORD commanded the children of Jacob, whom he named Israel (2 Kings 17:24-34).

The scripture in Kings finalizes the fulfillment of Hosea's prophecy (Israel's last prophet) concerning the dispersion of Israel: "I will utterly take them away." Hosea prophesied to the northern kingdom approximately 758–725 BC. He predicted the fall of both Israel and Judah. The last king of Israel was Hoshea; he ruled from 732–722 BC.

Dispersion and Return of Judah

God had mercy on Judah and temporarily saved them from their enemies (2 Kings 19:32–36). Subsequently, through King Manasseh, Judeans did evil from which they never fully recovered (2 Kings 21:1–17). They were eventually punished and scattered by Babylon, but they returned and were accepted during the Persian Empire. "But I will have mercy upon the house of Judah, and will save them by the LORD their God, and will not save them by bow, nor by sword, nor by battle, by horses, nor by horsemen." Finally, most of them were disposed of as "not my people" in the days of Jesus. The following quotes' pronouncement is the first capture of Judah by Babylon.

And Pharaohnechoh made Eliakim the son of Josiah king in the room of Josiah his father, and turned his name to Jehoiakim, and took Jehoahaz away: and he came to Egypt, and died there. (35) And Jehoiakim gave the silver and the gold to Pharaoh; but he taxed the land to give the money according to the commandment of Pharaoh: he exacted the silver and the gold of the people of the land, of everyone according to his taxation, to give it unto Pharaohnechoh (2 Ki 23:34-35).

Jehoiakim was twenty and five years old when he began to reign, and he reigned eleven years in Jerusalem: and he did that which was evil in the sight of the LORD his God (2 Chron. 36:5).

In the third year of the reign of Jehoiakim king of Judah came Nebuchadnezzar king of Babylon unto Jerusalem, and besieged it. And the Lord gave Jehoiakim king of Judah into his hand, with part of the vessels of the house of God: which he carried into the land of Shinar to the house of his god; and he brought the vessels into the treasure house of his god (Dan. 1:1-2).

And he carried away all Jerusalem, and all the princes, and all the mighty men of valor, even ten thousand captives, and all the craftsmen and smiths: none remained, save the poorest sort of the people of the land. And he carried away Jehoiachin to Babylon, and the king's mother, and the king's wives, and his officers, and the mighty of the land, those carried he into captivity from Jerusalem to Babylon... And the king of Babylon made Mattaniah his father's brother king in his stead and changed his name to Zedekiah (2 Kings 24:14, 15, 17; Jer. 40:7).

Notwithstanding what took place with Israel, the people of Judah and their king continued in disobedience. That gave God no option but to take them away. Their undoing resulted in Judah going into slavery under the Babylonian Empire. The following scripture reveals how they were taken into captivity.

Zedekiah was one and twenty years old when he began to reign, and reigned eleven years in Jerusalem. (12) And he did that which was evil in the sight of the LORD his God and humbled not himself before Jeremiah the prophet speaking from the mouth of the LORD. (13) And he also rebelled against king Nebuchadnezzar, who had made him swear by God: but he stiffened his neck, and hardened his heart from turning unto the LORD God of Israel (2 Chron. 36:11-13).

Therefore, he brought upon them the king of the Chaldees, who slew their young men with the sword in the house of their sanctuary, and had no compassion upon young man or maiden, old man, or him that stooped for age: he gave them all into his hand. (18) And all the vessels of the house of God, great and small, and the treasures of the house of the LORD, and the treasures of the king, and of his princes; all these he brought to Babylon. (19) And they burnt the house of God, and brake breakdown the wall of Jerusalem, and burnt all the palaces thereof with fire, and destroyed all the goodly vessels thereof. (20) And them that had escaped from the sword carried he away to Babylon; where they were servants to him and his sons until the reign of the kingdom of Persia (2 Chron. 36:17-20).

And as the evil figs, which cannot be eaten, they are so evil; surely thus saith the LORD, So will I give Zedekiah the king of Judah, and his princes, and the residue of Jerusalem, that remain in this land, and them that dwell in the land of Egypt: (9) And I will deliver them to be removed into all the kingdoms of the earth for their hurt, to be a reproach and a proverb, a taunt and a curse, in all places whither I shall drive them. (10) And I will send the sword, the famine, and the pestilence, among them, till they be consumed from off the land that I gave unto them and to their fathers (Jer. 24:8-10).

Although Judah went into captivity, Judeans had not faced the full wrath for their disobedience. Daniel prayed for the restoration of Israel. Daniel 8 speaks of an intervening temporal restoration from the disintegration imposed by a Grecian power. Before the Grecian corruption, Judah was restored through Persia after seventy years of desolation (Dan. 9:24–25). In his prayer, Daniel stated that the curses written in the law concerning Israel had been pouring partially yet uniquely on the people (Dan. 9:11–14). He made an inquiry concerning the seventy years of Jeremiah's prophecy. The time drew near, and something was about to happen. The following quotes revealed the answer to Daniel's prayer.

> Now in the first year of Cyrus king of Persia, that the word of the LORD by the mouth of Jeremiah might be fulfilled, the LORD stirred up the spirit of Cyrus king of Persia, that he made a proclamation throughout all his kingdom, and put it also in writing, saying, Thus saith Cyrus king of Persia, The LORD God of heaven hath given me all the kingdoms of the earth; and he hath charged me to build him a house at Jerusalem, which is in Judah (Ezra 1:1-2, cf. 2 Chron. 36:23, Dan. 9:2). c.f. Ezra 2:64, 65; 3:8.

God's prediction of Cyrus indicated that He would restore the Jews to the Promised Land. There were impediments to the progress of rebuilding Jerusalem. During the restoration process, the Jews had gotten comfortable in the kingdom of Persia. Internal and external social forces enshrouded those who desired to return. As they cried for deliverance, God strengthened their hands, and the city was rebuilt.

Gentiles Frustrated the Work

The innovation of Jerusalem grounding for the Messiah was inefficient at first. The Samaritans who frustrated the work were not ancestral to Israel. They were people from other nations who replaced Israel in Samaria. These new Samaritans had a partial conversion to the Judean religion, and they were political converts as recorded in 2 Kings 17. The following references illustrate the intermittent nature of the work.

> Now when the adversaries of Judah and Benjamin heard that the children of the captivity built the temple unto the LORD God of Israel; (2) Then they came to Zerubbabel, and to the chief of the fathers, and said unto them, Let us build with you: for we seek your God, as ye do; and we do sacrifice unto him since the days of Esarhaddon king of Assur, which brought us up hither" (Ezra 4:1-2).
>
> But Zerubbabel, and Jeshua, and the rest of the chief of the fathers of Israel, said unto them, Ye have nothing to do with us to build a house unto our God; but we ourselves together will build unto the LORD God of Israel, as king Cyrus the king of Persia hath commanded us. (4) Then the people of the land weakened the hands

of the people of Judah, and troubled them in building, (5) and hired counselors against them, to frustrate their purpose, all the days of Cyrus king of Persia, even until the reign of Darius king of Persia... (9) Then wrote Rehum the chancellor, and Shimshai the scribe, and the rest of their companions; the Dinaites, the Apharsathchites, the Tarpelites, the Apharsites, the Archevites, the Babylonians, the Susanchites, the Dehavites, and the Elamites, (10) And the rest of the nations whom the great and noble Asnappar brought over, and set in the cities of Samaria, and the rest that are on this side the river, and at such a time. (11) This is the copy of the letter that they sent unto him, even unto Artaxerxes, the king; Thy servants the men on this side the river, and at such a time. (12) Be it known unto the king that the Jews which came up from thee to us are come unto Jerusalem, building the rebellious and the bad city, and have set up the walls thereof, and joined the foundations. Be it known now unto the king, that, if this city be built, and the walls set up again, then will they not pay toll, tribute, and custom, and so thou shalt endamage the revenue of the kings.... Then ceased the work of the house of God which is at Jerusalem. So it ceased unto the second year of the reign of Darius king of Persia (Ezra 4:3-5, 9-13, 24).

Then the people of the land weakened the hands of the people of Judah, —Exasperated by this repulse, the Samaritans endeavored by every means to molest the workmen as well as obstruct the progress of the building; and, though they could not alter the decree which Cyrus had issued regarding it, yet by bribes and clandestine arts indefatigable plied at court, they labored to frustrate the effects of the edict (Jamieson, Fausset & Brown, 1997).

When interferences were reduced, and reformatory efforts bolstered the people's interest, the work resumed by the prophets God had raised. The time and purpose dawned for preparation for the coming Messiah. Yet, they were to wait 400 years before they can realize the promise. Daniel's prophecy in chapter 9 was written to establish this panorama.

Judah's Preparation for the Messiah

There were a few prophets under the Persian Empire who siphoned the work of transforming Jerusalem. The work progressed through the coalesced efforts of Haggai, Joshua, Zechariah, Nehemiah, Ezra, and Zerubbabel. Under the first return, several restoration officers were involved, namely Joshua, Haggai, and Zechariah. Their record is found in Ezra 1–4. Upon the second return, the restoration of the law was established under Ezra's ministry (Ezra 7–10). On the third return, the rebuilding of Jerusalem's walls took place through the leadership of Nehemiah, as attested to by the following:

> And the elders of the Jews built, and they prospered through the prophesying of Haggai the prophet and Zechariah, the son of Iddo. And they built, and finished it, according to the commandment of the God of Israel, and according to the commandment of Cyrus, and Darius, and Artaxerxes king of Persia. .... (21) And the children of Israel, which were come again out of

captivity, and all such as had separated themselves unto them from the filthiness of the heathen of the land, to seek the LORD God of Israel, did eat, (22) And kept the feast of unleavened bread seven days with joy: for the LORD had made them joyful, and turned the heart of the king of Assyria unto them, to strengthen their hands in the work of the house of God, the God of Israel (Ezra 6:14, 21-22). cf. Ezra 8:1, 15.

Key to the restoration was the purification of the Judean families exclusive to other nations. Ezra took on this responsibility to warrant that other nations' tainting impact would not remain a deterrent to the restoration. He instructed the people of God to divest themselves of strange wives and family ties that were askew with God's objectives. God did not want his people to marry across tribes while in their land, much less the heathens when they were scattered. As you can see, Ezra was flabbergasted by the level of dereliction the Judeans were in through the sin of amalgamation with other nations, as attested by the following:

Now when these things were done, the princes came to me, saying, The people of Israel, and the priests, and the Levites, have not separated themselves from the people of the lands, doing according to their abominations, even of the Canaanites, the Hittites, the Perizzites, the Jebusites, the Ammonites, the Moabites, the Egyptians, and the Amorites. (2) For they have taken of their daughters for themselves, and for their sons: so that the holy seed have mingled themselves with the people of those lands: yea, the hand of the princes and rulers hath been chief in this trespass. (3) And when I heard this thing, I rent my garment and my mantle, and plucked off the hair of my head and of my beard, and sat down astonied...(5) And at the evening sacrifice I arose up from my heaviness; and having rent my garment and my mantle, I fell upon my knees, and spread out my hands unto the LORD my God, (6) And said, O my God, I am ashamed and blush to lift up my face to thee, my God: for our iniquities are increased over our head, and our trespass is grown up unto the heavens. (7) Since the days of our fathers have we been in a great trespass unto this day; and for our iniquities have we, our kings, and our priests, been delivered into the hand of the kings of the lands, to the sword, to captivity, and to a spoil, and to confusion of face, as it is this day" (Ezra 9:1-3, 5-7).

Now, therefore, let us make a covenant with our God to put away all the wives, and such as are born of them, according to the counsel of my lord, and of those that tremble at the commandment of our God; and let it be done according to the law.... (10) And Ezra the priest stood up and said unto them, Ye have transgressed, and have taken strange wives, to increase the trespass of Israel. (11) Now, therefore, make confession unto the LORD God of your fathers, and do his pleasure: and separate yourselves from the people of the land, and from the strange wives. (12) Then all the congregation answered and said with a loud voice, As thou hast said, so must we do... (17) And they made an end with all the men that had taken strange wives by the first day of the first month (Ezra 10:3, 10-12, 17).

In dealing with the amalgamation, a thorough ablation needed to take place. Not only was the city to be rebuilt, but the people were to ablate for internal and external impurities. The children of Judah had to dispossess these strange wives taken from the surrounding nations. When the children of Judah gathered to rebuild dilapidated Jerusalem from the baleful acts of Babylon, they were met with staunch resistance from the false brethren of the Samaritans. Notwithstanding the encumbrance, God prospered the work, and the wall was finished. Another relevant factor in the restoration is: Israel was to segregate themselves from other nations and keep their lineage relatively pure. After removing this external impediment, success became pivotal in maintaining a continuous reformatory spirit, as seen in the following:

> But it came to pass, that when Sanballat heard that we built the wall, he was wroth, and took great indignation, and mocked the Jews. (2) And he spake before his brethren and the army of Samaria, and said, What do these feeble Jews? Will they fortify themselves? will they sacrifice? Will they make an end in a day? will they revive the stones out of the heaps of the rubbish which are burned?" (Neh. 4:1-2).
>
> But it came to pass, that when Sanballat, and Tobiah, and the Arabians, and the Ammonites, and the Ashdodites, heard that the walls of Jerusalem were made up and that the breaches began to be stopped, then they were very wroth, (8) And conspired all of them together to come and to fight against Jerusalem, and to hinder it (Neh. 4:7-8).
>
> So the wall was finished in the twenty and fifth day

of the month Elul, in fifty and two days. (16) And it came to pass, that when all our enemies heard thereof, and all the heathen that were about us saw these things, they were much cast down in their own eyes: for they perceived that this work was wrought of our God (Neh. 6:15-16).

And my God put into mine heart to gather together the nobles, and the rulers, and the people, that they might be reckoned by genealogy. And I found a register of the genealogy of them which came up at the first, and found written therein, (6) These are the children of the province, that went up out of the captivity, of those that had been carried away, whom Nebuchadnezzar the king of Babylon had carried away, and came again to Jerusalem and to Judah, every one unto his city (Neh. 7:5-6).

And the seed of Israel separated themselves from all strangers, and stood and confessed their sins and the iniquities of their fathers. (3) And they stood up in their place, and read in the book of the law of the LORD their God one-fourth part of the day; and another fourth part they confessed, and worshipped the LORD their God (Neh. 9:2-3).

The Jews were meticulous in recording genealogies. Ezra was concerned about the worshipers from other nations whose claimed lineage to Israel was apocryphal. Another point worth noting is that God had always warned His people about amalgamating the holy seed with other nations. So far, Israelite-Judean captivity was accomplished mainly by Egypt, Assyria, and Babylon. Following the grace period under the

Persians, Judah's kingdom and some Samaritan proselytes went through a series of persecution by the Grecians during the Intertestamental period. Ensuing the persecution was a mixed multitude in Palestine; the proselyte Jews of Samaria and some Greeks tainted the religion of the Judeans. During these encounters, Israel was at risk of losing track of the holy seed.

God announced the restoration of Israel in the book of Amos. Amos and Hosea were the last two prophets sent to Israel. Both the destruction and the restoration were outlined through these prophets. The same Old Testament quotations were used in the New Testament to underscore the plan. Therefore, the restoration spoken of through these pivotal prophetic utterances was predestined solely for New Testament fulfillment through Jacob's lineage.

For the first three and a half years after Christ's death, the messianic church was culturally Judeans. Remember, the negro Paul, was mistaken for an Egyptian. The early church was the identifying root and stump of the Jacobite tree, the literal house of Israel as messianic. They are the accepted house of Israel, "my people." The Judean Israelites who did not believe, temporarily became "not my people," spiritually blinded. They were scattered during the destruction of Jerusalem in AD 70. The believing Israelites had gone ahead of the unbelieving into Africa to escape the destruction. This scattering brought them to lower Africa and Saudi Arabia. They fled to the African Atlas Mountains. Others were captives of Rome. African history reveals that Israelites sojourned into Egypt and to the lower parts of Africa. There, they established the kingdom of Israel. In this new locality, they multiplied by the tens of millions. Says Windsor:

The pagans and the Romans attacked the Jews indiscriminately, both the Jewish soldiers and the uninvolved peaceful population, without mercy. Because of this merciless attack, many Jews fled to those parts of northwest Africa known as Tunisia, Algeria, Morocco, and Mauretania. Many other Jews fled to the areas where Rome did not have any jurisdiction, this was to the region of the south, the Sahara Desert and the Sudan. Grayzel says: "Such is the explanation of how the Sahara Desert first acquired Jewish tribes toughened by a fighting tradition and possessed of physical characteristics [blacks] which, it is said, still make them approximate very closely the original Jewish population of Palestine (Windsor, 1988, p. 86).

The Judean punishment was not over. When they said, "Let his blood be on us and on our children," they knew not of the baleful barbaric slave trade awaited them (Rom. 2:9). As Africans, they were captured and slain by Rome, Islam, and European Christians. Others were sold into slavery. They traversed by way of ships into many countries to become slaves once more. According to Daniel 9, they suffered the curses written in the law (Deut. 28; Dan. 9:27) until the consummation. Rome killed the lineage of Judean-messianic for Judaizing.

As the antitype, the church of the Messiah was wholly replaced by pagan rites. In most of today's Christianity paganism and unbiblical interpretation of the Pauline epistles are united. The messianic faith got baptized into the Holy Roman Empire. During our stay in that system, many messianic archetypes were converted to abet pagan and Gentile niches. Examples of these pagan cultural practices are: Sunday replacing Sabbath, all forbidden foods clean replacing Leviticus 11, baby baptism and sprinkling replacing personal accountability and immersion, saved by faith replaced by works of penance, praying to the Father in Jesus as mediator replaced by prayers to statues and Mary, the yearly frequency of the Passover replaced by indiscriminate timing and Easter, and the Feast of Dedication by Christmas. Not to mention Plutonic ideas about the afterlife replacing resurrection and the Old Testament's view of death. Considering this, there should be no doubt that the Christian church is a mixture of the concept of Judaism overrun by paganism. The call is to disown the hybrid Christianity and seek the laws of the Most High. God's call to Jacob is to accept the Messiah and cease the paganized form of Christianity. That may sound oxymoronic, but what better term can be employed? Thus saith the Lord:

> And what agreement hath the temple of God with idols? for ye are the temple of the living God; as God hath said, I will dwell in them, and walk in them; and I will be their God, and they shall be my people. Wherefore come out from among them, and be ye separate, saith the Lord, and touch not the unclean thing; and I will receive you (2 Cor. 6:16–17).

The converted doctrines are unclean things. To be enshrouded by everlasting righteousness is to cease touching the unclean thing. This purification must take place amid the people of God.

Israelites wheeled back and forth among the nations. Most of the ten tribes of Israel did not remain in Assyria but returned to Samaria by crossing "Euphrates by the narrow places of the river" from Gozan on the Northeast, to Westward, and continued South. Some of them established colonies in Judea. Others proceeded to Egypt and became aborigines of many uncharted lands of Africa, "into a further country, where never mankind dwelt." Their goal was to serve God in their traditional Israelite fashion, in lands "where no man dwelt" (2 Esd. 13:40–45 of the Apocrypha). Noteworthy is the work of Nahum Slouschz, which Windsor cites as tracing the path trod by ancient Israel in the following:

> In ancient times, the Carthaginians from North Africa penetrated the Sahara Desert and the Western Sudan during the second and third centuries B.C. When north and eastern Africa had amassed over a million Jews, these Jews began a continuous migration to the region of the Niger River. According to the researches of Nahum Slouschz: "The tradition of the Jewish traders in the Sahara stretches back to biblical times." Slouschz continues: "And it is not at all surprising to encounter in every part of the desert traces— and even survivals— of a primitive Judaism which at one time played an important role in the whole region of the Sahara from Senegal to the very borders of Somaliland *(Windsor, 1988, p. 88).*

Many kingdoms impacted Israel. As mentioned in scripture, the places of Israel's dispersion include Assyria, Babylon, Medo Persia, and Egypt, all of which were kingdoms of the colored (Black) people. Afterward, the Edomites sold some of Israel to the Grecians as slaves (Joel 3:6; 1 Macc. 8:18). Rome subsequently ruled these empires. In the early years (200–100 BC) of the Roman uprising as a world power, Rome did not intend to overthrow nations or change their political programming but to make them subservient to the Roman Republic. They were more into annexing nations by concessions rather than ruthless confrontations. The Roman Empire was a melting pot of diverse cultures, religions, and races, including Jews. For this reason, it was prophesied as a nondescript beast of Daniel's prophecy. The dispersed Jews were met with conflict and suffered cruel treatment by the Gentiles who conquered lands wherein they sojourned. Israelites suffered persecution at the hands of a myriad of people.

Chapter 12

—⊙⊙⊙—

The Restoration and the Time

The Messianic Restoration

I srael is not completely obliviated while among the nations. God has promised to preserve a remnant. The prophecies are concerned with both the genealogical and the spiritual aspects of Israel. God wants to institute reforms and redeem His original people. The early fulfillment of the following prophecy in Hosea began after Israel went into Assyria.

> For, lo, I will command, and I will sift the house of Israel among all nations, like as corn is sifted in a sieve, yet shall not the least grain fall upon the earth. (Amos 9:9)

From the return of the faithful among Israel, the following prediction tracks some as believers in Jesus.

> In that day will I raise up the tabernacle of David that is fallen, and close up the breaches thereof, and I will raise up his ruins, and I will build it as in the days of old. (Amos 9:11; cf. Mark 11:10, Act. 15:16)

This consolation was to initiate Israel's freedom. Israel long hoped for the Messiah's advent to save them from the nations that enslaved them. They did not realize that their restoration was to occur in stages. The first phase was reformation brought by the Messiah; afterward, God was to restore them as guardians of the Word, and through them, all nations would be blessed. These facts are underscored in the following:

> And she brought forth a man child, who was to rule all nations with a rod of iron: and her child was caught up unto God, and to his throne... And out of his mouth goeth a sharp sword, that with it he should smite the nations: and he shall rule them with a rod of iron: and he treadeth the winepress of the fierceness and wrath of Almighty God. And he hath on his vesture and on his thigh a name written, KING OF KINGS, AND LORD OF LORDS" (Rev. 12:5, Rev. 19:5, 6).
>
> He shall be great, and shall be called the Son of the Highest: and the Lord God shall give unto him the throne of his father David: And he shall reign over the house of Jacob forever, and of his kingdom, there shall be no end... To perform the mercy promised to our fathers, and to remember his holy covenant; the oath which he swore to our father Abraham, That he would grant unto us, that we being delivered out of the hand of our enemies might serve him without fear, In holiness and righteousness before him, all the days of our life. ... For mine eyes have seen thy salvation, which thou hast prepared before the face of all people; A light to lighten the Gentiles and the glory of thy people Israel. (Luke 1:32-33, 1:72-75, 2:29-32).

Behold, my servant shall deal prudently; he shall be exalted and extolled, and be very high. As many were astonied at thee; his visage was so marred more than any man, and his form more than the sons of men: So shall he sprinkle many nations; the kings shall shut their mouths at him: for that which had not been told them shall they see; and that which they had not heard shall they consider" (Isa. 52:13-15).

Behold my servant, whom I uphold; mine elect, in whom my soul delighteth; I have put my spirit upon him: he shall bring forth judgment to the Gentiles. (2) He shall not cry, nor lift up, nor cause his voice to be heard in the street. (3) A bruised reed shall he not break, and the smoking flax shall he not quench: he shall bring forth judgment unto truth. (4) He shall not fail nor be discouraged, till he has set judgment in the earth: and the isles shall wait for his law (Isa 42:1-4).

Simeon hath declared how God at the first did visit the Gentiles, to take out of them a people for his name. After this I will return, and will build again the tabernacle of David, which is fallen down; and I will build again the ruins thereof, and I will set it up: That the residue of men might seek after the Lord, and all the Gentiles, upon whom my name is called, saith the Lord, who doeth all these things...The Lord GOD which gathereth the outcasts of Israel saith, Yet will I gather others to him, beside those that are gathered unto him." (Acts 15:15–17, Isa. 56:4–5, 8).

Behold, the days come, saith the LORD, that I will raise unto David a righteous Branch, and a King shall reign and prosper, and shall execute judgment and justice in the earth. In his days [Messianic dispensation] Judah shall be saved, and Israel shall dwell safely: and this is his name whereby he shall be called, THE LORD OUR RIGHTEOUSNESS (Jer. 23:5–8).

From the preceding verses, there is no question as to the time of the restoration. Before the restoration, a righteous king shall arise. That righteous, noble king will build the house of the Lord. This house is initially a spiritual habitation, kingdom initiation. It is the kingdom of David reinstated. The kingdom comes in phases through its development. During the time of antitypical David (Jesus), salvation is open to both Israelites and Gentiles. They must embrace the New Covenant and its laws. Initially, the New Covenant comprises the four gospels, which tell of Jesus's life. The New Covenant was made by the life of Christ and sealed by His death. The book of Hebrews 1–8 delineates how the covenant was formed. This rebuilding of David's kingdom through the New Covenant allows salvation to reach those of non-Israelite lineage, the Gentiles. The kingdom is open to all who accept the Messiah. Before Edom is stricken, the "scepter" must first "rise out of Israel." This scepter is the promised Messiah of the New Covenant, as it is written:

> Therefore, behold, the days come, saith the LORD, that they shall no more say, The LORD liveth, which brought up the children of Israel out of the land of Egypt; But, The LORD liveth, which brought up and which led the seed of the house of Israel out of the north country, and from all countries whither I had driven them; and they shall dwell in their own land (Jer. 23:58).

Notice, the verse speaks of the seed of the house of Israel. This seed refers to the genealogical race of Jacob. In the latter-day fulfillment of the prophecy (Jer. 23:5–8, 58), the faithful remnant of Jacob returned to the Abrahamic promised territories during the Persian Empire days. They remained there for an everlasting covenant up to the first advent of the Messiah. Although the land acquisition was partially fulfilled in Joshua's days (Josh. 21:43, 44), Solomon's, and the Persian Empire, there is yet a greater fulfillment. From this latter return, they will never be removed. This latter return will embrace the entire Canaan-Arabian area from Kuwait to parts of Egypt. Israelites and Gentiles who keep God's Sabbath and take hold of the messianic covenant will be those whom God will accept. The prophecy continues:

> That they [Jacob's descendants] may possess the remnant of Edom, and of all the heathen, which are called by my name [non-Israelite Messianic], saith the LORD that doeth this. Behold, the days come, saith the LORD, that the plowman [servant] shall overtake the reaper [master], and the treader of grapes [servant] him that soweth seed [master]; and the mountains shall drop sweet wine, and all the hills shall melt. And I will bring again the captivity [free them from their masters] of my people of Israel, and they shall build the waste cities, and inhabit them, and they shall plant vineyards, and drink the wine thereof; they shall also make gardens, and eat the fruit of them. And I will plant them upon their land, and they shall *no more be pulled up out* of their land which I have given them, saith the LORD thy God. (Amos 9:12–15)

Obadiah 1 and Ezekiel mentioned the restoration. They show how God will overcome the heathen lands and give them to the faithful among the children of Israel. As you can see, the quote mentions the Gentiles as servants to a portion of saved Israel. These servants are fellow citizens of God's kingdom. As servants, they will be as people of the land, for the law says:

> Love ye, therefore, the stranger: for ye were strangers in the land of Egypt (Deut. 10:19). And if a stranger sojourn with thee in your land, ye shall not vex him. But the stranger that dwelleth with you shall be unto you as one born among you, and thou shalt love him as thyself; for ye were strangers in the land of Egypt: I am the LORD your God (Lev. 19:33-34).

> If ye oppress not the stranger, the fatherless, and the widow, and shed not innocent blood in this place, neither walk after other gods to your hurt: Then will I cause you to dwell in this place, in the land that I gave to your fathers, for ever and ever (Jer. 7:6–7).

> Thus saith the LORD; Execute ye judgment and righteousness, and deliver the spoiled out of the hand of the oppressor: and do no wrong, do no violence to the stranger, the fatherless, nor the widow, neither shed innocent blood in this place (Jer. 22:3).

> Is not this the fast that I have chosen? to loose the bands of wickedness, to undo the heavy burdens, and to let the oppressed go free, and that ye break every yoke? (7) Is it not to deal thy bread to the hungry, and that thou bring the poor that are cast out to thy house? When thou seest the naked, that thou cover him; and that thou hide not thyself from thine own flesh? (8) Then shall thy light

break forth as the morning, and thine health shall spring forth speedily: and thy righteousness shall go before thee; the glory of the LORD shall be thy rearward. (9) Then shalt thou call and the LORD shall answer; thou shalt cry, and he shall say, Here I am. If thou take away from the midst of thee the yoke, the putting forth of the finger, and speaking vanity; (Isa. 58:6–9).

The prophecy in Amos is a replica of another one in Numbers 24, the prophecy of Balaam:

And now, behold, I go unto my people: come therefore, and I will advertise thee what this people shall do to thy people in the latter days. And he took up his parable, and said, Balaam the son of Beor hath said, and the man whose eyes are open hath said: He hath said, which heard the words of God, and knew the knowledge of the most High, which saw the vision of the Almighty, falling into a trance, but having his eyes open: I shall see him, but not now: I shall behold him, but not nigh: there shall come a Star out of Jacob, and a Sceptre shall rise out of Israel, and shall smite the corners of Moab, and destroy all the children of Sheth. And Edom shall be a possession, Seir also shall be a possession for his enemies; and Israel shall do valiantly. Out of Jacob shall come he that shall have dominion [the Messiah], and shall destroy him that remaineth of the city (Num. 24:14–19; cf. Isa. 63:1–4).

Moreover, the assurance of the Promised Land to Abraham was confirmed to Isaac and Jacob. That confirmation includes the small strip of land along the East Nile branch (River of Egypt) to North Euphrates, which Israel gained during Joshua's days. The Abrahamic promised territory embraces land from East Euphrates near Kuwait and across Arabia to the Nile branch. That is the area in which New Jerusalem will claim as its capital as it descends from heaven. All the land described in the prophecy will be to the children of Israel and to all non-Israelites who join them (see Gen. 15). No one else but the faithful is admissible in the territory (Isa. 54). There will be a defense of formidable proportion that dares anyone to even think of trespassing. Neither will anyone be able to shoot an arrow there.

Restoration Preparedness

God planned to restore the kingdom of Judah and Israel into one messianic kingdom. At the onset, the kingdom was called the "Sect" by the Jews and "Christians" by the Gentiles. The order of the Old Testament laws, including the Sabbath and hygienic laws, will be restored.

Besides, this restoration includes healthy vegetarianism. If we are working toward that restoration, we should also be working toward healthy vegetarianism, the God-given original diet. We should not center our emotions, convictions, and spirit on the taste of food, "For the kingdom of God is not meat and drink; but righteousness, and peace, and joy in the Holy Ghost" (Rom. 14:17). For some people, losing the taste of some foods is like losing life itself. "They shall not hurt nor destroy in all my holy mountain: for the earth shall be full of the knowledge of the LORD, as the waters cover the sea" (Isa. 11:9). No animal will be killed there. Therefore, we can cool off about eating lamb chops or pork chops. It will be a vegetarian kingdom—Eden restored. Now is the time we must position ourselves to be on the right side.

We are not living in the days of the early messianic church where animal products were permissible. Besides, the way flesh food is prepared and consumed is against the Old Testament laws that the early church followed (Acts 15:20–22, 28–29, 17:11). However, given that some people are in short transitions of leaving flesh foods behind, which is important to kingdom-bound saints, in the provision that flesh is prepared correctly from the farm to the table, it is not a sin to consume it. Enlightened people will ask for the strength to copy God's Edenic ideals. We must not copy Gentile Christianity or elementary Judaism. Yes, we are passing on to a time where the laws are advanced. We are about to stand on the threshold of the dispensation of the Day of the Lord.

The restoration's initial base is Jacob. Jesus said to the disciples, "Go not into the way of the Gentiles, and into any city of the Samaritans enter ye not: But go rather to the lost sheep of the house of Israel" (Matt. 10:5–6). "But ye shall receive power, after that the Holy Ghost is come upon you: and ye shall be witnesses unto me both in Jerusalem, and in all Judaea, and in Samaria, and unto the uttermost part of the earth" (Acts 1:8). Here we see that the disciples were to witness to Israel preceding the Gentiles. As we shall see in the following quote, the believing Jews were not inclined to embrace the Gentiles.

> And he said unto them; Ye know how that it is an unlawful thing for a man that is a Jew to keep company or come unto one of another nation, but God hath shewed me that I should not call any man common or unclean. "Then

Peter opened his mouth, and said, Of a truth, I perceive that God is no respecter of persons: (35) But in every nation, he that feareth him, and worketh righteousness is accepted with him. (36) The word which God sent unto the children of Israel, preaching peace by Jesus Christ: (he is Lord of all·)" (Act 10·34–36).

Thus, the church commenced with the natural branches of Israel. It was God's purpose that original Israel were to administer God's Grace to the rest of the world. The Gospel started with Israelites, those of the original tree.

Provoking Israel to Jealousy

While provoking the Judeans to jealousy by accepting the non-Israelites, God did not have an uncompassionate concern for ancient Israel. As Gentiles came into the gospel in the apostles' day, jealousy was aroused among the Jews. This jealousy was the cause of some Judeans accepting the gospel. Although a Gentile can be a spiritual Jew (Rom. 2:28), God had not cast away Israel's genealogical line (Rom. 11:1, 4). God has held in reserve the lineage of Jacob for messianic faith. While a considerable number of Israelites had accepted the election, the rest were blinded spiritually (Rom. 10:7). James spoke of the twelve tribes scattered abroad (Acts. 26:7; James 1:1). Here he refers to those who had taken hold of the gospel away from the homeland.

Do the ancient prophecies point to the descendants of Jacob to whom the covenants were made? Is there a plan for the lineage of Jacob? Have their descendants become prophetically unimportant owing to messianic Judah? Have the blinded, unbelieving Israelites of Jesus's day stumbled so that God no longer regarded them as the people of the promise? God forbid (Rom. 11:11).

> And of Zion, it shall be said, this and that man was born in her: and the highest himself shall establish her (Ps. 87:5).

While explaining God's program, Paul stated that the non-Israelites accepting the gospel should respect the natural branches. Israel's lineage carries the Gentiles by right of the root. The tree is Israelite (Rom. 1:24). Paul wrote that Jacob would not be lost. He is blinded for a short time. He will take up the gospel work when the fullness of the Gentiles "be come in," the time when a significant part of Gentiles heard the gospel and had their chance of adherence. When God accomplishes the Gentiles' allotment to hear the gospel, the bridge will be rebuilt for the influx of Jacob's ancient lineage to become messianic. This homecoming was not to be apprehended until after their due course of chastisement through the odious slave trade. With the advancement of technology, we know that the gospel's general tenor has found its distribution among the Gentiles. That also allows for the warning to be declared to Israel in preparation for exiting their psychological captivity. Now is the time for the fullness of Jacob to turn to Jesus and to the Torah irrespective of whether they are found practicing Judaism. The call is to the seed, especially those whose lineage is historically, prophetically, and phenotypically traceable to ancient Israel. However, only a small remnant of them shall be saved.

In Romans 9:24–25, Paul quoted two verses of Hosea concerning the ingathering. He cited Hosea 2:22 first for the

Gentiles coming in, and then he quoted Hosea 1:10 for the influx of Jews into the gospel. While the Gentiles were never God's people, the Jews were temporarily considered "not my people." Some of the broken branches got reaccepted.

> Yet the number of the children of Israel shall be as the sand of the sea, which cannot be measured nor numbered; and it shall come to pass, that in the place where it was said unto them, Ye are not my people, there it shall be said unto them, Ye are the sons of the living God (Hos. 1:10).

This verse received its fulfillment in the church's early days when a multitude from Israel embraced the gospel. The next verse speaks of their election in Jesus as Lord. In proximity to the day of Jezreel, they will come out of the land of their modern captivity in the realization of gospel truth. The day of Jezreel starts just before God commences the final gathering. The election in Jezreel refers to Jesus as the seed sower. In the gospel's early days, this seed sowing was preparatory for the last ingathering, antitypical Feast of Tabernacles. Now is the time the message can reach the whole house of Israel. Now is the pre-ingathering harvest.

Indentured Servants of the Captivity

Before West Africans became the bulk of the slave trade, trading of slaves was transacted using indentured servants with a degree of sanity enveloped in biblical consciousness (1 Pet. 2:18; Eph. 6:5; Col. 6:22). At first, the slave trade appeared to be sober, but later, it spun out of control and corrupted with the Europeans' involvement. In its mild stage, the Africans were selling their people for gain to the Europeans as slaves. Afterward, when the demand became an issue, tribal wars among the West African tribes produced prisoners of war, a source feeding the slave trade. As greed became the norm among the Europeans, the concentration of slaves was focused on the West and Central Africa. The Negro slaves were treated as merchandise, property, and without a human soul. They were stripped of culture, descendants, identity, and class. Other factors included Europeans invading the West African Coast and Central Africa hunting for Negro slaves. An example of invasion is when King Leopold II of Belgium took over the Congo. He exploited it for riches, killing twelve million Negro Judean-Israelite natives. He reduced the entire population to servitude (Britainica, *2011*). Before infatuation of greed became the norm, the slave trade operated for centuries on a level of bearable consignment and was not racially tainted. The following explains how the trade transformed to what it is known as today.

> Slavery had existed in Africa and Asia for centuries. Long before the coming of the Europeans, Arabs in East Africa traded in slaves... This ages-old slavery had nothing to do with race. Black people in Africa were captured and sold into slavery by other Blacks. People of any race captured in war could be made slaves... However, after the Europeans entered the slave trade, the trade grew and attitudes toward slaves gradually changed ... Altogether, about 20 million Africans were shipped to the Americas... Conditions on the slave ships were so bad that one-fourth of the slaves died on the

voyages… Gradually many Europeans began to believe that Blacks were born to be slaves. Both Catholics and Protestants tried to use the Bible to prove that Black people were an inferior race and were normally right to make them slaves… For many Europeans, skin color became a sign of inferiority (Wallbank, Schrier, Maier Weaver & Gutierrez, 1977, p. 394–395).

As far as the English colonies to the north were concerned, the slave trade did not begin until 1619, when a Dutch man-of-war, probably a privateer sailing under letters of marque from the prince of Orange, put into the newly established colony of Jamestown with twenty Negroes, whom she may have "highjacked" from a Spanish merchantman in the Caribbean….Not until the latter part of the century [17th], the most important reason for the slow growth of the slave trade in the English colonies was the abundant use of indentured servants: … Since the bond of indenture was usually for five or ten years, the master did not need to worry about his servant's health, could work him harder, and did not have to provide for his old age. …. During the early period, there was no racial issue involved in slavery, although it aroused some religious questions. Generally, it was considered that enslaving heathens was more ethical than enslaving Christians. Negro slaves were simply listed as "servants" in the census of 1623–1624. The first Negroes were generally required to serve for a stipulated term but were then freed and given some land, as was done with the white indentured servants (Mannix & Crowley, 1962, pp. 54–58).

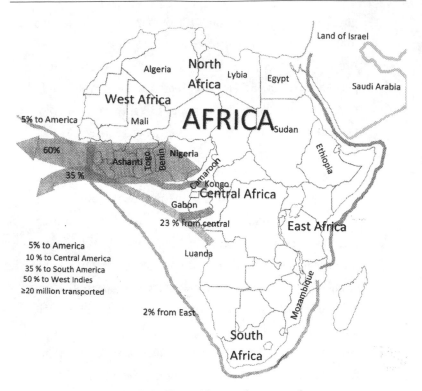

Figure 12.1 West Africa slave trade map

In an old history book used in high school, a Transatlantic Slave Trade map can be found. It shows a map like the one in figure 12.1 showing routes with percentages of slaves transported to different destinations. It states that those ships' conditions were so bad that one-fourth of the slaves transported died in transit. Africans were transported to the Americas and to the Middle East. It states:

> In the Trans-Atlantic slave trade, more than 20 million persons were taken from Africa between 1500 and 1800 about 75% came from West Africa, 23% from central Africa, and 2% from East Africa. Of those who survived

the crossing, about 60% went to the West Indies, Central America, and Spanish parts of South America, 35% went to Brazil, and 5% went to the United States. The slave trade also continued between East Africa in the Middle East (Wallbank, Schrier, Maier-Weaver & Gutierrez, 1977, p. 395).

The Captivity: People and Culture

As the years of the slave trade progressed, racism became the hallmark for eligibility in slave selection. Among the different classes in Africa, Negroes were the prime candidates due to their religion, strength, and ability to withstand long work hours. Negroes were the first choice. Although some of the slavers knew that the people who they were enslaving were, for the most part, Hebrews Israelites, they considered them as heathens. The strength of the Negroes was superior to other blacks in Africa. They were referred to as Negroes by the Spaniards. The following citations show how the races were differentiated.

Negroes could survive under conditions impossible for the Indians... Herrera also noted that the work of one Negro was more than equal to that of four Indians. As early as 1540 ten thousand Negroes a year were being imported to the West Indies (Mannix & Crowley, 1962, p. 5).

Africans south of the Sahara is divided by ethnologists into five main groups, only two of which played an important part in the slave trade. The most convenient names for the groups are Bushmanoid,

Pygmoid, Mongoloid, Caucasoid, and Negroid...In a long strip extending from Senegal, at the westernmost extremity of the African continent, to Ethiopia and northern Kenya on the east are the Caucasoid—formerly called the Hamitic— peoples. They have deep black to light brown skins, curly but not woolly hair, and thin lips and noses, and they tend to be tall, longlegged, and slender... Finally, on the west coast from the Gambia to southern Angola and stretching across the continent to Kenya and Mozambique, are the Negroids. The inhabitants of this vast area are often divided into two groups, the "true Negroes" in the northwest and the Bantu in the south and east, but this distinction appears to be more linguistic than truly racial. Both groups—although with more variation from tribe to tribe among the Bantu—have dark skins, woolly hair, thick lips, and broad noses, and are usually described as being of "average" height, that is, the height of average Europeans. Since the great centers of the Atlantic trade were on the west coast from Senegal to Angola, the vast majority of slaves shipped to the New World were Negroids ((Mannix & Crowley, 1962, pp. 7–8).

The Spaniards called the woolly-haired Jews Negroes because of what they were called in Spain, differentiating them from other blacks in Africa. In the book *The Hebrew Heritage of Black Africa*, Jacob Stevens writes, "'Negro' is a word of Spanish derivation ... rarely does the Black man think of himself as a descendant of the Ashanti, Fanti, Yoruba or other West African ethnic groups" (Jacobs & Farrar, 2016, p. 14). On pages 30 and 42 of the book, he stated that the official day of rest for these Negroes is Saturday, the seventh day of the week. A Ghanaian friend of mine said there are tribes in Ghana that maintained this tradition. He said that the tribes on the West Coast understand "Sunday worship" as coming from the white man. Though it existed elsewhere, Sunday sacredness did not reach far into Africa until the advent of the white missionaries and the slavers. The following tells of the Negroes having their own advanced and unique cultures.

> Most of the New World slaves came from tribes living within two hundred miles of the coast... A disproportionate share of them belonged to the Twi-speaking, Yoruba-speaking, or Ewe-speaking peoples living in what are now Ghana, Dahomey, and Nigeria (Jacobs & Farrar, 2016, p. 14).
>
> The West Africans had invented their own forms of architecture and their own methods of weaving. Many of them possessed flocks of donkeys and great herds of cattle, sheep, and goats. They were skilled workers in wood, brass, and iron, which last they had learned to smelt long before the white men came. Many of their communities had highly involved religions, well-organized economic systems, efficient agricultural practices, and admirable codes of law. We have only in recent years begun to appreciate West Africa's contribution to sculpture, folk literature, and music (Mannix & Crowley, 1962, p. 9, 12).
>
> The square breastplate worn by the Ashanti ambassador seated on the raft in the middle of the Prah River, in the very heart of Ashanti territory, is comprised of twelve parts or sections, just as was that

breastplate worn by the Biblical priests (Exodus 28:21)...
J. Leighton Wilson records in his book that 'there are
many obvious traces of Judaism, both in Northern and
Southern Guinea.' He says further that 'in Northern
Guinea paganism and Judaism are united (Jacobs &
Farrar, 2016, p. 40).

Clearly, the Bible states that the Israelites, for the most part, will
not continue to keep their religion pure while scattered among
the nations. They will worship wood, stone, and other gods
(Ezek. 20:32). While parts of their cultures are retained in some
cases, there may be no cultural retention in others. Because the
Gentiles see them as heathen in practice is not tantamount to
their racial lineage. There are those like the Ashanti and the
Lemba who sought to retain most of their cultural practices.
The Ashanti and the Lemba phenotype is exactly what Mannix
& Crowley describe in their book as Negroid. The Location
of the Lemba is in the Zimbabwe area (South Africa). Was
that area part of the slave trade? According to Maier-Weaver
(1977), yes!

Fate on the Coast

There are books and videos made to discredit the fact that
Israel was spread into Africa. They claim that Israel makes up
for the smallest part of Africa, and they were not a large part
of the slave trade. History seems to have a different record.
The claim of some African Americans to ancient Hebrew
Israelite ancestry is not without validity. Although the slave
trade involved many cultures, the concentration of slavery and
its brutality had been against the Negroes, those of Africa's

190

West Coast. And guess who was found front and center of the trade? Israel and Judah were at the epicenter. The following is an excerpt written by Jacobs who refers to Professor William's work explaining the connection.

> The ancient Hebrews are parent stock from, 'which the present Ashanti evolved; In fact, it was the "continuous influx of Hebrew settlers trekking up the Nile" which, he [Professor William] says "eventually spread itself clear across Africa to the Niger (river) and thence pretty much the whole of West Africa...Professor Williams, in his anthropological published by Boston College Graduate School in1936 and 1937, talks about a map published in the 1970 edition of the M*emoirs of the Reign of Bassa Ahadee, king of Dahomey*, by Robert Morris. It is an eye-witness account. The map which it contains designates the region surrounding the seaport town of Whydah as the "Country of the Jews." In fact, the name of the town very much sounds like Judah. The spelling usually found today is Ouidah, with the "o" sound dropped. Here we have an actual designation of a Hebrew population living in the very heart of the Black African slave coast. ....
> thirty years earlier... John. Atkins...says, "Whydah is the greatest trading place on the Coast of Guinea (as the area was called, in those days by the Europeans) (Jacobs & Farrar, 2016. pp. 21, 42, 43).

History has a way of losing identities when attempting to maintain the names of classes, cultures, and people. Alaezi (2013) traced the identity of the Nigerian Jews from imposed British nomenclature, which was later corrupted to "Ibos." He stated in his book, "On realizing their Jewishness, the British Colonial masters began to refer to the Nigerian Jews, the Ifites, as Hebrews ... a name that was corrupted as Heebo, Eboe and finally Ibo."(Alaezi, 2013, p. 20).

In his book, *Africa's Exodus to the Promised Land*, Pastor Sedenak Kojo Duffu Yankson explains many African tribes' Hebrew roots from various states. Yoruba Jews were known as B'nai or sons of Ephraim (Duffu-Yankson, 2010). The Yoruba Jews and the Igbos settled in Nigeria. The Ashantees of the Akan people settled in Ghana. Whyday, the country of the Jews, was among the coastal trading states of West Africa. Dahomey and Togo Jews called God as Mahu, Vodu, or Yehwe.

> Is Israel, a servant? Is he a homeborn slave? why is he spoiled (Jer. 2:14)?

Although nations enslaved God's chosen people, they further sought to extract every substance of their resources and give little or nothing in return. Pastor Sedenak Kojo Duffu Yankson noted this in his book. He explains that we were spoiled, but we worked counter-productively and were willing to forgive the foreigners while making it an arduous task to overlook our sister tribes.

> We Africans have been kind in sharing with everybody, but everybody did not treat us with kindness. Our forefathers (African republics) borrowed from their fathers (colonial masters) who now say we owe them. The ancestors borrowed gold, diamond, oil, timber, land and people and no one remember this huge indebtedness to African children! Whatever happened to restitution!

Time should have been made to relieve both the European and the African debt. But no! Time relieve one and not the other... The debt question is a theological issue, and the church cannot stand idly by and allow injustice to flourish. Interestingly, most of the people calling for justice in debt forgiveness are the so called secularist. Europeans got rich on the backs of African, and now they say we owe them and the church seem to be silent (Duffu-Yankson, 2010, p. 43).

These tribes were spread abroad in many of the sub-Saharan African countries of West and Central Africa. They were traded in the slave trade to different regions of the Americas and the West Indies. The Ashantees went to Barbados and Jamaica. The Dahomians went to Hispaniola, Cuba, and Trinidad. The Nigerians went to America and Trinidad. The Senegalese slaves went to Bermuda and South America. These destinations are approximations for most tribal groups that were transported to these regions. There were slaves taken from Haiti and Cuba to serve in America and Europe. This scattering is not a strict diasporan allocation. There was slave trading among the western nations, especially with the West Indies.

Although Israel went to many continents, their concentration was in the African continent. They were brutalized and shipped to other continents via ships. Israel is not only lost in different tribes and nations but also various denominations as well. They have, for the most part, lost their religious and national identities. This condition resulted from separating the parents from their children. God's promise is to regather them under the Messiah's gospel. Thus, it is that many Negroes have accepted the gospel.

Chapter 13

— ✦◉◉✦ —

The Messianic Church and the Decline

New Testament's Replacement Theology

The Christian church's replacement theology teaches that Israel is spiritual; accordingly, all the blessing promises will be fulfilled through the church. In my spiritual upbringing, I was trained in replacement theology. I was taught that the Gentile church replaced Israel in the scriptures. All of the covenant promises were to be fulfilled to the new Israel, the church. All the curses that are written to Israel were to be accomplished through the original descendants. Another type of replacement theology against the literal descendants of Israel was from Germany. The German Jews incidentally replacing Israel's actual descendants through political expediency adheres to a similar replacement theology as the Christian Church does. They implied that those who do not resemble them could not be accepted as Israel. This view was based solely on racial profiling. Although the church is drunken with this "cool-aid," there has been some anecdotal acknowledgment of this error. The German Jews were not aware that the real Jews, the Israelites were generally colored.

However, the validity of the church's deduction on Israel is drawn from the grafting process.

> For he is not a Jew, which is one outwardly; neither is that circumcision, which is outward in the flesh: but he is a Jew, which is one inwardly; and circumcision is that of the heart, in the spirit, and not in the letter; whose praise is not of men, but of God (Rom.2:28–29).

The above citation makes it appears that natural Israel is forgotten. Speaking to the Jews in Rome, Paul's disputation was, being a descendant of Jacob is inadequate for qualification as a spiritual Jew. One must exercise the faith of Abraham to become a spiritual Jew. This is the basis of replacement theology. Using Romans 2:28–29 and 10:11–13, there is a limited validity to replacement theology. However, in Romans 11, where Paul speaks of God's zeal in recognizing His ancient people's prominence, limitations exist. Those who feel that replacement theology is the whole truth have missed the point of Paul's theology. How about the remnant (children) of the fleshly lineage? Scripture declares:

> What mean ye, that ye use this proverb concerning the land of Israel, saying, The fathers have eaten sour grapes, and the children's teeth are set on edge (Eze 18:2)?
>
> The soul that sinneth, it shall die. The son shall not bear the iniquity of the father, neither shall the father bear the iniquity of the son: the righteousness of the righteous shall be upon him, and the wickedness of the wicked shall be upon him. (21) But if the wicked will

> turn from all his sins that he hath committed, and keep
> all my statutes, and do that which is lawful and right,
> he shall surely live, he shall not die. (Ezek. 18:20–21).

There is a notion that the Old Testament has little grace, while the New Testament is where grace is. The above verses have shattered that view (Heb. 10:28–31). The question to be asked is: Has God permanently rejected the ancient kingdom because of unbelief? In the above verses, God has promised that He will draw out a remnant from the descendant of ancient Israel of those who keep His Word, and He will bless them. There is a remnant of Israel's authentic lineage, which God considers according to the ancient prophecies. He will not forget those whom He foreknew. Since God's plan for ancient Israel is indispensable, it behooves us to study the correct interpretation.

Israel in the New Testament

The church's purity was degraded. That is a clear indictment of Hosea 2. This chapter applies to the ancient lineage of Jacob, both the early messianic and scattered Israel. The chapter opens with a plea to return to true messianic faith and culture. Although there have been some great self-sacrificing heroes of messianic faith in church history among the Gentiles, the general tenor had been a cesspool of problems. Seeing the advent of this deleterious condition, Paul was in tears for three years over the church's perilous future (Acts 20:25–38). There was lamentation after Paul's elocution of the demoralizing future. Their mourning resulted from more than Paul's imminent departure. They sobbed over the nefarious endangerment of messianic faith. Beyond AD 300, the Christian church was no less wicked than Manasseh's sins, which drove the Judeans into captivity. During that time, there was still a faithful remnant that strove to maintain pure messianic faith.

After extending the gospel to the Gentiles, corruption entered through the Holy Roman Empire. God allowed the original Israelites to be scattered after their abnegation of the gospel, at which time the Gentiles took full possession of Palestine (Luke 21:21; Rom. 11:22–25). Although some of the Europeans succeeded in restoring part of the gospel through the Reformation, it remained subject to corruption and misinterpretations, resulting in altering its original intent. Protestants who persisted in eroding biblical culture by their desired applications, omissions, additions, and distortions are removed from the Israelite tree.

One may say, "Isn't once saved always saved?" Yes, but there is what is called provisional salvation versus permanent salvation. Provisional salvation is when someone tries to get into the fold and has not made a complete surrender. They were not taught the Gospel correctly. They have hidden biases and unresolved prejudice toward the will of God. They may be loosely attached to the tree of Israel and can only be saved using special grace on a case-by-case basis predicated by God. If a complete commitment is not made, they will not be part of the Israelite tree (Rom. 2:28). Most of the Protestant Churches have provisional salvation, not real salvation. Many of them believe in a faulty version of "once saved always saved" salvation.

The Christian church, to some degree, has descended from grace. The truth is castrated, and evil reigns in most of church history. The church was downgraded by reverting to pagan practices of the heathen (days of Constantine). It rejected all the laws in the Old Testament and created its own new set of enchanting grace type of gospel. It became warlords, racist supremacists and inspired racist slavery. They inspired hatred for those who differ from them (Spanish Inquisition) and many other abominations falsely in the name of Jesus. Even now, many Christians are ignorantly and subconsciously indoctrinated with prejudices. Most church people are blinded to this condition. Here is some of what happened as recorded in the *New African* magazine (Femi, 2013, Art. Ugly-slavery-past).

The Netherlands, one of the smallest countries in northern Europe, was among the most enthusiastic of slave nations, but how to deal with this past is now a dilemma. As the historian, J. W. Schulte Nordholt, informs us in his seminal work, The People that Walk in Darkness: "The Dutch share in the slave-trade was large: in fact, in the 17th century, it was the largest. The Dutch West India Company had various settlements on the African coast, and millions of slaves were ferried from there, especially during the time of the Dutch occupation of Brazil. In 12 years (between 1637 and 1648), they transported no less than 23,163 slaves from Elmina and Loanda, for an amount of 6,714,423 guilders and 60 cents [the Dutch were very precise!]. They bought slaves from the Congo for 40 to 50 guilders and sold them in Brazil for 200 to 800 guilders. Certainly a worthwhile business.

Incredible as it may seem, the Christian church which today drips with brotherly love and all that, was at the forefront of the abhorrent trade in human flesh and received much of its inglorious wealth from this unholy trade. In 1452, Pope Nicholas V issued a papal bull, Dum Diversas, which granted the Portuguese King Afonse V the right to reduce any "Saracens, pagans, and any other unbelievers" to hereditary slavery, thus legitimizing the incipient trade in slaves.

Taking their cue from the Pontiffs, Christian theologians zealously published texts to justify the odious trade. As a result, few slave ships sailed without Christian priests on hand to bless them. Today, many Christians will feel discomfited by the fact that the first slave ship that actually took African slaves to the USA was named The Good Ship Jesus, which was lent to the pirate John Hawkins by the British monarch, Queen Elizabeth I.

For centuries, even up to the present day, the African continent is still in turmoil. The church is apologetic about its role in the slave trade. God allowed the slavers to punish the West Africans. But now, Islam and Christianity are widespread in Africa. There has been a number of political rivalries attempting to establish peace. True peace can only come with the advent of the Messiah.

Israel's Relations and Diversity

Concerning the race issue, the church of the first century is the opposite of the church now. It may be news to some that the early messianic Jews were mainly Negroes. According to Roman Emperor Tacitus, at the time of the early church, whom Joel Augustus Rogers quoted, the natural branches of Israel resembled Ethiopians (Amos 9:7).

Strabo (30 B.C.) says the people of western Judea were of part Egyptian ancestry. "But," he says, "although the inhabitants are mixed up thus the most prevalent of the accredited reports in regard to the temple of Jerusalem represents the ancestors of the present Judeans, as they are called, Egyptians." (28) Tacitus of about 90 A.D. says, "Many assert that the Jews are an Ethiopian race." (29) For Romans to have taken them for Ethiopians is clear indication of their color since the Ethiopians were definitely black to the Romans (Rogers, 1952, p. 123).

Although Israel had a minority of albinos among them, they were not a fan of whiteness. As reported by late Ivan Sertima, Jesus was not acquainted with white European Jew or a white European Israelite. However, skin color was not an issue. Color became an issue through some white Europeans. In his book, *From Babylon to Timbuktu*, Windsor says that the racism of the color line is fairly recent. He states:

Dividing the world along a color line was an idea that originated with the white supremists in Europe after the Renaissance. The Europeans did not have any great civilization immediately after the fall of Greece and Rome. During the Middle Ages, the black nations of Africa and Asia had the greatest political, economical, educational, and military influence in the world. At this time, Europe existed in a state of darkness for a thousand years. In the seventeenth century and later, Europe began to emerge out of the slough of ignorance, and certain Germans and others conceived of themselves as belonging to a superior race. Johann F. Blumenback, a

German (1752–1840), was the first to divide humanity on the basis of skin color. Up to this time, no such attempts had been made. His classification set up a color line, to the detriment of later generations. Mr. Blumenbach classified five chief races of mankind: the Caucasian, the Mongolian, the Ethiopian, the American (American Indians), and Malayan. Moreover, he considered the Caucasian to be the original race. Blumenbach, the anthropologist, named the whites after the Caucasus Mountains (these mountains are situated between the Black and Caspian seas), because he thought the purest white people originated there. Blumenbach was a racist and so was J. A. Gobineau. A third man by the name of H. S. Chamberlain wanted to advance the supremacy of the white Nordic race and its culture (Windsor, 1988, p. 21).

Christianity has little to no backbone regarding racial injustice. History reveals that the church was a champion of the slave trade. Since the church was under mystic grace, whatever was said in God's law concerning servants' handling was disregarded. That is not to ignore the work of godly white Christians who were abolitionists. Although the church is vocal about abortion and gay rights, it does very little against racial injustice. An increasing number of churches are becoming pro-homosexuality. The church fears the political repercussions stemming from a stance against racial prejudice. Presently, the church is under albinic domination. That is not to say it would be better under black domination. God has used the white people for His cause in two ways: To bless Israel with Bible messages through the Reformation and curse Israel by enslaving them physically and psychologically. They have been the messengers of God for His purpose. Instead of harboring bitterness, we should seek reconciliation while awakening from slumber.

The problem is rooted enough that some negroes have little appreciation for who they are. They want to change their skin, hair, the color of teeth, nails, eyelashes, and place graffiti on their skin. A church sister said she does the tattooing because others were doing it. After waking up, she learned about her Christian duty, and that God is concerned about the whole person and not just faith. They have been misinformed and mummified on many topics related to self-consciousness.

According to Moore (2002), the black family has been fed lots of myths concerning their capabilities. We have been nibbling on too many errors from the plate of lies at the slave master's table. Moore noted that in many studies, melanin is a key factor in children's psychomotor development (Moore, 2002, p. 95). A comparative study was done across the diverse socioeconomic line for this confirmation. This melanin, found in different parts of the body, has added benefits for black children in their psychomotor capacities.

There are social problems in the Black community that have led to additional underdevelopment of the Negro. Some of the ladies of Israel do not honor and respect their men, leading to divorces and single-family homes. Some of the men are not being good fathers and husbands. There are a number of caveats that must be adhered to maintain a healthy home relationship. One of the prime admonitions requiring attention is the manner of communication. Love and respect require good communication. Good communication requires a sense of humility and accepting and respecting roles. Good communication requires understanding, acceptance of one's limitations, and the fluidity of the expected. All this means is, always be a patient listener and allowing room for improvement. Sometimes you are in a situation where one's guess is as good as the other. Admitting this requires a sense of humility. Sometimes love requires a little give when compromise is not possible. Although experience is a good teacher, it cannot predict everything, and the claimant must leave room for development. Tone of voice, demeanor, and nonverbals all play a role in good communication. The tone must be graceful, even towards children. This is the training you must provide. The home environment should not be expected to be a battlefield. When you are together with someone as partner, you are expected to do things with unity. Good communication also requires setting short and long term goals. This helps eliminate knee-jerk decision-making. The leader in the circle is expected to communicate everything.

I was ignorant of myself and the plight of my people. Little did I know we were from similar tribes. Had I known, my approach to the situation would have been different. There is a great lack of education within the Negro family. We are so busy chasing the daily bread, Olympian pleasures, and demonic music that we remain ignorant of our roots and history. Our preachers are busy studying adaptability to the fluid nature of young people's culture. The young people are selling, and the church is buying. The church is not selling; they are adapting. The conversion is going in the wrong direction. Our white brothers' domination of the slave trade has caused long-standing trauma in the mind of black people. Although there are domestic problems in all groups of people, the need for reform among the Negro family remains paramount to their uprising.

The healing starts with love thyself. Then love thy people, and after that, love all others.

Windsor noted in the following that for superiority conquest, the Caucasians attempted a divide and conquer strategy by phenotypical classification or reclassification of blacks:

> Joseph Williams has this to say about the blacks of West Africa: "In most mixed group of Negroes a Songhois may be identified at first glance; his skin is black as theirs, certainly, but nothing in his mask conforms to their well-known characteristics. The nose of the Songhois is straight and long, pointed rather than flat; the lips are comparatively thin; and the mouth wide rather than prominent and broad, while the eyes are deeply set and straight in their orbits. A cursory glance shows that the profile resembles that of the European." Some European writers even penetrate into the blackest Africa and divide the blacks according to the shape of their noses and lips. Continues Williams: The Songhays, "though black-skinned and woolly-haired, their features are often of Caucasian cast." There are many colored people in the United States with straight noses and thin lips, even as black as tar; and the Europeans do not classify these colored people as belonging to the white race. After extensive research, my conclusion is this: Some European writers have classified certain tribes in Africa and Asia as belonging to the white race; they do this as long as it is psychologically advantageous, in order to inflate their ego, and to give them a prominent place in Afro-Asian history (Windsor, 1988, p. 105).

The divide and conquer strategy have worked well in Haiti. In that country, corruption and lack of oversight run rampant. Other nations prey on the weakness of leading citizens to disenfranchise their land. While Israel's true roots are being unearthed, its revelation is met with little enthusiasm by a significant number of blacks whose Judean-Israelite ancestors were scattered into Africa. Some Negroes are like Esau; they do not appreciate the treasure of their heritage. They are living in the obscurity of their heritage and identity.

The injury to the truth in the minds of mankind is difficult to reverse. As a college student at the beginning of my junior year, thirty years ago, my Caucasian literature professor, speaking on the history of the Christian church, stated to the class that Christianity is a religion from the black people. By this, she included Israel, from which the messianic church came. That came as a shock to me. After hearing her statement, I was a bit neutral on the issue, leaning toward albino domination. I was already brain conditioned and whitewashed to the European gospel. Like uninformed blacks and ignorant Muslims, I believed that Christianity was a religion of the whites handed down to the blacks. Upon learning that 95 percent of today's Jews of claimed Jewish ancestry are Caucasian and the whitest people on the planet, I thought her statement was suspect. I believed there must be some credibility to her comment, but I had no resource at hand to prove it. Being busy in my pre-med studies, I had not taken the time to do the research. I pondered the thought for a long time. Our bar of historical truth runs very low. We know a lot of things that aren't so. And there are two reasons for this. One, we don't want to know, and two, those who don't want us to know. When you are in the middle of a pack of wolves, and they make you feel that they are protecting you, do not wait until they are hungry.

Later, my black religion teacher said in a service that I attended that black people were once the ruler of all the world. Blacks ruled all the kingdoms, he said. That was harder to swallow, so I kept that in my rearview mirror. Based on my research, it is apparent that his claim has considerable credibility (Mc Cray, 1990, p. 9). Besides, it makes 100 percent scientific sense. The truth is that our real American racial and ethnic cleansing riot history, such as what happened in Tulsa, Oklahoma, and in many other places, is too barbaric and painful for most people to withstand. Unless we arm ourselves with the truth, both blacks and whites will forever be conditioned to believe a historical fairy tale.

History of Civilization and Race

Anciently, blacks were never a slave group of people. The Africans were warlords like those of every other continent. Blacks were rulers and conquerors of the then known world, as seen in the example below:

> Rome made anyone, who took a pledge to serve Rome, Roman citizens. Rome also created armies out of these new Roman citizens and set them apart from Rome's own army. In 193 A.D., a black man named Septimius Severus (descendant of the Phoenicians), as a General in the Roman army, aided by the black men under his command, conquered Rome beginning the time period referred to as the Dark, or Middle Ages. According to Carl Roebuck, "The Roman Empire passed through a

crucial period of internal anarchy and foreign invasion which transformed its nature. The death of Commodus in 192 was followed by civil war, from which Septimius Severus, the commander of the Danubian legions, emerged as victor and established the Severan Dynasty of Rulers." From this period on, black people began to rule in different parts of Europe at different times during the Middle Ages (Horton, 1999, Art. misrep.htm).

The Hebrew Israelites claim does not arise from an inferiority complex, to surface above white supremacy. Inferiority may be an issue for some. The fact is blacks (Egyptians) were the producers and rulers of the ancient world and taught the world many things to advance civilization. The Blacks (Moors) were inventors of firearms and many other things, which I will not take the time to mention. A note from the historian, Sertima attests to some accomplishments as follows:

When Count Volney stood under the shadow of the great Sphinx in 1783 and looked at these man-made mountains stretching across the western desert, he was startled and confused. A strange guilt troubled Count Volney. It was so natural to think of blacks as "hewers of wood and drawers of water." When did this curse begin? "How we are astonished," he later wrote, "when we reflect that to the race of Negroes, at present our slaves, and the' objects of our contempt, we owe our arts, sciences..." This rediscovery by Europeans of ancient Egypt and the disclosures of a powerful Negro-African element in the ancestry of a civilization to which Europe owed so much came as an embarrassment. It came also at a most inopportune time. It threatened to explode a myth of innate black inferiority that was necessary to the peace of the Christian conscience in a Europe that was then prospering from the massive exploitation of black slaves.

The Christian conscience of slave-trading Europe had been assuaged for a while by a myth which drew its inspiration not from the Christian Bible, as some theologians of the day then thought (for the Bible makes no distinctions between black and white), but from a very arbitrary interpretation of a biblical story, the story of Ham, which appeared in the Talmud, a collection of Jewish oral traditions, in the sixth century.

When, however, the Napoleonic expedition uncovered the splendors of ancient Egyptian civilization, a new version of history was urgently required. The myth of blackness as a curse had backfired. How could a black, and accursed race have inspired or contributed greatly to the development of a pre-European civilization? An ingenious new version was not long in the making. Political necessity, then as now, is the mother of historical invention. Christian theologians began to suggest that Noah had cursed only Canaan, one son of Ham and that therefore the curse lay only on his progeny, the black race. Another son of Ham, Mizrairn, had not been cursed. From him issued the marvelous Egyptians, the creators of the greatest of early civilizations. The Christian conscience could sleep peacefully.

The American anatomist Samuel Morton—-the Shockley of the nineteenth century—using pseudoscientific criteria flattered and delighted his Negrophobic listeners by demonstrating to their satisfaction that the Egyptians were a Caucasoid race and indigenous to the Nile valley. This finding flatly contradicted the claim of the historian Herodotus that the Egyptians, compared to the Greeks and other European Caucasoids, were for the most part "a black-skinned and wooly-haired" people (Sertima, 1976, pp. 110–113).

Those who say that blacks can only use religion to express their importance have missed the mark of history untainted with racism. Regardless of religion, blacks had a far more prominent place in history than most people imagine. Now, let us consider black religious history from a biblical perspective. The Bible discredits the claim that Israel did not go into Africa to live among Ham's sons.

From beyond the rivers of Ethiopia my suppliants, even the daughter of my dispersed, shall bring mine offering. (11) In that day shalt thou not be ashamed for all thy doings, wherein thou hast transgressed against me: for then I will take away out of the midst of thee them that rejoice in thy pride, and thou shalt no more be haughty because of my holy mountain. (12) I will also leave in the midst of thee an afflicted and poor people, and they shall trust in the name of the LORD (Zep.3:10–12).

And it shall come to pass in that day, that the Lord shall set his hand again the second time to recover the remnant of his people, which shall be left, from Assyria, and from Egypt, and from Pathros, and from Cush, and from Elam, and from Shinar, and from Hamath, and from the islands of the sea. (12) And he shall set up an ensign for the nations and shall assemble the outcasts of Israel, and gather together the dispersed of Judah from the four corners of the earth (Isa. 11:11–12).

The history of our white brothers is not entirely clear. The Bible divides Noah's descendants according to where they took residence, not along with racial designations. Those of the North were sons of Japheth (Gen. 10:5). In this table of nations, the place in the North is called the "isles of the Gentiles." The Northern nations were not to be highly populated. The others of the South and the lower East were the descendants of Ham and Shem. They populated the motherland of nations. Our white (pale) brothers were fewest in history; they were not on favorable or close terms with the Israelites.

It is said that the oldest known genes are from the San people of South Africa. Everyone has some African DNA. The color range has been from reddish-brown to dark brown or "black." Apparently, the Sans are the precursors of the black mongoloid race of Asia. While Indian albinism became commonplace, from them arose European albinos. Some of the Shem line produced the wooly haired Israelites and other nations. The claim that Dravidians and black Africans have produced albino Caucasian-like children is another part of the mystery of the Caucasian albino's origin. The albino migration path was from Africa to Asia, Europe, then Greece, and eventually to Rome. The albino Indians who came from Africa migrated to Europe and became white Europeans. Thus, pale-skinned people are children of blacks. It is not clear precisely when our white brothers' race originated. According to Abernethy (1910), it is estimated that whites began about 3000 BC. Some claimed that the albino origin is from the black San people in Africa. There are two circulating theories: some say whites are from Albino Indians from India or Australia, and others say from an admixture of the Neanderthal (so-called) race.

> It is widely accepted that our early human ancestors migrated out of Africa to colonize Europe and Asia, with a general view that this group of hominids replaced earlier Neanderthal populations throughout Europe. Despite some interactions and possible admixture between Neanderthals and early modern humans, the consensus opinion, based on mitochondrial DNA and Y chromosome sequences, is that Neanderthals did not contribute appreciably to the modern human gene pool. The MC1R sequences of the two Neanderthal fossils support the latter view, but in association with the data on MC1R variants in different human populations, they also suggest that there may have been advantages to the acquisition of fair skin in Europe (Healy, 2008, p. 340).

Up until the 1500s, Rome had more blacks than pale. The invasion of barbarians before AD 476 ended the Roman Empire. Albino Caucasians and other white Europeans infiltrated Rome. This infiltration was more commonplace during the 1600s. This condition on the Holy Roman Empire was a precursor of whitening Rome. Grecian whiteness is estimated to have begun during the fifth century BC. Although Greece was mainly black, as the years progressed, mulattos resulted from the admixing. The Grecians were the first group to assimilate and classify albinos. In Daniel's prophecy, they are the goat empire.

Walking in the Image of Jesus

God loves people of all races, colors, and defects. While the internal persons are almost identical, color is a deception of external appearance. Dr. Martin Luther King said that people should be judged, not based on their skin color but on the content of their character. We are all of one blood. "Color does not matter," said the black Christian man. The white Christian man said to himself, "Color does matter, but Jesus is colorless or pale mulatto, leaning toward white." A colorless or mulatto Jesus is necessary for the continuing psychological captivity of the black man. The white man forcibly teaches the black man that nothing good can come out of the negro. The Church had been silent on that myth. Silence against the truth as myth prevails in the court of public opinion constitutes collusion. To love the black slave-shipped Africans (Afro-American, Haitian, Brazilian, Mexican, Cuban, Jamaican, etc.) is to teach them their roots and historical importance related to God's prophetic program and about the pre-colonial African civilizations. To hide or to keep them in ignorance concerning this is the curse of perpetual slavery. We are fast to teach the white proselyte Jews of their importance to the land of Israel, right? Why not teach the black lost tribes of original Israel of their importance to the same?

We do not have to be ashamed of worshipping the black Jesus. He was far from looking handsome like your Negroes (Isa. 52, 53). Jesus' appearance, being Isaiah's doctrine, is part of our basic messianic lesson. The claim of the irrelevance of Jesus's earthly appearance is not Biblical. It is a doctrine not inspired by Isaiah's God.

Why should black Africans have such rich antiquity of Palestine and Egypt associated with their history? Have you ever wondered why God did not refer to the lands of Shem and Ham as "isles of the Gentiles?" He knew that Israel would sleep in the tents Ham and produce populous nations. Jesus came from a line of Negroid people who did not prefer albinism or vitiligo. Jesus came from a race of people who considered albinism (*albus* or *album* in Latin) a sickness, and *scientifically*, it is. That does not make the white man any less a person or any less important in any way than the black man. Again, the color line is a deception. Although color has a physiological advantage, it cannot be used to establish personal value. Today's Edomites and Ishmaelites in the Middle East are a mixture of white Europeans who embraced Islam. Yahawahsha (Jesus) was not a so-called light-skinned modern-day "Middle Eastern."

Jesus had Ethiopians' appearance (Amos 9:7) and ancient Egyptians, which was the same as Israel. The modern-day Middle Easterners and some people in Egypt are prodigiously albinos with a minor shade of light brown. They may have had some mixture with Edomites and Ishmaelites who lived in the area who were black. The so-called light brown or light-skinned Middle Eastern Jesus is an invention to suppress the truth about Jesus's external identity. When it is belittling to one's ego to worship the Negro Jesus, the need for a little whitewashing is profitable.

Is the external appearance of Jesus significant? Yes, only to the need of a racist society. Because there has been a need for some to falsify the record, it should not be surprising that this is a salvific issue. Just as there was a need for the whites to break off the noses of many Egyptian statues so that they don't resemble blacks, likewise, there is the need to whitewash. "They laid open the book of the law, wherein the heathen had sought to paint the likeness of their images" (1 Macc. 3:48). Sure, God can create or choose whatever appearance He wishes, but we cannot have another Jesus in mind than the one spoken of in history and scripture (Dan. 7:9; Heb. 2:17).

In their ignorance, black people, for the most part, had no problem worshipping a straight-haired, blond, blue-eyed leper (white) "Jesus" whose image ubiquitously portrayed worldwide. However, some Christians find God offensive in discovering that Jesus was a black man with woolly hair. If the white man or the whitewashed black man sees no light in disabusing the minds of those they teach false history, color inevitably becomes an ethical, moral issue. It is racially and morally unethical (uncleanness) to have a "white" (pale) supremacist Jesus portrayed since the original was black. Rather than teaching about an unscriptural Roman Jesus or praying to an albino image in mind, shouldn't the true Jesus be lifted up, not with an image but with the truth? It is true that some paint Jesus according to their image. How about when that image sent to Africa and to those whose congregations are racially black? The facts about the Jesus of scripture should be taught as precepts. Here is what the historian Joel Augustus Rogers (1952) had to say about Jesus as he quotes Josephus, the Roman Jewish historian who lived about the time of Jesus:

> The earliest traditions of the 'Saviors of Mankind' from the Buddhas to Jesus depict them as black, or dark-skinned (see *Sex and Race*, Vol. 1 pp. 273-83. 2ed. 1940). Eisler R. says that Josephus, the Jewish historian of the first century said that Christ 'was a man of simple appearance mature age, dark skin, with little hair, about 4½ feet, 54 or 58 inches (tall), hunchbacked, with a long face.... and underdeveloped beard.' He says this

appears in the reconstructed original—(*Halosis, II,* 174 et seq.) The early Christians, he says, accepted that picture, including Tertullian and Augustine but that the Halosis underwent the usual 'corrections at the hands of Christian copyists with a view to embellishment.' The Christians had gained power; they had become mighty; Jesus had become a king, and it would no longer suit to portray him as unimpressive in appearance. The original text, says Eisler, 'would give offense to believing Christians and their Hellenistic ideal of male beauty,' therefore, they changed the pen-picture of Jesus 'ruddy, six feet high, well-grown, venerable, erect, handsome.... blue eyes...copious beard.' (*Messiah Christ*, pp. 411, 421-442). See also F. Hertz *Race and Civilization*, p. 183, 1928 on this.

A portrait of Christ, entirely apocryphal and with absolutely no foundation in truth, was conceived somewhere along the line by a European artist according to European ideals of beauty and that seems to have served as concept for thousands of pictures that since followed. Since the first one, or ones, were entirely the product of imagination, it follows that all the rest are. Their only value is artistic.

Peigot says, 'there remains nothing authentic upon the exterior appearance of Christ.' *Recherches His sur la personne de Jesus Christ*, p. 2 1829. He says also that neither St. Augustine nor Tertullian thought Jesus [was] good-looking (Rogers, 1952, pp. 40-41).

The scriptures are not silent about the outward appearance of Jesus. We have hints in Daniel's revelation (Dan. 7:9, 10:6; Rev.

1:15). Back in the day, most Middle Easterners were black. Degrading the Negro reflects on one's difficulty in worshipping God, besides being discourteous to his black ancestors. The Bible and history declare that the Israelites, with few exceptions of leprosy, were predominately black.

Science and Diversity

Most of the nations' aborigines, in the days of Noah and Abraham, were naturally melanin laden. Without much effort, healthy skin with sufficient melanin and mineral capability will acquire minor changes of color in response to the sun's rays. The tendency to acquire mineral is based on the soil and diet. Melanin is controlled mainly by genetics and the Pineal gland (Moore, 2002). Color production is very complicated. There are many independent factors and a series of events that give rise to a carbonated hue. The more natural and healthier one eats, the healthier one's body is, and with few exceptions, the faster color change can occur. As scripture states, nutrition affects one's color (Lam. 4:8).

The genes control the amount of change. The genes permitting a color change in a white person are too distant ancestrally for retrieval use. Distant genes rarely show up phenotypically. Atavism is the term used when distant genes show up phenotypically after a long period. Most albinos' polygenic genes are so mutated that retrograding to blackness is extremely difficult irrespective of sun exposure. On the other hand, black people will not turn mulatto-like or white if they live in the Earth's frigid zones. Although black people may lighten up slightly, blacks will still retain their genetic color. As they lose skin cells, the new cells will produce a little less melanin. The damaging ultraviolet rays from the sun are not absent in cold regions. These rays are of varying concentration in different areas, giving rise to a slight skin hue variation. There are some rare cases of people capable of drastic change in skin color dependent on sun exposure. This is due to people's admixture of skin color's polygenic nature which allows for the range of mulatto phenotypes we have today.

Mistaken views are circulating about the terms used in scripture concerning the external nature of the ancient people. Natural human skin color consists of varying mid-brown hue shades, from reddish-brown to actual dark brown, known as black. A melanin goddess type of black is not very common in our Western society. Fair in the Bible refers to a person with a beautiful countenance. It does not refer to "alba," white, or leprous as assumed. By modern definition, the term "fair" has been used to replace leprous (whited) skin. The children of Israel considered whiteness a curse, the curse of leprosy (2 Chron. 26:20–21). Biblical "ruddy" is a deep brown with a reddish tone. For example, a black person's back being clothed can exhibit reddish brown and dark brown face from sun exposure. However, light brown is a level of albinism passed on from generations. In different UV radiation levels, natural human color changes from the middle brown (reddish) to the dark brown (black) end of that color spectrum.

Paleness (white) results from the black man's physical decadence (a harmful mutation) of the genome. A scientific report mentions an impediment to the trafficking of intracellular tyrosine, which gives rise to albinism. "The issue remains; why is the skin affected in some cases and not the hair, is still in research" (Oetting, Fryer, Shriram, & King, 2003, p. 308). Naturally, a white person will never be black though he may have brown freckles (acidified destroyed cells). A black person can turn white or leprous (vitiligo) through disease (Num. 12:10–12). The skin that is incapable of adapting to natural sun protection is defective or mutated.

Contrary to popular beliefs, there are varying expressions of Albinism in the human race. The P gene on chromosome 15 and tyrosine processes play a crucial role in determining cutaneous color. Most white people today have OCA2 (Oculocutaneous Albinism II). OCA1b are albinos who have recent ancestral black in their lineage and can tan a little over time. Those with OCA1a are completely albino (Oetting, Fryer, Shriram, & King, 2003). There is only one race of people on Earth (Acts 17:26). All people are of the human species, descendants of Adam and Eve and Noah's three sons.

An Israelite maternal DNA of the mitochondrial genes and the X chromosomes from either gender does not establish male lineage from the biblical perspective. However, the connection does exist between autosomal DNA and the X chromosomes. The purpose for this is that a large part of the autosomes and the X chromosomes makeup the male constitution, though not male characteristics (Miller & Levine, 2012). This fact seems to imply that the first man had both X and Y chromosomes without the female characteristics on the X chromosomes until the creation of Eve. A Male's Y chromosomes have a dominant effect on the female's X characteristic genes. Biblically speaking, women do not carry male lineages though they are blood relatives. This is more of a social construct than pure genetics. Male hormones are carried by women but in different concentrations. An Israelite woman may be from Jacob's family but may not identifiably carry that unique genetic marker. Yes, they do carry autosomal DNA from the male. Unless there is a marker or peculiar alteration, it is difficult to trace ancestry by autosomes. In Israel, the female is important for establishing a phenotypical identification. God has promised Israel to see himself in his children. This identification should not be lost through the admixing among other nations. Therefore, a male Gentile who mixes with an Israelite woman can only have non-Israelite (Gentile) children. Dinah, Jacob's daughter, was excluded from carrying her father's lineage. Although she was inextricably part of the nation and identified with it, she cannot carry the lineage. The daughters of Lot did the unthinkable to carry their father's seed to future generations. They knew that their father's lineage would cease unless they had a male from the core family.

For those of you interested in the haplogroup genetic identification and the history of the white race, a detailed explanation is provided by Ronald Dalton Jr. in his book, where he elaborates on the Egypt connection about the genesis of our white brothers. Even in those early days in antiquity, the mystery of white people's origin persisted (Dalton, 2016). In some sections of the book, the emphasis is placed on the nations' and Israel's genetic markers.

Today's definition of leprosy as a bacterial infection (*Mycobacterium leprae*) is partially true. There has been tunnel-visioned campaign for that definition. White, vitiligo and leprous are the same except that leper had subclassifications in ancient times. There were clean lepers and unclean lepers in Israel. Those who were clean were born lepers. For example, Gehazi's descendants were clean lepers. Some whose whole body became leprous were also considered clean lepers. Those who had partial discoloration were deemed to be unclean. Most skin infections were viewed as a form of leprosy. An autoimmune process that extends to the skin can cause partial discoloration. An allergic reaction is an example of an autoimmune process that can be partially suppressed by anti-inflammatory agents. The world is flooded with only one leprosy definition, thus setting the stage to obscure the term's biblical, etymological nuances.

Although all black people are not Israelites by ancestry, there are valid reasons for slave-trade Negroes and other aboriginal Negroes in the world to consider Israelite ancestry. Israelites or not, blacks or whites, everyone whom God has called will play an important role in His kingdom, and the love of God will be in them, and he will be their God.

A messianic remnant of Jacob's male diaspora with or without their female counterpart in many countries of the Americas, Asia, Europe, Australia, West Indies, and especially in Africa, are waiting on both the Second Coming of the Messiah and their return to the Promised Land. God made irrevocable prophecies concerning the ingathering of Israel with blessings. The proof of Israel's identity can be investigated through cultural, historical, and prophetic signs. Regional ancestry and haplogroup mapping may, in some cases, provide clues of Israel's stock. However, in tracing the modern Judean diaspora, the Spanish Inquisition study provides useful insight into the identity and demise of Jews and Judiazers.

Historical Mapping of Israel

Judah and Israel were considered outsiders in some foreign lands where the Most High had driven them. The tribes of Israel migrated to Africa before and after AD 70. From there, they spread into the lower parts of Africa (sub-Saharan). Their land in Africa was called Negroland. There was an area in Negroland called the kingdom of Judah. Some claim that the tribes in Africa worship foreign gods; they could not, therefore, be of Israel. Those who draw this conclusion have missed the parts of the Bible about Israel's idolatry. Second, the tribes of Israel living in Africa go back to BC times, at least from Solomon's time. Although the Africans saw Israel as African neighbors (outsiders), the white European Christians, European proselyte Jews, and Islam knew that they were the children of Israel, fit for slavery. The African Israelite kingdoms went into slavery more frequently than regular Africans because of their sturdiness for service. The warlords were Christians, Islam, and the European Jew who hated Israel. Christians and Islam demanded their conversion or the sword or slavery. For detailed proof, refer to the slave-trade section at the end of chapter 11. In some cases, their culture and religious practices were a source of betrayal to their enemies. Besides, they were strong, industrious people.

Judah's kingdom heavily populated the lower parts of Africa (sub-Saharan) before and after the AD 70 exile. The people of the exile, though mainly Judah, included all the tribes and went toward the south into Africa. They were referred to as the Bantu (Congolese), Ewe, Yoruba, Whydah, Falasha, Lemba, Ibos, and the Ashanti, to name a few. This diaspora resembles what Steven Jacobs noted in the following quote concerning the Bantu and the Ashanti:

> They both came, it is thought, from the northeastern part of the African continent. The Ashanti eventually migrated to the west coast roughly parallel to the southern edge of the Sahara Desert. The Bantu, by contrast, moved mainly to the south, so that today they occupy nearly the entire southern half of the continent from the

Congo Republic and Zaire on the west to Mozambique on the east and southward to the very southernmost tip called the Cape of Good Hope...Israelites already inhabited the inland heart of black Africa is recorded by John Africanus, a famous 16th-century geographer and historian. He records in his book, which in translation is entitled A GEOGRAPHICAL HISTORY OF AFRICA, "There inhabiteth a most populous nation of Jewish stock" located west of the Nile and below the Sahara in a region between Abassin [Ethiopia] and Congo (Jacobs & Farrar, 2016, pp. 51, 59).

Subsequently, many were scattered via slave ships to the Americas, Europe, Asia, the West Indies, and South America. However, the 721 BC Assyrian dispersion of Israel took them to inhabited lands of Africa and Asia, and they became aborigines of some uninhabited portions of those continents. Some escaped the sword (Ezek. 6:8–9). It is important to note that their northeastern path to Babylon and Assyria or their westward path to Phoenicia did not change their racial appearance. For the scriptures said:

> Therefore, thus saith the LORD, who redeemed Abraham, concerning the house of Jacob, Jacob shall not now be ashamed, neither shall his face now wax pale. (23) But when he seeth his children, the work of mine hands, in the midst of him, they shall sanctify my name, and sanctify the Holy One of Jacob, and shall fear the God of Israel. (24) They also that erred in spirit shall come to an understanding, and they that murmured shall learn doctrine (Isa. 29:22-24).

In Israel, it was shameful but acceptable for someone to become pale (white). Although Israel can have different appearances, the general features of the genetic phenotype was reflected, if the stranger's descendants remains in the congregation (Duet. 23:8). This is where the maternal line becomes important. The above quote does not negate a minority of albinos among the children of Israel. If most of one's genes come from a certain race, he will be classed with that race. I'm sure when Ezra segregated the mixed people among the children of Israel, the phenotype was considered, and he devalued the genotype of the children who were authentically Israel among the mixture. He sent them away with their mothers to be Gentiles. These children were from men who desired to have strange women. They are those who knew better.

On the other hand, Ruth, a Gentile woman, entered Israel by personal conversion and produced authentic lineage through her male Israelite counterpart. Some of Israel nowadays have lost their sense of the importance of generational and cultural roots.

Stemming from the early messianic church, Judah and Israel had a good mixture of converts from the Gentiles. Such an event made it difficult to trace them by racial lineage. Most of the messianic Jews of the early church died by the sword or fled to Africa just before Jerusalem's destruction.

Conservative Israelites who were scattered into the nations in colonies are mentioned in the regathering prophecies. Israel was cast out of God's sight during the earlier dispersion into the nations. "Then said the LORD unto me: Though Moses and Samuel stood before me, yet my mind could not be toward this people: cast them out of my sight, and let them go forth" (Jer. 15:1). Those of His people who did not regard the gospel were "let go" to be scattered. The children of Israel and messianic Israel left Jerusalem never to return by covenant until the ingathering time. What are the biblical waymarks of African-Judean ancestry? Because of Israel's moral decadence, Jeremiah asked if they were born just to be slaves (Jer. 2:14).

All the countries mentioned in Isaiah 11 were of people of color. Concerning the Roman captivity in AD 70, some Israelites were captured and placed on ships destined for Rome as slaves, and others went to Egypt on foot. Many were already in Egypt and in lower parts of Africa (Acts 2). The region beyond Ethiopia is primarily West Africa and secondarily South Africa. Beyond (*ayber* in Heb. means opposite side) the rivers of Ethiopia are where the majority of Judah and Israel were dispersed after AD 70 and from there to the islands of the sea by slave ships (Deut. 28:64, 68). Scripture says this is one of the signs of their identification among all the things written concerning the curse (Deut. 28:45–46).

While it is verifiable that many Israelites were taken into captivity in the northeast areas, many returned to Palestine during the days of the Persian Empire. The Israelite family is in almost all corners of the earth. Region, culture, group migration, and prophetic disposition all play a role in the identification. None fits the narrative like the diaspora from West and Central Africa.

The Lord promised to speak to His people in a foreign language, not Hebrew (Deut. 28:49; 1 Cor. 14:21). This language can be diverse languages manifested in the church at Pentecost and represent the English language through which the ingathering message is dispersed to Israel. That is not disbanding the study of Hebrew. Modern Hebrew is simply that. Paleo-Hebrew is yet another. We are grateful to our brothers who have compiled dictionaries assisting in the acquisition of biblical languages.

Today, many Israelites have recognized Jesus (Yahuwahsha) as the Savior of the world, and He is the blessed one to return and take them home. Millions of them have been converted and accepted Jesus as their personal Savior and not subject to the papal-rooted Christianity of the Middle Ages. As Torah-abiding citizens of Jesus's kingdom, they keep biblical laws, timely applicable biblical feast, and the seventh day Sabbath.

Chapter 14

The Prophecies Concerning Israel

I n this chapter, I will quote the different passages that refer to Israel's dispersion and regathering. Israel was scattered in both Testament times. Even to the year AD 2000, Israel is still scattered. But now, they are being regathered under the call for truth in the inward parts. "Whom shall he teach knowledge? And whom shall he make to understand doctrine? Them that are weaned from the milk, and drawn from the breasts" (Isa. 28:9). "And I will give you pastors according to mine heart, which shall feed you with knowledge and understanding" (Jer. 3:15).

The Dispersion in Prophecy

Behold, the LORD makes the earth empty and makes it waste, and turns it upside down, and scatters abroad the inhabitants thereof" (Isaiah 24:1; cf. Mic 3:12; Ezekiel 36:19; Jeremiah 9:16).

And I will deliver them to be removed into all the kingdoms of the earth for their hurt, to be a reproach and a proverb, a taunt and a curse, in all places whither I shall drive them (Jeremiah 24:9).

Son of man, when the house of Israel dwelt in their own land, they defiled it by their own way and by their doings: their way was before me as the uncleanness of a removed woman. (18) Wherefore I poured my fury upon them for the blood that they had shed upon the land, and for their idols wherewith they had polluted it: (19) And I scattered them among the heathen, and they were dispersed through the countries: according to their way and according to their doings I judged them. (20) And when they entered unto the heathen, whither they went, they profaned my holy name, when they said to them, these are the people of the LORD, and are gone forth out of his land (Eze. 36:17–20).

Conditions of Disobedience in Prophecy

But if ye will not hearken unto me, and will not do all the commandments; And if ye shall despise my statutes, or if your soul abhor my judgments, so that ye will not do all my commandments, but that ye break my covenant: I also will do this unto you; I will even appoint over you terror consumption, and the burning ague, that shall consume the eyes, and cause sorrow of heart: and ye shall sow your seed in vain, for your enemies shall eat it. And will set my face against you, and ye shall be slain before your enemies: they that hate you shall reign over you, and ye shall flee when none pursueth you. And ye will not yet for all this hearken unto me; then I will punish you seven times more for your sins (Leviticus 26:14–18).

Cursed shalt thou be in the city, and cursed shalt thou be in the field Curse shall be thy basket and thy store (Deut. 28:16–17; 28:22). And thou shalt grope at noonday, as the blind gropeth in darkness and thou shalt not prosper in thy ways: and that shalt be only oppressed and spoiled evermore, and no man shall save thee (Deuteronomy 28:29).

The stranger that is within thee shall get up above thee very high, and thou shalt come down very low. He shall lend to thee, and thou shalt not lend to him: he shall be the head, and thou shalt be the tail (Deuteronomy 28:43–44). (Deuteronomy 28:46; cf. Jeremiah 15:2–4).

For these be the days of vengeance, that all things which are written may be fulfilled. But woe unto them that are with child, and to them that give suck, in those days! for there shall be great distress in the land, and wrath upon this people. And they shall fall by the edge of the sword, and shall be led away captive into all nations: and Jerusalem shall be trodden down of the Gentiles until the times of the Gentiles be fulfilled (Luke 21:22–24).

Regathering in the Promised Land

In that day, saith the LORD, will I assemble her that halteth, and I will gather her that is driven out, and her that I have afflicted. And I will make her that halted a remnant, and her that was cast far off a strong nation: and the LORD shall reign over them in mount Zion from henceforth, even forever (Mic 4:6–7).

In those days and in that time, says the Lord, The

Children of Israel shall come. They and the Children of Judah together; With continual weeping, they shall come, And seek the Lord their God (Jeremiah 50:4).

For the children of Israel shall abide many days without a king, and without a prince, and without a sacrifice, and without an image, and without an ephod, and without teraphim: Afterward shall the children of Israel return, and seek the LORD their God, and David their king; and shall fear the LORD and his goodness in the latter days (Hosea 3:3–4).

The New Testament Gospel - the Restoration

Behold, the days come, saith the LORD, that I will make a new covenant with the house of Israel, and with the house of Judah: (32) Not according to the covenant that I made with their fathers in the day that I took them by the hand to bring them out of the land of Egypt; which my covenant they brake, although I was an husband unto them, saith the LORD: (33) But this shall be the covenant that I will make with the house of Israel; After those days, saith the LORD, I will put my law in their inward parts, and write it in their hearts; and will be their God, and they shall be my people. (34) And they shall teach no more every man his neighbour, and every man his brother, saying, Know the LORD: for they shall all know me, from the least of them unto the greatest of them, saith the LORD: for I will forgive their iniquity, and I will remember their sin no more any more for ever (Jer. 31:31-34).

But in the last days it shall come to pass, that the

mountain of the house of the LORD shall be established in the top of the mountains, and it shall be exalted above the hills; and people shall flow unto it. (2) And many nations shall come, and say, Come, and let us go up to the mountain of the LORD, and to the house of the God of Jacob; and he will teach us of his ways, and we will walk in his paths: for the law shall go forth of Zion, and the word of the LORD from Jerusalem. (3) And he shall judge among many people, and rebuke strong nations afar off; and they shall beat their swords into plowshares, and their spears into pruninghooks: nation shall not lift up a sword against nation, neither shall they learn war anymore. (4) But they shall sit every man under his vine and under his fig tree, and none shall make them afraid: for the mouth of the LORD of hosts hath spoken it. (5) For all people will walk everyone in the name of his god, and we will walk in the name of the LORD our God forever and ever (Mic 4:1–5; cf. Eze. Eze. 37:24–28.).

Let both grow together until the harvest: and in the time of harvest I will say to the reapers, gather ye together first the tares, and bind them in bundles to burn them: but gather the wheat into my barn. ...The Son of man shall send forth his angels, and they shall gather out of his kingdom all things that offend, and them which do iniquity; And shall cast them into a furnace of fire: there shall be wailing and gnashing of teeth. Then shall the righteous shine forth as the sun in the kingdom of their Father. Who hath ears to hear, let him hear (Matt. 13:30, 41–43).

For thou shalt break forth on the right hand and

on the left; and thy seed shall inherit the Gentiles, and make the desolate cities to be inhabited... (7) For a small moment have I forsaken thee; but with great mercies will I gather thee. (8) In a little wrath I hid my face from thee for a moment; but with everlasting kindness will I have mercy on thee, saith the LORD thy Redeemer. (9) For this is as the waters of Noah unto me: for as I have sworn that the waters of Noah should no more go over the earth; so have I sworn that I would not be wroth with thee, nor rebuke thee. (10) For the mountains shall depart, and the hills be removed; but my kindness shall not depart from thee, neither shall the covenant of my peace be removed, saith the LORD that hath mercy on thee... (Isa. 54:3, 7–10, 13–17).

I say then, Hath God cast away his people? God forbid. For I also am an Israelite, of the seed of Abraham, of the tribe of Benjamin. (2) God hath not cast away his people which he foreknew. Wot ye not what the scripture saith of Elias? how he maketh intercession to God against Israel, saying, (3) Lord, they have killed thy prophets, and digged down thine altars; and I am left alone, and they seek my life. (4) But what saith the answer of God unto him? I have reserved to myself seven thousand men, who have not bowed the knee to the image of Baal. (5) Even so then at this present time also there is a remnant according to the election of grace. (7) What then? Israel hath not obtained that which he seeketh for; but the election hath obtained it, and the rest were blinded. (11) I say then, have they stumbled that they should fall? God forbid: but rather through their fall salvation is come unto the Gentiles, for to provoke them to jealousy (Rom. 11:1–5, 7,11).

Now if the fall of them be the riches of the world, and the diminishing of them the riches of the Gentiles; how much more their fulness... (25) For I would not, brethren, that ye should be ignorant of this mystery, lest ye should be wise in your own conceits; that blindness in part is happened to Israel, until the fulness of the Gentiles be come in. (26) And so all Israel shall be saved: as it is written, There shall come out of Sion the Deliverer, and shall turn away ungodliness from Jacob: (27) For this is my covenant unto them, when I shall take away their sins (Rom. 11:12, 25–27). This is in reference to Jeremiah 31; cf. Heb. 8:7–12).

Having never received their complete fulfillment in the Old Testament, these above-quoted verses are eschatological.

Let My People Go

Israel is still in exile in the lands of the Gentiles. Their exile is worse than ever before. Only in this modern exile are they stripped of their ancestral lineage, culture, identity, and possession (Jer. 17:4). Most of God's original people are lost and are entirely disconnected from His purpose. They are ceased from being a nation (Ps. 83:3–6). The land of Palestine to them is a foreign land. The land of the Gentiles has become their new habitation. They are taken for Gentiles by the world's religious standards though they are of Jacob to whom the promises were made. Israel has embraced all manner of evil, and they know not the way of their feet. Most of them are caught in socially and spiritually arduous situations, such as addiction, single-parent homes, extreme poverty, atheism, no self-respect, Broadway Christianity, Islam, witchcraft, Egyptology, and other religions. They worship "wood, stone, and other gods" (Deut. 4:28, 28:36, 64). Concerning them, the Lord saith:

> Then he said unto me, Son of man, these bones are the whole house of Israel: behold, they say, Our bones are dried, and our hope is lost: we are cut off for our parts. Therefore, prophesy and say unto them, Thus saith the Lord GOD; Behold, O my people, I will open your graves, and cause you to come up out of your graves, and bring you into the land of Israel. And ye shall know that I am the LORD, when I have opened your graves, O my people, and brought you up out of your graves, And shall put my spirit in you, and ye shall live, and I shall place you in your own land: then shall ye know that I the LORD have spoken it, and performed it, saith the LORD (Ezek. 37:11-14).

Coming to America on slave ships, the Negroes were "sore oppressed." Reflecting on ancient Israel's enslavement in Egypt, they found a parallel: the old Negro spiritual written in 1862 by the contrabands. It reveals their cry in the song, "Oh Let My People Go." The song was written in response to their experience in slavery compared to ancient Israel. According to Wikipedia:

> Although usually thought of as a spiritual, the earliest recorded use of the song was as a rallying anthem for the Contrabands at Fort Monroe sometime before July

1862. Early authorities presumed it was composed by them. Sheet music was soon after published, titled "Oh! Let My People Go: The Song of the Contrabands", and arranged by Horace Waters. L.C. Lockwood, chaplain of the Contrabands, stated in the sheet music the song was from Virginia, dating from about 1853. The opening verse, as recorded by Lockwood, is:

> The Lord, by Moses, to Pharaoh said:
> Oh! let my people go
> If not, I'll smite your first-born dead—
> Oh! let my people go
> Oh! go down, Moses
> Away down to Egypt's land
> And tell King Pharaoh
> To let my people go

In the song, "Israel" represents the African-American slaves, while "Egypt" and "Pharaoh" represent the slave master. Going "down" to Egypt is derived from the Bible; the Old Testament recognizes the Nile Valley as lower than Jerusalem and the Promised Land; thus, going to Egypt means going "down" while going away from Egypt is "up." In the context of American slavery, this ancient sense of "down" converged with the concept of "down the river" (the Mississippi), where slaves' conditions were notoriously worse, a situation which left the idiom "sell down the river" in present-day English (Wikipedia, 2018, Art. *Go down Moses*).

In addition to displacement and slavery, captivity has harnessed a psychological effect. Most of Israel today does not ask to seek the laws of the Lord their God. They are not your typical Jews. Most of Israel today does not seek Torah. Today's taskmasters are religious. They keep the deception of Pharaoh on par through religious captivity, teaching those whose descendants from beyond the rivers of Ethiopia that the promises and the laws of God are not for them. This psychological captivity aims to destroy Israel by the roots, to cease being the people to whom the promises were made. During these times of the Gentiles, the replacement of literal Israel by the Europeans seems to make prophetic sense, "times of the Gentiles." The European Jews had refused to accept the Negro people as original Israel until recently when the facts *forced* them to do so. Even then, they hesitantly accepted them with reserves. Why did they accept them with reserve? In light of the facts presented, it is not rocket science to see that Israel is disconnected from their heritage, parts, and purpose.

The messianic truth delivered to Israel two thousand years ago was from the white man, so most people thought. The gospel fed to the black man from Christianity is a far cry from that the apostles and prophets left. The cry is even more pertinent than ever: "Let my people go!"

Some of our leaders, unwittingly, have kept the Negro in darkness concerning their ancient Judean-Israelite roots. Some think they are doing God a favor by teaching the remnant of the ancient people the Christian religion without Old Testament principles. Most Christian churches today are established on meticulously cherry-picking portions of the Bible that is culturally friendly. This "Christian" version is supersaturated with the "let my ego go" type of teachings. The outcome of such teachings makes Christians just a little better than if they made no profession.

The Hebrews find themselves in diverse cultural settings. A few Israelites from America and Africa have repatriated to Palestine. After discovering their roots, with all good intentions, some African Americans attempted to establish God's ideal in Dimona, Israel, as a vegan society of peace. If everyone in the area respects their neighbor and kills no animals except pest, it is indeed a village of peace. The key to peace is how the middle and the high schoolers are raised to understand society's ideals and the anchor of their religious belief. If that process is not harnessed, it's only a matter of time before it's over. True, everlasting peace is a messianic promise that must be done by God himself. Going to the land of Israel today, though it won't fulfill Bible prophecy, could be a good beginning for some.

I think going back to Africa is also great. "Beyond the rivers of Ethiopia," in the tents of Ham, is where most of the remnants of Israel and Judah are. God's call to Israel is to receive the Messiah and the Torah. The call is to those whose parts are broken and have lost all hope of being the remnant of God's chosen people. Israel in captivity finds himself worshiping at the shrine of self, celebrities, and other gods. They are lost among the Gentiles. They are lost in Islam, Christianity, and heathenism. God is looking to regather them through repentance. He will save Israel from the land of their captivity and bring them back to their land. Then shall be fulfilled: "And they [the enemies] went up on the breadth of the earth, and compassed the camp of the saints about, and the beloved city: and fire came down from God out of heaven, and devoured them" (Rev.20:9).

There is little progress in the Christian understanding of the biblical prophetic program. To be alert is to be in tune with the prophetic Word. If our understanding stops with the people's limits in Jesus's day, then stagnation and inadequacy are the hallmarks of our prevalent unfamiliarity.

The key to initiating the restoration is teaching Torah to the lost family. Israel is troubled because many of them have little or no family structure, nor do they know their roots. Parents are satisfied with ignorance, and children are set to dance to demonic music and profanity. Many parents are religiously educated by those who misused the Pauline epistles, keeping them in darkness in the conveniences of sin. They are set to worship at the shrine of Olympia, where their focus, time, and energies are. Some churches dismiss their members early just to have time to feed their addiction to the games. It's not elusive that the for-profit wind of prophets, preaching an incomplete gospel, breaks hearts. Jacob today faces three problems: ignorance, slumber, and captivity. They are in captivity from God's promises of tranquility in the land of promise. Although some Israelites are waking up from slumber, the clear majority are still in dreamland with hopeless hope. They are battered on every side. There is work yet to be done. God has said he will gather his people (Isa. 27:12):

> Therefore, will I cast you out of this land into a land that ye know not, neither ye nor your fathers; and there shall ye serve other gods day and night; where I will not shew you favour. (14) Therefore, behold, the days come, saith the LORD, that it shall no more be said, The LORD liveth, that brought up the children of Israel out of the land of Egypt; (15) But, The LORD liveth, that brought up the children of Israel from the land of the north, and from all the lands whither he had driven them: and I will bring them again into their land that I gave unto their

fathers. (16) Behold, I will send for many fishers, saith the LORD, and they shall fish them; and after will I send for many hunters, and they shall hunt them from every mountain, and from every hill, and out of the holes of the rocks. (17) For mine eyes are upon all their ways: they are not hid from my face, neither is their iniquity hid from mine eyes. (18) And first I will recompense their iniquity and their sin double; because they have defiled my land, they have filled mine inheritance with the carcasses of their detestable and abominable things (Jer. 16:13-18).

Although this prophecy received fulfillment in the Persian days, it remains to repeat itself today. Since the new kingdom of Israel was established in Africa in Negroland after the AD 70 dispersion, the remnant should remain there until the return of Jesus. The repatriation of some Ethiopian Israelites by the American and Israeli operation through "operation Moses" and "Solomon," is a gesture of goodwill. It must be commended. When Jesus comes to execute judgment, He will do the separation and gather His people into the final phase of His kingdom (Matt. 25:32–46). The work to be done now is to accept Yahawahsha (Jesus) into your life as Lord and Savior and be ready for the separation. Be on the right side!

We are all appointed unto violence and death by our initiatives. Regardless of color, race, or national identity, God loves all people. All seeds are naturally evil. Both the Bible and history bear evidence that no group of people is any less barbaric and wicked than another. We are all children of wrath (Job 15:14–16; Ps. 10:4, 14:2–4; Jer. 17:9).

God does not look on the outward appearance to determine

His love toward anyone. God has sent His Son to rescue you from yourself that you may have a place in His kingdom. Jesus lights every man who comes into the world. He is the light to the Gentiles and glory to the children of Israel. Everyone willing to be saved through Him can have a place in his kingdom. He loves all the creation dearly (Matt 10:29; Rom. 8:21). God will not leave the faithful African, European, or Asian of non-Israelite ancestry out of salvation.

> Moreover concerning the stranger, which is not of thy people Israel, but is come from a far country for thy great name's sake, and thy mighty hand, and thy stretched out arm; if they come and pray in this house; Then hear thou from the heavens, even from thy dwelling place, and do according to all that the stranger calleth to thee for; that all people of the earth may know thy name, and fear thee, as doth thy people Israel, and may know that this house which I have built is called by thy name (2 Chron. 6:32–33).
>
> Wherefore remember, that ye being in time past Gentiles in the flesh, who are called Uncircumcision by that which is called the Circumcision in the flesh made by hands; That at that time ye were without Christ, being aliens from the commonwealth of Israel, and strangers from the covenants of promise, having no hope, and without God in the world: But now in Christ Jesus ye who sometimes were far off are made nigh by the blood of Christ (Eph. 2:11–13).
>
> How that by revelation he made known unto me the mystery; (as I wrote afore in few words, Whereby, when ye read, ye may understand my knowledge in the

mystery of Christ) Which in other ages was not made known unto the sons of men, as it is now revealed unto his holy apostles and prophets by the Spirit; That the Gentiles should be fellowheirs, and of the same body, and partakers of his promise in Christ by the gospel (Ephesians 3:3–6).

And to make all men see what is the fellowship of the mystery, which from the beginning of the world hath been hid in God, who created all things by Jesus Christ (Ephesians 3:9).

God has a graceful position for everyone in his kingdom. All will accept the position God assigns them, and all will work harmoniously for the common good.

Chapter 15

The Feasts of The Lord

The Nature of the Festivals

Although I dealt with the feast topic in part one of this book, this sequel is synoptically added for further development and elucidation. The feasts had not only a religious import but were part of Israel's culture as well. From a cultural perspective, the Israelites are justified in celebrating the feasts. The feasts were celebratory holy days that shed light on the plan of redemption. The early church Judeans who believed in the Advent of the messiah realized the fulfillment of the feasts. Who can deny that Christ fulfilled the Passover, and the Spirit's descent fulfilled the Day of Pentecost? Who can deny that the Lamb slain (Jesus Christ) represents what happened with the two goats on the Day of Atonement to atone for Israel's sins? Are we saying the atonement of the Messiah had no typical preparatory event to represent it? Was not *Rosh Hashana* appointed for announcing the new civil year, in preparation for the atonement? Was not John the Baptist, the trumpet blown to publicize the new era of the antitypical atonement of the New Covenant?

With this light now shining on our pathway, the messianic believer celebrates the appointed times with the new purpose and delineations. For example, one should not celebrate Passover with the old concept of being liberated from Egypt because of the Messiah's sacrifice, gives a more significant and spiritual liberation. Jesus said, do this (Passover) in remembrance of him. The appointed feast times were not abolished as it may appear in Paul's writings in Col. 2:16. Paul states, they are shadows of Christ who had to come. The impractical shadows, in the messianic sense, are the rituals of the appointed time, not necessarily the appointed time itself (Heb. 8:5, 9:10, 10:1).

The appointed times are the basis of Israel's calendar. Every seventh month there is a remembrance of the ancient calendar and time. The biblical calendar is recognized by the cyclic nature of the events being celebrated. Biblically speaking, the day is the emblem of the event. The blowing of the Shofar recognizes each New Moon. This event was a national ritual to mark the new month, a timekeeping mechanism. It cannot be abolished (Isa. 66:23). The rituals for welcoming the new moon is what could be term as shadows that are abolished or altered to suit the dispensation. New month cycle rituals are not particularly useful while dispersed among the nations. We need to exercise caution in our interpretation of Col. 2:16; we have to rightly appropriate Paul's elucidation.

Inextricable to national design is the inherent nature of why some feasts are provisionally challenging to replicate. For example, consider the wave-sheaf and the Feast of Tabernacles. Jesus and those resurrected with Him are the first fruits of the wave-sheaf. To celebrate this feast, one must carry his naturally grown raw harvest to his congregation's leaders on the Sunday following the first day of Unleavened Bread. If you are not a farmer, replication of this ritual is difficult if not impossible.

The Day of Atonement is permanently canceled due to Messianic once and for all offertory sacrifice. Jesus bore "Azazel," the curse of sin, upon himself and away from God's people. Jesus was delivered to the Romans to be crucified on Golgotha (out of the camp), to die a criminal's death. This act completed the work to be done in the antitypical atonement.

The Feast of Tabernacle, the wave sheaf, and the wave loaves all commemorated the harvest. These feasts are best celebrated when Israel live as one nation in their land. These feasts are associated with raising crops, presenting the first fruits in the spring (Ruth 1:22), and the second fruits offered in the fall. As Israel scattered among the Gentiles and living in city life, presents a challenge to these feasts celebrations in their intended fashion. Today, we can commemorate them with times of convocations.

The people of God often crave times to celebrate and have a social affair. What better times can be imported other than the times prescribed in the scriptures? Why celebrate the pagan holidays and neglect the holy times prescribed? The holy days can be used to celebrate and learn about the spiritual and natural aspects of the feasts.

The Day of Atonement

The Day of Atonement, by definition, is fused with Christ's death during Passover week. Antitypically, the Day of Atonement spans from the cross to the time of sins' eradication. In ancient times, the Day of Atonement was accompanied by fasting and a Sabbath. These two requirements were valued pending on the high priest's work on that day. Only the Israelite who has a high priest representing his sins in a yearly earthly sanctuary service needs to fast and keep a Sabbath. This is the prescription in the Torah. Back in the day, some Judeans were fasting with or without a sanctuary service. That act was not scripturally based and was not law-based for the day of Atonement. Atonement fasting was done for the cancelation of sins at the appointed time by the high priest. These sins were previously transferred to the sanctuary. In the Messianic sense, events of that appointed time happened at Passover. The once-a-year selected time of this event was substituted by Christ's sacrifice (Heb. 9). This day is not about a person getting his life in order with God, but rather hopes that God accepts his past service, and his sins are forgiven. Christians cannot think that way about salvation. That would indicate a qualm in faith. This day can be memorialized by using that time to plan for Passover or to contemplate on Jesus's Passion Week. His sacrifice is our atonement.

The change in the covenant also requires a shift in the priestly law (Heb. 7:12). The Day of Atonement was all about the priestly work and order. It is not a day to institute a fast or a Sabbath, but the fasting was for a priestly ministry's sacredness. This appointed time inevitably applied to the ancient earthly sanctuary service. Whether Old or New Testament times, any scriptural validation model necessitates a yearly earthly sanctuary service.

To Aaron, the Lord said:

This shall be an everlasting statute unto you, to make an atonement for the children of Israel, for all their sins once a year. And he did as the LORD commanded

Moses (Lev 16:34). On the tenth day of this seventh month there shall be a day of atonement: it shall be a holy convocation unto you, and ye shall afflict your souls, and offer an offering made by fire unto the LORD (Lev. 23:27). And ye shall do no work in that same day: *for it is a day of atonement, to make an atonement for you before the LORD your God* (Lev. 23:28).

There is an assumption that after the Lord's supper and before the crucifixion, fasting took place among Jesus and His disciples. This fasting day was not instituted biblically but was circumstantial to the events that took place that week. It is becoming of spiritual demarcation for Christians to institute a semi-fast on the fourteenth day.

Catholics use this one day of fasting from the early Christians as a premise for Lent. It was reported that fasting was observed by a reporter who witnessed it occurring in Jerusalem. This fasting took place after the day of the crucifixion, as "Lent." Lent was extended for forty days of fasting before the resurrection and included the day after the crucifixion. The post-apostolic church had created its holy days just as the Judeans did with Hanukah and Purim.

Lent probably developed from a fusion of the 40-day catechumenate with the fast that preceded Pasha [Passover]. This fast-preceding Easter was originally one day (Saturday), but it soon developed into two and then three days...The first indisputable reference to Great Lent is from St. Athanasius, the great theologian-bishop of Alexandria (died AD 373). In one of his "festal letters," which announced the date of Easter [Passover] each year to all the churches of the world, he speaks of a 40-day Fast beginning the sixth week before Easter and including "Holy Week," which he called "Holy Paschal [Passover] Week...The North-African theologian Tertullian (c. AD 225) refers to vigils and fasts in preparation for Paschal baptism." (Findikyan, 2006)

This attests to the fact that the early believer's most significant holy day was the days of Passover in place of the Day of Atonement. The Lord's Passover signifies the day God wipes out Israel's sins by accepting the Great Messianic Atonement. The "end of the world" mentioned in Scripture (Heb. 9) is a period concerning the old world when the old covenant terminated with Christ's appearance. The new period or the later period is typified by the fall feasts (Heb. 9:26). He appeared at the end of the old period to put away sin. Sin was put away, and Satan was defeated (Rev. 12).

The Type and Antitypes

The spring and the fall feasts have their antitypical significance. The fall feasts are prototypes of the spring feasts: the atonement and the Passover overlap in meaning. The Feast of Tabernacle and Pentecost intersect in their significance. Spiritually speaking, the Holy Spirit's abiding in us signifies a new way of life where comfort comes under subjection (feast of sukkot). Furthermore, the Old Testament period represents the spring feasts, while the New Testament period represents the fall feasts. Messiah's week of passion was the closing of the old world and the beginning of the new.

The Judean Calendar

According to scholarly sources, the Judeans' civil calendar was used by the nations before Israel ever used it. The Israelites kept the old calendar configurations in common with the other countries. They called the old calendar the civil calendar. The civil calendar accounts for birth dates, agricultural systems, and other civil matters. God commanded the religious calendar, which was also in common with the other nations. This calendar was used for religious ceremonials and predicted the beginning and end of religious celebrations. The harvest rites beginning with the spring calendar came into being as God commanded Moses to make that time the beginning of their year.

> This month is called Abib (lit., fresh young ears of, e.g., barley). This was when barley was to be harvested (March–April). With a new calendar, the Israelites were to receive a new identity as the favored people of the true God (Hannah, 1985, p. 126).

The initiation of the month in the history of the Jews was known as the new moon. The beginning of the month was marked by celebration among both the Israelites and the heathen nations. The new moon was identified by lunar sightings rather than by astronomical calculations. Researchers have written and testified concerning the procedure by which the new moon was recognized and announced. Recognition of the new moon was known by the following:

> The testimony of messengers appointed to watch the first visible appearance of the new moon, and then,

the fact was confirmed by the official and announced through the whole country by signal-fires kindled on mountain tops. The new-moon festivals having been frequent among the heathen, it is probable that an important design of their institution in Israel was to give the minds of that people a better direction. (Jamieson, Fausset & Brown, 1997, p. 114)

The Harvest rites were calculated according to the following events in their times. Below is a summary of the harvest rite and their times.

Beginning Civil Year, 2 Harvests)
1. Begin of the civil year
August/ September
Summer Fruit (qayiṣ) 2 Sam 16:1–2; Isa. 16:9; Jer. 40:10–12; 48:32; Amos 8:1–2; Mic. 7:1. This time begins in mid-August for figs and continues until mid-September for grapes.

2. Second fruit harvest
September/October
The fall. Exod. 23:16; 34:22; These are months of ingathering. The Hebrew term *ʾāsīph* (ingathering) is for grape harvesting.

3. **Soil preparation and seed time.**
November to January early seed planting
January to march late seed planting
Winter, Seed time. The Hebrew *zerāʿ* ("seed"). Seed time is referred to in Gen. 8:22 and Lev. 26:5. This included diverse crop seeds from legumes, to vegetables, etc. Hebrew, *leqeš*, referrers to crops in the spring (Amos 7:1).

Beginning Religious Year (3 harvests)

4. Passover and Wave Sheaf (first of first fruits)
March/April
Spring time Cut flax stalks, first fruits Ex.9:31. The seventh month in the spring is devoted to the flax harvest. It is the first month of the religious calendar.

5. One month of the barley harvest
April or early May
(2 Sam 21:9; Ruth 1:22, 2:23). The harvest of wheat and barley depended on the location at the time.

6. Pentecost Harvest – Firstfruits
May to early June
Wheat harvest. One month was for the wheat harvest and large-scale trade and taxation. Measuring (*kayil*) may include taxation.

7. Pruning times
February- March, and July- August.
This pruning type of work was purposeful for increasing the yield of the crops by removing unnecessary and dormant areas of the plant. Soil enrichment was enhanced while pruning.

To understand Paul's statement in Col. 2:14–17, we must have a clear view of the importance of the Judean calendar and its relation to the religious with the civil aspects of daily life. The above exposition lay bare the appropriations of the Hebraic calendar to Judaic life. Being away from our homeland makes it challenging to observe all the harvest rites. Today's diverse factions and scattered Messianic Hebrews Israelites may find a spiritual application and different mode of use by which these appointed feast times can be celebrated.

Paul's Difficult Statements

According to the commandment, there were required offerings for the Sabbaths, the new moons, and the three annual convocational festivals —the festival of unleavened bread, weeks, and booths. Because the Lamb took away Israel's sins, Christians do not offer these offerings in honor of the feast days.

Colossians 2 speaks of "wiping out of the handwriting of ordinances" and "Let no man, therefore, judge you in eating, or in drinking, or with respect to a feast day or a new moon or a Sabbath day" relates how one recognizes the days with special services or respects for the times or events being celebrated. The handwriting against us was the sentences for violations and the oblations done for them. Those feasts times were sanctified by oblation rites, which were "payments" for the sentences levied against us. There were three things against us: sacrifices of animals, the sentence for sinning, and our inherent weakness to meet God's demands. All these were nailed to Messiah's cross. The times were shadows of impending events that, without improvising them, are weak versions of the light.

Christians did not observe the Judean feast days' offerings. Christians were to remember the appointed feasts' times in the light of the Messiah's work. Messiah commanded them to keep the Passover in His remembrance, not another day, but the appointed time. This command shows that the festivals were not abolished, but only some directives associated with them. In Hebrews chapter 9, Paul could have well been saying that the festival's rituals are shadows to the exclusion of the appointed times by which Israel identifies calendric time and agricultural eventualities.

There is "a change in the law" associated with stripping "the principalities and the powers." What did Christ do to tear the principalities and powers? To strip the powers, He upheld the "Israelite moral law" as a guide to overcoming the powers of sin in human flesh. Israel used sacrifices, special food offerings, and solemnity of days to celebrate forgiveness, thankfulness, and past events. The entire sanctuary service, its Day of Atonement, and directives, served strictly as tutors until the arrival of the first advent of the Messiah. Their purpose was to show how the powers of darkness were to be stripped by the Messiah.

The same concept can be adopted for the Passover, which Christians celebrate under other names, such as communion, the holy meal, Eucharist, and the Lord's Supper. Why do Christians continue to celebrate this, which served as tutors and shadows and was superseded by the Messiah? The reason is, they received new directives from the Messiah to continue this feast in the light of His sacrifice. In truth, it is the new Passover. The early church celebrated this feast once a year with a potluck at the appointed time to remember the Messiah's week of passion. The Early Christians celebrated this festival in memory of Jesus' broken body, and it was celebrated in the evening, annually. A change in the conditions under which the law was executed applies here.

The males among the Children of Israel were to present themselves as a congregation three times a year. These times were the Passover (feast of unleavened bread), the feast of Weeks, and the feast of Booths. The feast of booths, like the Passover, requires some days to solemnize it. It involves sacrificial tutors. Since we were instructed about the change in celebrating the Passover and not the feast of booths, as we are in exile, we may not have a cohesive procedural method for this celebration (Zech. 14). This feast cannot be celebrated in a hotel or in someone's home. It is make-shift dwellings, camping in tents. It is not that the feast days are abolished, but new provisions must be adopted.

The feasts do not have the moral effect as the seventh-day Sabbath and other laws as some people would like to make of them. This does not mean that they should be neglected. Unlike the Ten Commandments and other laws, they are for national jubilation in design.

The Feast of Weeks likewise has the same sacrificial elements of meats and drinks as do the others. It is celebrated in one day, commemorating the giving of the Ten Commandments and the Spirit on the Day of Pentecost. According to Hebrews chapter 8, these events are part of the belief system of the Messianic Israelite. Therefore, the Day of Pentecost can be partly commemorated by a festive gathering like the early Christians did after the resurrection (Acts 2). Pentecost is celebrated on the fiftieth day, beginning the Sunday following the first day of Unleavened Bread. In seeking the same unity of the Spirit, we should follow the example of the early church. Because the church was still in the Promised Land, it was easy for them to be engaged in whatever their customs were.

In Neh. 8:15–18, we see how Israel was to keep the Feast of Tabernacle. They were to keep it as a national holiday collectively, and they had not done so for a long time. This undoing was not due to flagrant discard of the law but due to inconveniences mounted by the protracted captivity. The feast days were not undesirable commandments, as were the "moral" law. They were not a daunting task for Israel to observe. Israel lived in a setting that facilitated these celebrations. At times, Israel was asked to stop the celebrations predicated on moral corruption. The feast of Tabernacles represents the last ingathering of the religious year and the second harvest of the civil year in the antitype. Zechariah chapter 14 states how this feast will be celebrated during the Christian era. Although this feast remains current, it is not presently regulated due to captivity and lack of applied Christological implications. Paul's negation of feast in Col. 2:15, 16 is related to unwarranted salvific consequences under which they were submerged. As a means of punishment, captivity has had an adverse environmental effect on Israel's national holidays (Hos. 2:11). Once in captivity, the feasts seem to be subject to ones' possibilities.

"You observe days, months, seasons, and years. I am afraid for you that I might have wasted my labor for you" (Gal 4:3, 8–11). Back in the day, the Judeans, the Messianics, and the proselytes were infatuated with observing extra-biblical times. There are reasons to believe that Paul could have been referring to other factors than biblically appointed times, or simply refers to the infatuation itself.

Change in Calendric Times

Various nations had their calendar from which they calculated time. Back in the Old Testament time, most of the world was ruled by empires having vast domains embracing most nations. The calendric influence of these empires successively rules their term on the world stage.

The religious calendar of Israel was identical to that of

the Babylonians. Apart from what is known from Leviticus 23 by the hand of Moses, the first written calendar for Israel is known as the Gezer calendar at Solomon's time. The most ancient calendar is that of the Babylonians from Mesopotamia (2000 BC). Israel's calendar was lunisolar. It was lunar from the point of the beginning the crescent moon ("Hodesh") for new monthly ("Yereah") cycles, and solar form the effects of the sun on the Barley grain ripening at the beginning of the liturgical year in the spring.

The Egyptians, Phoenicians, Assyrians, and Persians had their new year in the fall equinox (Britannica, 2002), which Israel adopted for the Feast of Trumpets. The Roman Republic's New Year was on March 1, similar to Jew's religious year. In 153 BC, the Roman new year was changed to January 1. The Julian calendar followed suit in honor of Janus, the god of the doorway and new beginnings. This change was later bolstered through the introduction of the Gregorian calendar (1582). Before the Gregorian calendar was imposed on the nations by the Papacy, most of Christendom celebrated the New Year in the spring. Modern nations today hold to the Roman custom of the New Year celebration in January (Britannica, 2002).

I hope you have received a better understanding of the Lord's feasts, without which an adequate illumination on their settings and statements made by Paul becomes difficult to comprehend. Paul's statements contain an incomplete elaboration of the conditions under which he spoke about the feasts. This cloudy world view prevents clear attainment of concepts intended. Much of the understanding can be acquired through the inspiration of the Holy Spirit. The feast days must have had continued recognition among Judeans and Messianics in post-apostolic days. We should use the feast days as times for spiritual reinforcement and for celebrating spiritual values of the Judaic messianic culture.

Israel's Diaspora and Return

Israel is scattered (Hos. 3:4). "For the children of Israel shall abide many days without a king [no kingdom], and without a prince [no future king], and without a sacrifice [no temple services], and without an image [no representation or culture or identity], and without an ephod [no priest or services], and without teraphim [no substitute]."

During the AD years, the children of Judah and some of the children of Israel began to lose some of their cultural practices as they were scattered among the nations. At that time, the Gentile, proselyte Samaritans remained in the land of Israel. Jerusalem had both proselytes and original Judeans. But when AD 70 came, a prodigious cleansing of the land took place. It was an unfortunate, unprecedented event of destruction. "And he shall confirm the covenant with many for one week: and in the midst of the week he shall cause the sacrifice and the oblation to cease, and for the overspreading of abominations, he shall make it desolate, even until the consummation and that determined shall be poured upon the desolate" was fulfilled (Dan.9:27).

Jesus said: "O Jerusalem, Jerusalem, thou that killest the prophets, and stonest them which are sent unto thee, how often would I have gathered thy children together, even as a hen gathereth her chickens under her wings, and ye would not! Behold, your house is left unto you, desolate. For I say unto you, Ye shall not see me henceforth, till ye shall say, Blessed, is he that cometh in the name of the Lord" (Matt 23:37–39).

With the Christian message's acceptance by scattered Israel and Judah, these negroes were forced to shed their ancestral Judaic religion, thus fulfilling the scriptures:

> And they shall fall by the edge of the sword, and shall be led away captive into all nations: and Jerusalem shall be trodden down of the Gentiles until the times of the Gentiles be fulfilled (Luke 21:24).
>
> For I would not, brethren, that ye should be ignorant of this mystery, lest ye should be wise in your own conceits; that blindness in part is happened to Israel until the fulness of the Gentiles be come in. And so, all Israel shall be saved: as it is written, there shall come out of Sion the Deliverer and shall turn away ungodliness from Jacob (Rom. 11:25, 26).
>
> Afterward shall the children of Israel return, and seek the LORD their God, and David their king; and shall fear the LORD and his goodness in the latter days (Hos. 3:5).

During the latter diaspora, most of Israel and Judah found themselves deep in Africa. Some went to Assyria, Babylon, and Spain. Some had gone as far as Russia and made converts in the land of Ashkenazi (Germany). Some of the scattered Israel and Judah were soon to lose their identity as they face the Roman dragon of the inquisition. The Roman church was bent on destroying all of the roots of Israel, who were a large population of "true negroes." Their color served as an appointed demarcation for their demise. Israel was in double jeopardy. To Rome, skin color and religious beliefs of Israel were at the apex of offense. Judah was driven out of Spain and Portugal and was made slaves. Most of them were sent to Africa and became the main part of the transatlantic slave trade. Many were forced to convert to either Islam or Christianity, thus losing their identity, further masking them from their heritage of the promised land (Ps. 83:1–6).

> And the LORD shall scatter thee among all people, from the one end of the earth even unto the other; and there thou shalt serve other gods, which neither thou nor thy fathers have known, even wood and stone (Deut. 28:64,). *And thou, even thyself, shalt discontinue from thine heritage that I gave thee;* and I will cause thee to serve thine enemies in the land which thou knowest not: for ye have kindled a fire in mine anger, which shall burn forever. Thus, saith the LORD; Cursed be the man that trusteth in man and maketh flesh his arm, and whose heart departeth from the LORD" (Jer. 17:4,5). "And he said, I will hide my face from them, I will see what their end shall be: for they are a very forward generation, children in whom is no faith. They have moved me to jealousy with that which is not God; they have provoked me to anger with their vanities: and I will move them to jealousy with those which are not a people; I will provoke them to anger with a foolish nation...I said, I would scatter them into corners, *I would make the remembrance of them to cease from among men*: Were it not that I feared the wrath of the enemy, lest their adversaries should behave themselves strangely, and lest they should say, Our hand is high, and the LORD hath not done all this" (Deut. 32:20-21, 26-27).

The Scriptures trace some of Israel on the West coast of Africa thus:

> "Therefore wait ye upon me, saith the LORD, until the day that I rise up to the prey: for my determination is to gather the nations, that I may assemble the kingdoms, to pour upon them mine indignation, even all my fierce anger: for all the earth shall be devoured with the fire of my jealousy. For then will I turn to the people a pure language, that they may all call upon the name of the LORD, to serve him with one consent. From beyond the rivers of Ethiopia, my suppliants, even the daughter of my dispersed, shall bring mine offering" (Zep. 3:8-10).

Pray for the Peace of Israel

It is certain if there is a blessing to receive, nobody wants to be left out. When Jacob received the blessing from his father Isaac, his brother Esau, who felt cheated of the blessing, beg to be blessed. But this could not happen. Only one of the opposing characters could lead in spiritual things. While Esau was unwilling to be deprived of the physical to secure the spiritual, Jacob took the opportunity to help himself with the occasion he yenned to grasp. He wanted Esau's birthright, and Esau was willing to trade it for food. Little to Esau's expectation, the trade deal was to become perpetual. After completing the deal, Esau regretted it so much that he hated his brother (Gen. 27). In the end, God protected Jacob and promised him great blessings.

> Let people serve thee, and nations bow down to thee: be lord over thy brethren, and let thy mother's sons bow

down to thee: cursed be every one that curseth thee, and blessed be he that blesseth thee (Gen. 27:29).

He couched, he lay down as a lion, and as a great lion: who shall stir him up? Blessed is he that blesseth thee, and cursed is he that curseth thee (Num. 24:9).

A similar blessing was formerly given to Abraham, then passed on to Jacob. For Jacob to escape the curse and get the blessing, he must be faithful and accept the "star that rises out of Israel." This Star is the ruler whom God appoints. This Star is the Beloved Son, the Messiah to Israel. The time of the blessing follows the time of the curse. Israel had been under the curse of slavery throughout his sojourn among the nations. His brief return to Jerusalem for accepting the messiah was the opportunity to obtain the prophesied blessing. When most of Israel failed, they returned head-long into destruction, captivity, and slavery until recently. Israel was in the transition period as he was led to accept the messiah through the force of slavery, then to accept the call voluntarily before acquiring all the blessings attached. Their rejection was temporary until these last days, said Paul: "For I would not, brethren, that ye should be ignorant of this mystery, lest ye should be wise in your own conceits; that blindness in part is happened to Israel until the fulness of the Gentiles be come in" (Rom. 11:25).

Pray for Israel to accept the humility that the Messiah affords them. When Israel fled from Jerusalem, Spain, and Portugal, most went into Africa, and many were overcome by the Islamic religion (Windsor, 1988). There has been an increasing number of Israel coming out of Islam into the Messiah's kingdom. "Pray for the peace of Jerusalem: they shall prosper that love thee. Peace be within thy walls, and prosperity within thy palaces.

For my brethren and companions' sakes, I will now say, Peace be within thee. Because of the house of the LORD our God I will seek thy good" (Psalm 122:6–9).

The value of prayer

> Prayer is the opening of the heart to God as to a friend. Not that it is necessary in order to make known to God what we are, but in order to enable us to receive Him. Prayer does not bring God down to us but brings us up to Him.
>
> Perseverance in prayer has been made a condition of receiving. We must pray always if we would grow in faith and experience. We are to be "instant in prayer," to "continue in prayer, and watch in the same with thanksgiving" (Romans 12:12; Colossians 4:2). (White, 1892, p. 60).

God specializes in helping us overcome our difficulties, according to His foreknowledge. Prayer is not intended to replace what we can do for ourselves. When there is incompetence, we go on our knees, in faith, knowing that God will supply the need according to His will. He will also provide our wants if they are for our good. Even if there are doubts about His will for you concerning a particular thing, you can still go to God on your knees, as did Jesus, asking in faith, knowing that God will withhold nothing good from those who love him and keep His commandments. Answered prayer is not always a meritorious result from an impeccable lifestyle. Our God is the all-powerful, merciful, and compassionate One, forgiving iniquity and sin of those who love Him. As a sinner who craves repentance, you can go to God with humility, asking for what you desire.

The truth treated herein is knocking at your door. If you have not accepted Jesus as your Savior, you can pray for His peace and Spirit to enter your life and forgive you for all your sins. Start anew in His name. What you need is an efficient cultural relationship with Jesus. I hope that you make time for prayer and study and are filled with the Spirit of Jesus. God loves all His children, and He longs to save you.

> "Now, unto him, that is able to keep you from falling, and to present you faultless before the presence of his glory with exceeding joy, to the only wise God our Savior, be glory and majesty, dominion and power, both now and ever. Amen."—Jude 1:24–25.
>
> May the truth be taught, and may the people take hold of it.
>
> I hope this reading has been a blessing to you and your family.

Appendix A

———⊙◉⊙———

The Times of the Passion

The following is a timetable of the events of Christ's Passion Week. These times are approximate for managing crowds. Remember, in the last part of the trial; the whole city was involved (Luke 24). Distances are significant while considering times. From Herod to Pilate was approximately three city blocks long; from Sanhedrin to Pilate was six city blocks long, and from Pilate to Golgotha was five city blocks long. This approximation was calculated using the *Holman Bible Atlas* (Brisco 1998). The trial's great mystery is whether it took just three to four hours to go through civil aspects or nearly two days? It appears logical to say if the trial is to be done without rush and through the public system, each segment could take hours.

Which time column below is the most probable?

Event	10 hours rush trials	No rush in civil court Two days
They probably had about 2.5 hours of sleep at the most. Matt 26:54	About 2.5 hrs	

Event	10 hours rush trials	No rush in civil court Two days
1) John 18:3 Judas then, having received the band of soldiers	*about 11 PM*	
2) Went to Annas first. John 18:13	*11:30: PM*	
3) then to Caiaphas. See John 18:28	*Midnight*	
4) Mt 27:1. In the morning, they took counsel against Jesus to put him to death:	*5:30-6:30 Am-*	6 AM
5) "Then led they, Jesus, from Caiaphas unto the hall of judgment: and it was early." (John 18:28.) -- Mt 27:2 and they bound him, and led him away, and delivered him up to Pilate, the governor.	*7:30 Am Early For government*	6:30-7:00
6) Luke 23:6. And when he knew that he was from Herod's jurisdiction, he sent him unto Herod	*8:30 AM*	8:00-8:50
7) Lu 23:11. And Herod, with his soldiers, set him at naught and arraying him in gorgeous apparel, sent him back to Pilate.	*8:00 Am-8:15*	9:15-10:00
8) John 19:4 And Pilate went out again, and saith unto them, Behold, I bring him out to you, that ye may know that I find no crime in him. Luke 23:17 Now he must need release unto them at the feast one prisoner. Isa 53:8	*8:25- 9:15*	Resume 12:15 p.m. –Pilate's wife had a dream
9) John 19:9 and he entered into the Praetorium again, and saith unto Jesus, Whence art thou? But Jesus gave him no answer.	*9:17-9:25*	His wife related the dream.

Event	10 hours rush trials	No rush in civil court Two days
10) Luke 23:16. I will, therefore, chastise him. John 19:2; and the soldiers platted a crown of thorns, put it on his head, and then put him in the penitentiary. 11) Mt 27:31 And when they had mocked him, they and led him away to crucify him.	*9:30-9:45*	8:00 AM
12) Mrk. 15:22 And they bring him unto the place Golgotha, which is, being interpreted, the place of a skull.	*10:00*	9:00
13) Mrk 15:25 And it was the third hour, and they crucified him.	*10:15*	9:05-9:15
14) Mrk 15:33 And when the sixth hour came, there was darkness over the whole land until the ninth hour. 12-3: PM	*12:00-3:00*	12:00- 3:00 Preparation for 7th day Sabbath and the feast Bread
15. Burial	*4-5 pm*	4-5 pm

For the two-day event, it is not certain when the events of the next day begin. However, the recess could have begun after Christ was scourged and placed in the penitentiary.

Appendix B

―――◆◉◆―――

A Study in Typology

Passover - protection from the death of the firstborn Egyptians

Symbol	Old T Description	Christian NT description
1. Passover - Abib –Nisan April	Protected from the death of the firstborn in Egypt	1 Cor. 5:7 Christ is our Passover Sacrificed for us
2. unleavened bread April –Matzoth	Affliction in Egypt and rushing out	The life of Christ; truth and sincerity without hypocrisy; The affliction of Jesus for us. Yahawasha is the bread of life. 1 Cor. 5:7, Isa. 53:5, 7,10,11; John 6:32-35.
3. Wave Sheaf April (Sunday)	Thanking God for arriving in the new land for its harvest presented the stalk of grain	Jesus's resurrection on Sunday to a new life. Mark 14:58. Christ, firstfruits of them that slept 1 Cor. 15:20; also, those that rose with him. Mat. 27:53-53.

Symbol	Old T Description	Christian NT description
4. Wave loaves Feast of Shavuot (weeks) 50 days later Pentecost, Giving of the Law	Thank offering for the first major harvest loaves of bread -time of giving of the law at Sinai, The Spirit on Judgment comes	Second of the First harvest; 120 disciples, Acts 1:20, Act.1:15, Acts 2. Church starts pure later degraded. During the period of wheat and tares (leaven). James 1:18. The Spirit of God –brings the law to convict of sin and Judgment.
5. Trumpets Tishri (Ethanim) Use for Sabbatical and Jubilee years September Feast of Shofar, Rosh HaShanah (Civil New Year)	The blowing of trumpets (Announces the advent of the Law a memorial of a Spring event -- Ex.19:18-22).	Announces Advent of Messiah– John the Baptist ministry (Luke 2:15-17; 3:4-6). The Advent of the Law in human form (Isa. 9:7, Luke 1:76-79;2:34). Post antitypically, the trumpets Announce the readiness of the church and judgments to follow. Rev. 8-9.
6. Atonement Yom Kippur Feast of fasting October	The day of atonement – the time of forgiveness of sin by the hand of Moses as mediator Ex. 32:29-Ex. 34:12, Lev. 16	Jesus– Mediator -- the life, the death, and the Resurrection into heaven. Bears sins of many. Rom 5:8-21, 8:34. Heb. 9:25-26. 2 Cor. 5:18-19. Heb. 1:3, 8:1, 10:12. The day of atonement is at the cross. Post antitypical is at the fulfillment of Zech 12:7-14.

Symbol	Old T Description	Christian NT description
7. Tabernacles Feast of boots Sukkot, tents ingathering	Celebration for having completed the last harvest of the year. Also, Israel dwells in tents in the wilderness of wandering for 40 years.	God dwells with us by the first advent of Christ. Rome scattered the early church in the wilderness (Rev. 12:6, 12). Post antitypical fulfillment is seen in Zech 14:16,18-19, Celebration of the last ingathering of the people of God

Appendix C

The Terms of Ancient Feasts

The Feast in the Old Testament, feasts, and presentations seven in all.

The Spring Festival
- Passover, Unleavened bread, wave sheaf presentation, and Pentecost (wave loaves or weeks)

10th day of the 1st month
- Take a young lamb of the first year according to his eating, hold for four days Ex 12:3-6

14th day of the first month Abib or Nisan--Passover (exemption) Lev 23:5 Duet. 16:1 Feast Passover preparation.
- Kill the lamb that was kept alive to the 14th day in the evening, and eat it that night with unleavened bread Ex. 12:6-8.
- Lamb died where Lord chooses for his Name Duet. 16:2, 5.
- Any remaining part of the feast shall be burned up with fire. Ex. 12:9-11.

- Put leaven out of houses Ex 12:15
- Purpose: In haste out of Egypt and was afflicted in Egypt. Duet 16:3

15ᵗʰ day -21ˢᵗ day (7 days) of the first month ---Feast of Unleavened Bread. Lev. 23:6

- Fifteenth and 21ˢᵗ day a Holy convocation, and a Sabbath of no regular work Lev 23:6-7-8
- Seven days Feast of unleavened bread Lev 23:6-7. For having left Egypt Ex 12:17
- No leaven should be found in houses for all the seven days. It begins 14ᵗʰ day at even Ex.12:18-20 Ex 34:25
- Offer two bullocks, one ram and seven young lambs as burnt offerings and one goat for atonement for seven days Num. 28
- Offer burnt offerings as regular every morning and evening
- No uncircumcised shall eat thereof, the circumcised can. Ex 12:48-49.
- **On Sunday, harvest presentation,** the next day after the Sabbath, priest wave firstfruits sheaf of harvest – Lev 23:10-11.
- Shall wave the sheaf on Sunday and a young male lamb offering
- Meal offering of flour, oil, and wine, bring to the Lord before you eat anything of it. Lev. 23:13-14
- The day to put the sickle to the corn count seven weeks. Deut. 16:9

Fifty days from Sunday to Sunday – after seven Sabbaths – the feast of Pentecost (weeks). Lev. 23:15-16 (when coming into the land)
- Bring a new meal offering to the Lord
- Bring two leavened loaves for a wave offering to the Lord. Lev. 23:17
- Present seven young lambs, one bull, and two rams as a burnt offering. Lev. 23:18
- A Sabbath of no regular work and a Holy Convocation. Lev. 23: 21
- Two bullocks, one ram, seven lambs, and one goat for atonement. Num. 28:26-30

Fall festival

1st day of 7th month, the blowing of Trumpet
- A Sabbath of no regular work solemn rest Lev. 23:24-25
- Memorial of trumpets blown when they left Egypt. Lev. 23:24
- Meal offering presented offering made by fire to the Lord. Lev 23:25
- One bullock, one ram, seven lambs, and one goat for atonement. Num. 29:2-5

10th day of 7th month Day of Atonement –to make an atonement for you, not judgment but salvation by justification, followed by your sanctification –your self-denial. Lev. 23:27-32.
- A holy convocation. Lev 23:27
- Atonement is to be made. Lev 23:27
- Afflict your soul, self-denial, Lev 23;27
- Offering by fire to God. Lev. 23:27

- Solemn Sabbath, no type of work. Lev. 23:28-32.
- One bullock, one ram, seven lambs, and one goat for atonement. Num. 29:8-11

The 15th to the 22nd day of the 7th Month is the feast of tents (booths or tabernacles). Lev. 23:34-36
- 15th and the 22nd day shall be a Sabbath of no regular work, the eighth day a solemn assembly Lev. 23:36
- Offerings made by fire on all days (seven and one)
- Seven-day feasts after the 15th day after the harvest Lev 23:39
- Make boots out of good trees and palm branches. Lev 23:40
- All Israel born shall dwell in booths. Seven days. Lev. 23:42-43
- Sets of bullocks, ram, lambs, and goats for each day. Num. 29:12-38
- Because God has blessed all thy works and thy increase. Duet 16:13-16

The males were to appear before the Lord during three feasts and not come empty. Deut. 16:16-17
- Unleavened bread (Accepting Yahuwahshua as Savior)
- Weeks (Receiving the gift of the Spirit of Christ)
- Tabernacle (The ingathering and indwelling of the Spirit)

One feast that we did not expound on is the Feast of Dedication, called the Feast of Lights. This feast is mentioned in the New

Testament. It is a feast of the Jews. Although it was not one of God's appointed times, this feast was instituted by the Jews to commemorate the cleansing of the temple that was defiled by Antiochus Epiphanes IV. This cleansing or restoration of the temple took place during the inter-Testamental period. The dedication happened in December 165 B.C. In memory of this special occasion, the Jews created a special candlelight vigil called Chanukiah. This candle has nine lights. The ancient sanctuary candle, however, has seven lights, and it is called the Menorah. According to some, this event has deep prophetic implications in the book of Daniel. The account is found in the first three chapters of the first book of the Maccabees in the Apocrypha.

The ancient Jews maintained a seven-candlelight vcalled the Menorah when celebrating Temple dedication. Our bodies are the Temple of God. We should have a special temple dedication every year at this time of the year. Our bodies should be cared for as a living sacrifice to God. What we eat and wear or how treat our bodies should be a sacrificial feast of dedication.

-------------------------the End -----------------------------

Appendix D

The Judean Calendar

Judean Months	Sacred/Civil/ Event	English Months	Crops/antitype
Aviv/ Nissan	1/7 Passover/ Unleavened Bead First of first fruits	March/ April	Latter rains; barley harvest, flax, chickpeas, grapes, eggplant, and garlic (Exodus 9: 31, 2 Samuel 21: 9). Death, purity, and resurrection of Christ
Ziv/ Iyyar	2/8	April/May	The dry season begins; papaya, cherry, plum, nectarine, squash, watermelon.
Sivan	3/9 First fruits Pentecost	May/June	Wheat harvest; early figs, apricot, pineapple, okra (Exodus 9:31). First major harvest of the early church, the Spirit's outpouring
Tammuz	4/10	June/July	Hot season; grape harvest and figs.

Av	5/11	July/August	Pruning season; summer fruits, olive harvest, avocados, dates, grapes
Elul	6/12	August/ September	Pruning continues; summer fruits continue, dates, and summer figs.
Ethanim/ Tishri	7/1 Trumpets -Rosh Hashanah Yom Kippur Feast of Tabernacles	September/ October	Former Rain; plowing time. Perennial fruit Harvest, and grapes Opening of major events, the Atonement by Christ; final harvest of the second fruits
Bul/ Heshvan	8/2	October/ November	Year's end ingathering; rains, sowing of wheat, custard apple, Kiwi, olive, and guava.
Kislev	9/3 Hanukkah	November/ December	Winter begins; strawberries.
Tebeth	10/4	December/ January	Rains
Shebat	11/5	January/ February	Almond trees blossom, asparagus, peas, beans, and Bok choy.
Adar	12/6 Purim	February/ March	Pruning; Latter Rain, citrus harvest, flax budded by June.

Concept Reflection

Chapter 1

1. Make a list of the appointed times and name each event.
2. Elucidate how the feasts corroborate the plan of redemption.
3. In what setting were the feasts best celebrated?

Chapter 2

4. How has Passover changed since the days of the Apostles?
5. Which two feasts can be represented and celebrated with the same meaning?
6. What parts of the Jewish feast celebration can be omitted from the Christian feast?

Chapter 3

7. Describe how Christian feast keeping is a ceremonial practice.
8. Why is it incorrect to conclude that Paul's statements in Colossians 2:and Galatians 4:8--were meant to abolish all feast days' celebrations? (Also, see chapter 15). Explain your answer.

9. What can be concluded from history about the Apostolic understanding concerning feast applications?

10. Explain why the feast sabbaths and the 7th day Sabbath are in different subcategories.

Chapter 4

11. How were Jesus's suffering and death celebrated in Apostolic times?

12. How is feast keeping today different from the Apostolic times?

13. What symbolic ritual celebrates Christ's resurrection during Apostolic times?

14. What significant event co-occurred with the time that Christ ate the Passover?

15. Describe the event in the antitype that was prefigured by "the heart of the earth" and the "belly of the fish."

Chapter 5

16. Which biblical statement implies that Christ was not buried before the feast started?

17. Which type of Sabbath did the disciples rest "according to the commandment" (Luke 56)?

18. List the facts indicating that a day does not always require a 24-hour reckoning.

19. According to scripture, on what date of the month does Passover and the Feast of Unleavened Bread (Communion) begin?

Chapter 6

20. List the events that occurred from Jesus' first appearance before Pilate to the crucifixion.

21. What spiritual indication shows that "unleavened bread' and "Passover" are used interchangeably?

22. What issue do the Muslim apologists present against Christians' mistakes about the "three days and three nights" application?

Chapter 7

23. Is the Sabbath a special day? If so, how and why? If not, explain.

24. What biblical factors separate the weekly Sabbath from the lunar sabbaths?

25. Explain what the 7th day Sabbath and the lunar sabbaths symbolize concerning salvation and transformation.

26. What indications show that Jesus did not abolish the Sabbath?

27. Summarize how the church came to accept Sunday in place of the Sabbath.

Chapter 8

28. What difficulty was presented with understanding the Pauline Epistles?

29. How do we know that all the laws of the Old Testament have categories?

30. What are the three timeless laws in Genesis?

31. How did Paul describe the decalogue in the Old Testament?

32. What can we conclude about spiritual rest from the Old and New Testaments?

Chapter 9

33. What are the three classifications in the law? How do they apply?

34. What do people who dislike the ten commandments often say about them?

Chapter 10

35. What commonality exists between ancient Israel and the Egyptians?

36. Under what condition can a Jew be accepted in the covenant promises?

37. Which scripture teaches that God still has a covenant plan for the descendants of ancient Israelites?

Chapter 11

38. How many times was there a mass emigration of Israelites from their kingdom? Can you give the scriptures for your answer?

39. According to Daniel, how long did the curses against Judah continue?

40. List some changes the Roman church instituted into the Christian faith.

Chapter 12

41. When did the first phase of the kingdom restoration begin?

42. What verses show that God accepts both the Jews and the Gentiles in His kingdom?

43. According to history and scripture, on which continent was most of Israel finally scattered?

Chapter 13

44. What historical and scriptural evidence indicates the resemblance of the people of Israel as Ethiopians?
45. What does the scripture teach about the external appearance of Jesus?
46. How many types of albinism exist in science?
47. What did the Israelites classify general skin disease to be?
48. Where did the Bible say that many of the scattered remnants of Israel were found?

Chapter 14

49. Concerning teaching, what is God looking to do today?
50. What are the three dilemmas Jacob faces today?

References

Abernethy A. T. (1910), *The Jew, A Negro.*

Alaezi, O. (2013), *Ibos: Hebrew Exiles from Israel*, American Edition.

Aquinas, T. (2007) *Article four: Question 122: of the Precepts of Justice*, New Advent, Knight, Kevin, Electronic Edition

Brisco, T. C. (1998). *Holman Bible Atlas*, Broadman & Holman Publishers, Nashville, Tennessee 37234

Britannica, online (n.d.), Art. *Congo free state.* Retrieved from https://www.britannica.com/place/Congo-Free-State 10/2018

Britannica, online (n.d.), Sabbatarianism, Definition & Views Britannica.com. Retrieved from https://www.britannica.com/topic/Sabbatarianism

Catholic Encyclopedia, (2007*), Synod of Laodicea Canon 16;* New Advent, Knight, Kevin Electronic Edition

Catholic Encyclopedia, (2007) Art. *"Constantine the Great."* New Advent, Knight, Kevin, Electronic Edition

Dalton, R. Jr. (2015), *Hebrews 2 To Negroes*, Vol. 2, G Publishing; USA. (Ch. 7,11-12.)

Duffu Y. S. K (2010); *Africa's Exodus to the Promised Land*, Roots in God. Sankofa Heritage Books U.S.A.

Encyclopedia Britannica (2013) Art. *"Sabbath"* Retrieved from CD set Electronic Edition.

Femi, A. (2013), Dutch trouble with ugly slavery past *"New African"* IC Publication London, Retrieved from http://newafricanmagazine.com/dutch-trouble-with-ugly-slavery-past/ 9/2018

Gill, J (1746-1763), Deuteronomy 16:3 *Exposition of the Entire Bible.* Retrieve from: http://biblehub.com/commentaries/gill/deuteronomy/16.htm

Grundmann, W., van der Woude, A. S., Hesse, F., & de Jonge, M. (1964–). χρίω, χριστός ἀντίχριστος, χρῖσμα, χριστιανός. G. Kittel, G. W. Bromiley, & G. Friedrich (Eds.), *Theological dictionary of the New Testament* (electronic ed., Vol. 9, p. 494). Grand Rapids, MI: Eerdmans.

Hardinge, L. (1973), *The Celtic Church in Britain*, Teach Services Inc. Brushton, NY.

Healy, E. (2008), Neanderthal man's MC1R plays fair. *Pigment Cell & Melanoma Research*, 21(3), 340. doi:10.1111/j.1755-148X.2008.00465.x).

Hefele, K, V. (1876), *History of the Councils of the Church*, Vol. II Book 6, 1876, Sect. 91 (A History of the Councils of the Church; E-catholic 2000. (n.d.). Retrieved from https://www.ecatholic2000.com/councils/united-21.shtml)

Hindson, E. (2003), *Courageous Faith: Life Lessons from Old Testament heroes*, p. 62; AMG Publishers; Chattanooga, TN 37421

Horton, D., (1999), *Western Misrepresentation of The Jews*, *Retrieved from* http://timbooktu.com/horton/misrep.htm 9/2018

Houteff, V, T. (1942), *The Sign of Jonah*; Universal Publishing Association, Mountaindale, N.Y. 12763

Jacobs, S., Farrar, M., (2016) *The Hebrew Heritage of Black Africa*, African Tree Press, Clifton New Jersey.

Jamieson, R., Fausset, A. R., & Brown, D. (1997). *Commentary Critical and Explanatory on the Whole Bible* (Vol. 1, p. 290). Oak Harbor, WA: Logos Research Systems, Inc.

Jones, T. P. (2009), *Christian History Made Easy*; Rose Publishing, Carson, California

Martyr, J. (A.D. 130-165), *First Apology ch 67*, Knight, Kevin, Electronic Edition

Mannix, D. P., Crowley, M. (1962), *A History of the Atlantic Slave Trade Black Cargoes,* The Viking Press Inc. New York, NY 10022,

Mc Cray, W. 1990, *The Black Presence in the Bible*. The Black Light Fellowship. Chicago, IL. 60680. (9).

Miller, K. & Levine, J. S. (2012), *Biology (Florida),* Pearson Education, Saddle River, New Jersey 07458. Pp. 392-395.

Moore, O. (2002), *The Science and the Myth of Melanin*, A&B Publishers Group Brooklyn, NY.

Neander, A., Terrey, J., (1847-1853), *The history of the Christian Religion* volume one, Sixth American Edition, Boston: Crocker & Brewster. London: Wiley & Putnam G. Bohn, York-street, Covent Garden., pp 186-187, 410

Oetting, W. S., Fryer, J. P., Shriram, S., & King, R. A. (2003). Oculocutaneous Albinism Type 1: The Last 100 Years. *Pigment Cell Research*, 16(3), 308. doi:10.1034/j.1600-0749.2003.00045.x).

Pick, A (1977), *Dictionary of Old Testament Words for English Speakers*, Kregel Publishers. Grand Rapids, Michigan.

Resse, E., Klassen, F. R. (1977), *The Reese Chronological Bible*, Bethany House Publishers, Bloomington, Minnesota 55438.

Richards, H.M.S. *Christmas Catechism*, (1953), The Voice of Prophecy Inc.

Rogers, J. A., (1952), *Nature Knows No Color-Line*, Helga M. Rogers St. Petersburg, Florida 33175,

Ryrie, C. C. (1999); *Basic Theology*, Moody Publishers, Chicago IL. 60610.

Shelley, B. L. (2008), *Church History in Plain Language*; Thomas Nelson, Nashville Dallas Mexico City.

Sertima, I. V. (1976), *They Came Before Columbus*; Random House Trade Paperback, USA

Steven L. C, Kendall H. E. (2003), *Harmony of the Gospels* Holman Bible Publishers.

Strong, J. (1990). *The New Strong's Exhaustive Concordance of the Bible. The Jewish calendar* (Sect. Miscellaneous). Thomas Nelson Publishers.

Wallbank, W. T., Schrier, A., Maier-Weaver, D., Gutierrez, P. (1977), *History and Life, The World, and Its People*. Scott, Foresman and Company, USA.

Westcott and Hort (2002). *Greek New Testament with morphology*. (Col 2:16). Bellingham, WA: Logos Bible Software

Whiston, W. (1987), *The World of Josephus* (XVI, 6:2). Hendrickson Publishers Inc. Peabody, MA.

Whitaker, R., Brown, F., Driver, S. R. (Samuel R., & Briggs, C. A. (Charles A. (1997). *The Abridged Brown-Driver-Briggs Hebrew-English Lexicon of the Old Testament: from A Hebrew and English Lexicon of the Old Testament*. Oak Harbor WA: Logos Research Systems, Inc.

White, E. G. (1888), *The Great Controversy*, Light House Digital Library 1998.

Wikipedia (2018), Art. *"Go Down Moses"* Retrieved from https://en.wikipedia.org/wiki/Go_Down_Moses 10/2018

Windsor, R. R. (1988), *From Babylon to Timbuktu*, Windsor Golden Series, Atlanta, Georgia 30331.

Zondervan Cooperation (1975), The Zondervan Parallel New Testament in Greek and English, Iverson-Norman Associates; Zondervan Bible Publishers, New York, New York.

Graphic credits:

Africa Map, chapter 12: Retrieved from https://pixabay.com/en/africa-map-african-political-35742/

Index

Printed in the United States
by Baker & Taylor Publisher Services